POSTCARDS
FROM THE TRENCHES

POSTCARDS
FROM THE TRENCHES

NEGOTIATING

THE SPACE BETWEEN

MODERNISM

AND THE FIRST WORLD WAR

Allyson Booth

NEW YORK   OXFORD
OXFORD UNIVERSITY PRESS
1996

Oxford University Press

Oxford   New York
Athens   Auckland   Bangkok   Bogota   Bombay
Buenos Aires   Calcutta   Cape Town   Dar es Salaam
Delhi   Florence   Hong Kong   Istanbul   Karachi
Kuala Lumpur   Madras   Madrid   Melbourne
Mexico City   Nairobi   Paris   Singapore
Taipei   Tokyo   Toronto

and associated companies in
Berlin   Ibadan

Published by Oxford University Press, Inc.,
198 Madison Avenue, New York, New York 10016

Oxford is a registered trademark of Oxford University Press

Library of Congress Cataloging-in-Publication Data
Booth, Allyson.
Postcards from the trenches : negotiating the space between
modernism and the First World War / by Allyson Booth.
    p.   cm.
Includes bibliographical references and index.
ISBN 0-19-510211-8
1. English literature—20th century—History and criticism.
2. World War, 1914-1918—Great Britain—Literature and the war.
3. War stories, English—History and criticism.   4. War poetry,
English—History and criticism.   5. Modernism (Literature)—Great
Britain.   I. Title.
PR478.W65B66   1996
820.9'358—dc20   95-47921

Page v constitutes an extension of the copyright page.

9 8 7 6 5 4 3 2 1

Printed in the United States of America
on acid-free paper

For Mom and Dad

ACKNOWLEDGMENTS

For anyone who knows her work, my intellectual debt to Elaine Scarry is conspicuous. The shocks and delights of her teaching, writing, and warm encouragement can hardly be overstated, and I am deeply grateful for the scrupulous care with which she helped to shape and to sharpen this study as a dissertation at the University of Pennsylvania. Vicki Mahaffey, who codirected the dissertation, has been similarly influential in both eloquently Joycean and utterly practical ways. Her teaching rendered the modernist canon at once luminous and understandable, while her coaching navigated me through the quicksand of writing. Susan Greenfield, who for years has read the most and the roughest drafts of my work, has shepherded this project from its earliest confused beginnings with an uncanny gift for filling in conceptual blanks and connecting psychological dots. Her friendship has been a quirky and steadfast joy.

Many other wonderful teachers have participated, mostly unwittingly, in this book. Long before it ever occurred to me to go to graduate school, the daily classroom energies of Norman Stewart, Ross Murfin, Joseph Gordon, and Harriet Chessman opened door after magical door of literary possibility. Later, authors Paul Fussell, Modris Eksteins, Stephen Kern, Eric Leed, and Samuel Hynes presided over the space of the library for me. Their books, each of which attends differently to the cultural implications of World War I, sketch out an imaginative landscape that makes this book possible.

The Naval Academy has supported my work both institutionally, in the form of Naval Academy Research Council and Faculty Development Fund grants, and locally, in the form of an extraordinarily generous and good-natured English department. I would like especially to thank (former and current) chairs Charlie Nolan and Mike Parker and Associate Chair John Thomson for their many acts of personal and bureaucratic loyalty and my colleagues Anne Marie Drew and Molly Tinsley for their intellectual animation and frank dependability. Thanks also to Flo Todd at Nimitz Library for handling hundreds of interlibrary loan requests with patience and skill.

I am a moody writer, susceptible to mental bogs but remarkably fortunate in the friends who surround me and, literally, make work possible. Wendy Wall, Laura Tanner, James Krasner, Jenny Green-Lewis, Greg Bredbeck, Anita Tien, Margie Wing Hirsch, Carolyn Carlson, and Jesse Shafer provided me with a wonderfully reliable, funny, and tolerant community in Philadelphia—a community that made possible both my escapes from and my returns to this project and that has stuck with me imaginatively even as it has dispersed geographically. Joan Raiselis and Deb Golden have shared their abilities to see the world architecturally; Jerry Case and Barbara Greenberg have been free with their publishing expertise and their encouragement. Thanks especially to Jerry for making this book in particular.

My sister, Carlye Booth Case, and her husband, Chris, have not only supplied and repaired the array of computers on which this manuscript was written but also loaned me money for its permissions and illustrations. That I have a key to their house and know the code that disables its security system typifies their blanket and matter-of-fact generosity. My brother, Grant Booth, has been a treasured and affectionate listener, equally openhanded with his perceptiveness and his exuberance; his wife, Kristen Ludgate, has been a staunch ally and trusty source of E-mail. My parents, Ed and Dottie Booth, who read to us every night while we ate orange sherbet out of yellow cups, taught me to love words. Their house on Crea Street and the family they created in it have always constituted the imaginative space and emotional safety in which this project, or any other, could be undertaken. This book is for them.

Washington, D.C.   A. A. B.
September 1995

CONTENTS

POSTCARDS
FROM THE TRENCHES

And what we said of it became

A part of what it is . . .

Wallace Stevens,
"A Postcard from the Volcano"

INTRODUCTION

In the middle "Time Passes" section of Virginia Woolf's *To the Light-house* (1927), the narrator tells the death of Andrew Ramsay:

> [T]here came later in the summer ominous sounds like the measured blows of hammers dulled on felt, which, with their repeated shocks still further loosened the shawl and cracked the tea-cups. Now and again some glass tinkled in the cupboard as if a giant voice had shrieked so loud in its agony that tumblers stood inside a cupboard vibrated too. Then again silence fell; and then, night after night, and sometimes in plain mid-day when the roses were bright and light turned on the wall its shape clearly there seemed to drop into this silence, this indifference, this integrity, the thud of something falling.
>
> [A shell exploded. Twenty or thirty young men were blown up in France, among them Andrew Ramsay, whose death, mercifully, was instantaneous.] (200–201)

This passage essentially constitutes the novel's attention to the Great War: textually bracketed, numerically limited, and architecturally contained. War is reported by an ambiguous narrator lodged in an empty house; the report relies on no witness, details no wound, and elicits no response. War here is the sound of hammers dulled on felt, the vibration of tumblers in a cupboard, the thud of something falling. Yet despite Woolf's positioning of it at an extraordinarily complicated remove from both narrator and reader, the first time I read *To the Lighthouse*, Andrew's death made me gasp.

This book grew out of questions surrounding what seemed to me the peculiar shock produced by telling war from inside an empty house. Was

3

it possible that the elaborate set of circumstances within which Woolf's narrator seems nested actually conspired to intensify rather than muffle that shock? What was the point of imaginatively positioning "twenty or thirty" shattered young bodies in an uninhabited building? How centrally or peripherally did the war figure in this and other of Woolf's novels? In other canonical modernist works? Did explicit accounts from the spaces of war—trenches, hospitals, and the infamous no man's land—have any relation to the literary spaces of Woolf's modernism? To the built spaces of modern architecture?

I argue in this book that they do—that even at moments when the spaces of war seem most remote, the perceptual habits appropriate to war emerge plainly; that the buildings of modernism may delineate spaces within which one is forced to confront both war's casualties and one's distance from those casualties; that the dislocations of war often figure centrally in modernist form, even when war itself seems peripheral to modernist content. The patterns I trace here are familiar aspects of modernism—the dissolution of borders around the self, the mistrust of factuality, the fascination with multiple points of view. But placing such familiar patterns in a broad cultural context uncovers not only their frequent overlaps with the writing of combatants but also, at moments, their frictions with the verbal tactics endorsed by governments or with the imaginative structures relied on by military leaders.

In Wallace Stevens's declaration that the poet "creates the world to which we turn incessantly and without knowing it . . . giv[ing] to life the supreme fictions without which we are unable to conceive of it" ("Noble Rider" 31), he posits a deep and unconscious relation between the "real world" we believe ourselves to be inhabiting and the fictive structures invented by poets. Hayden White makes a similar claim about the relation between history and fiction when he asserts that "historical documents are not less opaque than the texts studied by the literary critic. Nor is the world those documents figure more accessible" (*Tropics of Discourse* 89). The patterns I analyze in this book both depend on and justify just such mixtures of category: modernism and realism, history and fiction, imagination and reality. The materials I handle here include novels, buildings, newspapers, poems, letters, monuments, and documents of architectural criticism and military history. What emerges from this crossing of discourses is an expansive conception of modernism—literary and architectural—that displays itself as deeply engaged in a broader Great War culture.

Because it is purely conceptual and largely retrospective, modernism is of course not locatable in any one text, any one architectural structure. It can only be understood as a pattern that gradually emerges across a series of words and buildings, visible only because we make precise decisions about those details to which we will attend. Other critics have attended to modernism's participation in cultural discourses about sexual politics, technological innovation, the theories of Freud and Darwin, the visual tactics of postimpressionism and cubism, or any of a number of other cultural pressures. By attending strictly to the Great War, I do not mean to suggest that I see these other elements as peripheral or unengaging—only that they are beyond the scope of this project. A canonical modernist text, like any other work of art, will reconfigure itself depending on the lens through which one peers, and there are any number of narratives that can be constructed from the numerous forms of representation that provide us with our only access to the past. I posit just one of those possible narratives.

That many of the representational strategies I identify as linked to the war preceded the war should come as no surprise. War does not happen in a vacuum: men and women venture into it provided with the same perceptual equipment that they rely on to understand and articulate any other experience. In attempting to express war, they draw on the idioms and representational techniques that seem to fit best. Some conceptual categories and verbal methods will lend themselves to the problem of articulating the new experience and be pressed into service frequently; others will seem less useful and be discarded. The ghosts of "dead ideas" that Mrs. Alving feels wrapped in and oppressed by in Henrik Ibsen's *Ghosts* (1881) suggest a set of images that writers could have drawn on in discussions about the ghosts of dead soldiers thirty-five years later, yet few seem to have moved in the direction of the ghost story. However, the family history made palpable in the objects and architecture of Henry James's "The Jolly Corner" (1909) and E. M. Forster's *Howards End* (1910) sketch a relationship between the past and the material world that, as I argue in chapter 6, writers like Rebecca West and Ernest Hemingway draw on in their postwar accounts of veterans attempting to place the experience of war firmly behind them.

My categories are thematic rather than chronological. I do not pretend to diagram specific cause-and-effect relationships between modernism and the First World War. No doubt well-educated junior officers incorporated lessons they had learned from prewar poets into their descriptions of the war: Wilfred Owen reaches backward to an ancient tradition to produce the bitter effect of his famous "*Dulce et Decorum Est*" (1917). No doubt soldiers taught postwar poets lessons as well: T. S. Eliot's *The Waste Land* (1922) is commonly understood to incorporate the sounds and images of trench warfare and its aftermath. What I'm interested to trace is not the particulars of those exchanges but the patterns that emerge as appropriate to both the experience of war and the experience of a world shaken up by war—patterns that both soldiers and civilians seem gradually to have internalized as fitting the disconcerting worlds of both combatant and civilian modernism. To focus on these habits of perception suggests at once that the Great War was experienced by soldiers as strangely modernist and that modernism itself is strangely haunted by the Great War.

More than twenty years ago, Paul Fussell, in *The Great War and Modern Memory,* talked about the tension between capitalized abstractions like Heroism and the concrete details of trench warfare—a tension largely unfamiliar to inhabitants of the prewar world:

> [T]he Great War took place in what was, compared with ours, a static world, where the values appeared stable and where the meanings of abstractions seemed permanent and reliable. Everyone knew what Glory was, and what Honor meant. It was not until eleven years after the war that Hemingway could declare in *A Farewell to Arms* that "abstract words such as glory, honor, courage, or hallow were obscene beside the concrete names of villages, the numbers of roads, the names of rivers, the numbers of regiments and the dates." In the summer of 1914 no one would have understood what on earth he was talking about. (21)

More recently, Samuel Hynes has documented what he calls the "Myth of the War" by which he means "not a falsification of reality, but an imaginative version of it, the story of the war that has evolved, and has come to be accepted as true" (xi). Hynes's outline of the war's familiar "myth" incorporates the shift into concreteness to which Hemingway and Fussell refer; Hynes's book *A War Imagined: The First World War and English Culture* sketches the myth's "collective narrative of significance" as follows:

> [A] generation of innocent young men, their heads full of high abstractions like Honour, Glory, and England, went off to war to make the world safe for democracy. They were slaughtered in stupid battles planned by stupid generals. Those who survived were shocked, disillusioned and embittered by their war experiences, and saw that their real enemies were not the Germans, but the old men at home who had lied to them. They rejected the values of the society that had sent them to war, and in doing so separated their own generation from the past and from their cultural inheritance. (xii)

Hynes charts the development of this imaginative version of the war, emphasizing the gap the war was understood as constituting: a gap between past and present, between combatant and civilian, between the generation that engineered the war and the one that was swallowed up in its casualty lists. From the complicated process that resulted in this myth of the gap came the gradual emergence of a new soldier's vocabulary of war—stripped down, concrete, and pitched in tense opposition to the abstractions that hitherto had constituted war's verbal convention. While it is difficult not to see this transformation as a move from inaccuracy to accuracy, from gleaming illusion to gritty clear-sightedness, Hynes's careful identification of this version of events as myth reminds us that the replacement of one convention with another, no matter how much more honest the new one seems, does not bring those of us at a remove from war any closer to the physical experience of it.

Hynes points out a number of ways in which the myth of the war simplifies a situation that was not that simple. There were young men, as well as old, who were ignorant of the war yet insisted on its continuance; all soldiers did not lose their idealism; many cultural traditions survived intact. Although the myth of the war contends that soldiers became cynical while civilians continued on their blithe and patriotic way, Hynes demonstrates that there were plenty of soldiers who felt as if *they* were the ones who clung to idealism while civilians gave it up. He cites, for instance, a soldier named R. H. Tawney, who charges that "you [civilians] seem—forgive me if I am rude—to have been surrendering your creeds." Tawney argues that despite the vast difference in experience that the war represented, soldiers and civilians shared for a time the idealistic patriotism of its early months: "[O]ur foreground may be different, but our background is the same. It is that of August to November, 1914. We are your ghosts" (qtd. in Hynes 118–19). This soldier challenges the myth of the war by suggesting that it was not soldiers but civilians who became disillusioned; he serves as a reminder to us that any pattern, no matter how pervasive it seems, is always a simplification of reality.

Most of the veterans upon whose work I draw are men and women whose voices helped to constitute what Hynes identifies as the war's myth, rather than people like Tawney who resisted it. To some extent, then, my version of modernism participates in the version of the war that Hynes documents. But just as Hynes is careful to point out that the oppositions implied by his myth (a raw and concrete soldier's sensibility versus an idealistic and abstract civilian's; old men versus young veterans, and so forth) are not stable oppositions, I don't set out in this book to construct rigid categories of modernist versus antimodernist texts or expressionist versus international-style buildings. Too much evidence militates against such rigidity, for even individual writers fluctuate back and forth along the spectrums that roughly delineate the differences between Hynes's myth and the forms of representation that contradict it, between modernism and the forms that might seem to constitute its opposite. Ford Madox Ford produced propaganda for C. F. G. Masterman's Department of Information but also wrote a modernist war tetralogy; Rudyard Kipling was one of the "pillars of the Edwardian literary establishment" (Hynes 26) who agreed to write on behalf of the government, yet his story "Mary Postgate" exemplifies a modernist handling of architecture; Vera Brittain veers back and forth in *Testament of Youth* between earnest abstraction and grisly concreteness. Architectural history is similarly messy: Ludwig Mies van der Rohe designed what seemed to be expressionist buildings before he designed what Philip Johnson and Henry-Russell

MODERN HISTORIOGRAPHY

Hitchcock later decided were modern, international-style ones; Erich Mendelsohn moved away from the molded expressionist forms of his Einstein observatory toward much more rectangular designs. I am concerned here not to shore up binary categories, but rather to explore the multiple positions that modernism made available to inhabitants of a culture over which the Great War loomed.

Andrew Ramsay is not the only family casualty of time's passage in *To the Lighthouse*. His mother also dies—"rather suddenly" (194) but from unspecified causes, and his sister Prue dies "in some illness connected with childbirth" (199). Virginia Woolf's narrator reports the fates of various family members from inside a house where they lived together, surrounding Andrew's death with the deaths of his mother and sister, collapsing the distance between a French battlefield and an English bed. Lily Briscoe levels the import of the three deaths by lumping them all together: "Mrs. Ramsay dead; Andrew killed; Prue dead too—repeat it as she might, it roused no feeling in her" (219). Of course, the death that does eventually rouse real feeling in Lily is the death of Mrs. Ramsay, not that of Andrew. But for the moment, at the breakfast table, Lily decides that Cam and James (not Andrew) are the tragic characters, for they are the ones subject to a father looking "like a king in exile," forcing them to submit to his will. "And it struck her, this was tragedy—not palls, dust, and the shroud; but children coerced, their spirits subdued" (222). Mrs. Ramsay's death has left her children more vulnerable than before to the tyranny of her husband; the tragedy is not her death but its effect on them. Prue's death "was indeed a tragedy, people said" (199). Andrew's death, however, is never mentioned in tragic terms.

This kind of attention to the gendering of tragedy (a mode typically bestowed with generosity on men at war) distinguishes female modernist writers like Woolf from some modernist soldiers who are not above lapsing into ugly misogyny, prompted at least partly by the fact that during the Great War women were a protected category—safe from conscription yet frequently willing to pressure men to enlist. Siegfried Sassoon's poem "Glory of Women" skewers women specifically for a rhetoric that was certainly not limited to women; Richard Aldington's *Death of a Hero* is trenchant in its attitudes about women: George Winterbourne chides the narrator, charging that "the War had induced in [him] a peculiar resentment against women," which the narrator admits "was probably true" (233). Many feminists argue that female writers should be understood as producing texts that differ from those produced by men, and if I were going to make that kind of argument, these are the kinds of distinctions with which I would begin. Shari Benstock states her premise that "[m]odernist writing by women is significantly unlike that of men" (32); Sandra Gilbert and Susan Gubar's important three-volume investigation of modernism begins with a similar claim: "[M]odernism, because of the distinctive social and cultural changes to which it responds, is differently inflected for male and female writers" (xii).

While I agree that in some ways, and in many cases, the battle of the sexes was waged in the textual territory of literary modernism (early twentieth-century architecture seems to have been so male-dominated that it presented no forum for such struggles), to begin with the premise, as Gilbert and Gubar do, that modernism "is itself . . . a product of the sexual battle" (xii) would make it difficult for me to attend to the perceptual patterns that most concern me—patterns that frequently link, for example, the writing of female nurses to that of male soldiers, or even the works of civilian women like Virginia Woolf to those of combatant men like Edmund Blunden. Despite the sometimes markedly divergent concerns of male and female writers, I attend more to their overlaps, so that I present here a version of modernism constituted not so much in the space between men and women as in the space between civilians and combatants—or, more precisely, in the surprising array of imaginative methods that begin to bridge that space and to delineate a cultural and imaginative landscape that could take both combatant and civilian experience into account.

I tend to move as freely across national borders as I do between books by men and women, drawing most frequently on British culture and British writers but also incorporating works by German, French, and American authors: Erich Maria Remarque's *All Quiet on the Western Front,* Henri Barbusse's *Under Fire,* Willa Cather's *The Professor's House.* I would argue that, however small the sample of non-British works on which I draw, the texts I have encountered that were written by German, French, and American authors tend consistently to confirm the patterns I trace in British texts. Even more important, I draw on Wallace Stevens and Ernst Jünger, on Willa Cather and T. S. Eliot, because their works, as surely as those of Virginia Woolf, E. M. Forster, and D. H. Lawrence, have taught me what I know about modernism, influenced my own perceptual habits, and shaped the imaginative categories I bring to this project.

In a 1917 letter to her brother-in-law, Virginia Woolf remarked that "[i]ts [*sic*] an absorbing thing (I mean writing is) and its [*sic*] high time we found some new shapes, don't you think so?" ("To Clive Bell"). E. M. Forster worried in 1920 that "[o]ur 'own' times, as they are ironically termed, are anything but ours; it is as though a dead object, huge and incomprehensible, had fallen across the page, which no historical arts can arrange, and which bewilders us as much by its shapelessness as by its size" (qtd. in Hynes 324). Ten years later, Mary Borden described a French territorial regiment straight from the trenches: "And they were all deformed, and certainly their deformity was the deformity of the war. They were not misshapen in different ways. They were all misshapen in the same way. Each one was deformed like the next one" (27). Woolf, writing from the middle of war, looked for new shapes; Forster, trying to imagine a world after war, felt bewildered by its shapelessness; Borden, remembering the bodies of war, claims that "[t]hey were all misshapen in the same way."

War alters the world's shape in numerous ways, but in her analysis of its structure, Elaine Scarry cites three major "arenas of alteration": "embodied persons," "aspects of national consciousness," and "material culture" (114). This book is organized according to those categories: part I, "The Shapes of Bodies"; part II, "The Shapes of Countries"; and part III, "The Shapes of Objects." In each part, I investigate both the ways in which war distorted previously existing shapes—ways of thinking—about death, national borders, time, military spaces such as battlefields, and civilian spaces such as buildings—and the ways in which modernism accommodated and articulated those distortions, developing, painfully and erratically, the new shapes for which Woolf called.

In part I, "The Shapes of Bodies," I am primarily concerned with the space between western front and home front, the space that protected civilians from the casualties of war.[1] In Britain, what Paul Fussell has called the "ridiculous proximity" of Great War combat zones to Trafalgar Square meant that Monday's *Daily Mail* reached the front by Tuesday, that an officer could breakfast in the trenches and dine at his club in London, that the flash of a large explosion in Messines was visible across the Channel in Kent (64–69). Soldiers frequently made the trip home and back, becoming familiar with the absurdly narrow gap that separated duckboards from carpets, barbed wire from stone walls and stiles. But thousands of British civilians—coached by a government whose versions of events were reiterated in newspapers and whipped up by cartoon propaganda—were deeply invested in a war that compelled them to offer up an entire generation of sons, husbands, and fathers. They inhabited a relatively unambivalent rhetorical world in which the Great War was patriotic, all Germans and all things German were wicked (German music was for a time banned from Sir Thomas Beecham's Promenade Concerts), and exhibition trenches, "clean, dry, and well furnished" (Fussell 43), wound neatly through Kensington Gardens.

Meanwhile, soldiers were telling of trenches "carpeted at bottom with a layer of slime that liberates the foot at each step with a sticky sound" (Barbusse 5). They were traversing landscapes in which they had no choice but to "trample soft bodies underfoot, some of which [were] moving and slowly altering their position" (Barbusse 262). Here, a combatant might (as Robert Graves once did) refrain from shooting an enemy soldier because that enemy is taking a bath. And an officer might order his troops forward, berating them for being "bloody cowards" when they fail to stir, only to have his platoon sergeant "gas[p] out: 'Not cowards, sir. Willing enough. But they're all f——ing dead'" (Graves, *Good-bye* 191).

In the context of these radical fractures between spaces, my chapter 1, "Corpselessness," analyzes the empty spaces created by absent bodies, both in England—where governmental policy dictated that corpses would not be shipped home for burial and that photographs of corpses would not be circulated—and at the front, where shell explosions "could disintegrate a human being, so that nothing recognizable—sometimes apparently nothing at all—remained of him" (Keegan 269). Focusing most explicitly on Woolf's *Jacob's Room* (1922), but citing examples from a number of other writers (Henry James, D. H. Lawrence, Rudyard Kipling, Willa Cather), I argue that the houses of modernist fiction attend to the problem of corpselessness, as do architectural memorials to the missing. Chapter 2, "Corpses," handles the problem of the body at the front, arguing that the corpses with which soldiers had to live generated a surprisingly "modernist" conception of character—an instability with which writers like T. S. Eliot (*The Waste Land*), Katherine Mansfield ("The Daughters of the Late Colonel"), James Joyce ("The Sisters," *Finnegans Wake*), and D. H. Lawrence (*Women in Love*) have made us familiar through their representations of civilian corpses.

All countries narrate their wars, but, as Samuel Hynes has pointed out, several factors made the narrative of the Great War particularly crucial to the British government. Britain needed the support of its citizens both politically and militarily, so that voters would support the war and civilians would enlist to fight in it (conscription was not introduced until 1916). In addition, as Paul Fussell has explained, the British population in 1914 was more literate and literary than it had ever been. In part II, "The Shapes of Countries," I investigate some of the problems of narrating the spaces of the Great War: competing descriptions of national borders; difficulties in determining facts; battlefields on which it was hard to gain a visual perspective; and battles which, because nobody seemed to move and nothing seemed to happen, did not lend themselves to the conventions of narrative. In each of the chapters of part II, I pair the difficulties of narrating war with their attendant manifestations in civilian modernism.

Chapter 3, "Physical Borders," begins with a discussion of the competing nationalist discourses of August 1914, in which Germany insisted that its invasion of Belgium was prompted by a fear of "encirclement" and Britain insisted that it entered the war because of the "rape" of Belgium. I examine these conflicting formulations in terms of Elaine Scarry's analysis of what is at stake, imaginatively, for countries at war. Scarry argues that war exposes the constructed nature of the very beliefs for which a population is fighting, for "[i]n a dispute that leads to war, a belief on each side that has 'cultural reality' for that side's population is exposed as a 'cultural fiction'" (Scarry 128). War may thus, Scarry explains, be understood as generating terrifying tension around the categories of fact and fiction. With that tension in mind, I argue that the British discourse that superimposed the physical borders of a woman's body onto the national borders of Belgium may be understood as creating a verbal construct confirming the British belief that the national borders, as they existed prior to Germany's invasion, were "natural" (not invented). This same tension between fact and fiction is visible in a number of civilian and combatant texts that I go on to discuss, especially in the alleged assault on Adela Quested in Forster's *A Passage to India* and in the fierce written debate between Robert Graves and Siegfried Sassoon regarding their respective narratives of war and the facts of combat.

Because the weapons with which the Great War was waged increased the dimensions of the battlefield at the same time that the philosophy of military leadership positioned generals in offices far behind the lines, the military narratives of war were produced by men who rarely, if ever, visited the front line. In chapter 4, "Maps," I look at some of the results of this new spatial organization of war, arguing that because generals were physically so removed from the battlefield, their discourse relied on imaginative principles that may be traced back to maps: the line, the synecdoche, and a singular point of view. I suggest that the metaphorical maps of Joyce's *Finnegans Wake* and Mary Borden's *Forbidden Zone*, along with the multiple perspectives employed by such writers as Wallace Stevens, Helen Zenna Smith, Edmund Blunden, and Ford Madox Ford, confirm the insights of soldiers who became convinced that these map-related principles were representationally flawed and militarily irresponsible.

Chapter 5, "War Calendar," takes as its starting point the tension between the Victorian belief in progress and the immobility for which World War I is infamous. I link the narrative consequences of the policy of attrition, which accepted war as a condition rather than plotting it as a story, to modernism's disruptions of narrative convention in such works as Siegfried Sassoon's *Memoirs of an Infantry Officer*, Enid Bagnold's *A Diary without Dates*, Virginia Woolf's *The Years*, and Ellen La Motte's *The Backwash of War*. Given the ways in which both combat's inevitable physicality and modernism's focus on psychic interiority resist the conventions of linear movement forward, I suggest that war books tend to be understood as written in a realist style not so much because they differ from modernist works as because civilians are willing to see war—but not peace—as a fundamentally disordered and unpredictable experience.

Although part III, "The Shapes of Objects," depends conceptually on Scarry's assertion that war alters material culture, I modify her structure slightly in the process of investigating modernist architecture.[2] When Scarry refers in her analysis of war to the alteration of material culture, she is speaking about the destruction that happens inside war: damage to embodied persons and damage to material culture "are the means for determining which of the two sides will undergo" alterations of national consciousness; damage to bodies and to objects "function as an abiding record" (114) of collective imaginative alterations imposed upon the losing country. I adapt Scarry's structure by extending my examination of material culture beyond the end of the war, in order to investigate not the destruction of material culture that happens during war but rather the construction of material culture that happens afterward. Thus, part III deals with how war affected the design and construction of architectural spaces and material artifacts and the ways in which those buildings and objects were understood by the architects who designed them, by the architectural historians who positioned them in architectural history, and by writers who incorporated buildings and objects into their own works.

In chapter 6, "Forgetful Objects," I argue that both literary and architectural objects were frequently understood as enacting an erasure of an explicitly wartime past. I trace this studied forgetfulness in the architectural history of the international style as documented both by critics (Nikolaus Pevsner, Reyner Banham) and by architects themselves (Le Corbusier, Walter Gropius), paying attention at the same time to their opinions about how war warped the designs of expressionists like Hermann Finsterlin, Erich Mendelsohn, and Hans Poelzig. I then examine the objects in such literary texts as Ernest Hemingway's *A Farewell to Arms* and Rebecca West's *The Return of the Soldier,* suggesting that here, too, artifacts become implicated in the disposal of an ugly wartime past.

Chapter 7, "Glass Objects," examines the use of glass in both buildings and texts. I suggest that because glass, like language, can glide back and forth between transparency and opacity, it lends itself to both expressionist architects and modernist writers as an opportunity to explore the fracture that may separate perceptual from physical experience. I trace the tendency in both modernist literature and expressionist architecture to portray interior and exterior reality with equal vividness, arguing that the modernist attention to interior experience springs at least in part from an awareness that only when the lessons of war are rendered in imaginative terms can modernism teach the lessons of war without participating in it. This chapter draws on the architecture and ideas of Paul Scheerbart, Ludwig Mies van der Rohe, Bruno Taut, Philip Johnson, and Henry-Russell Hitchcock and on the literary work of Virginia Woolf (*The Waves, Mrs. Dalloway*), Katherine Mansfield ("Bliss," "Prelude"), Tennessee Williams (*The Glass Menagerie*), and Wallace Stevens ("The Glass of Water," "Asides on the Oboe").

Paul Fussell has explained how the Field Service Post Card allowed soldiers to supply their families and friends with the reassurance that civilians seemed to want during the war. "If a man was too tired to transcribe the clichés of the conventional phlegmatic letter" (183), he could always resort to the government-generated postcard, which required only enough energy to cross out the inappropriate sentences and to affix one's signature to the card (figure 1). Thousands of these postcards were sent to relatives after battles, when soldiers would cross out everything except "I am quite well," thus informing their families that they were still alive. Fussell goes on to note that these postcards constituted the first widely used "form": "Infinite replication and utter uniformity—those are the

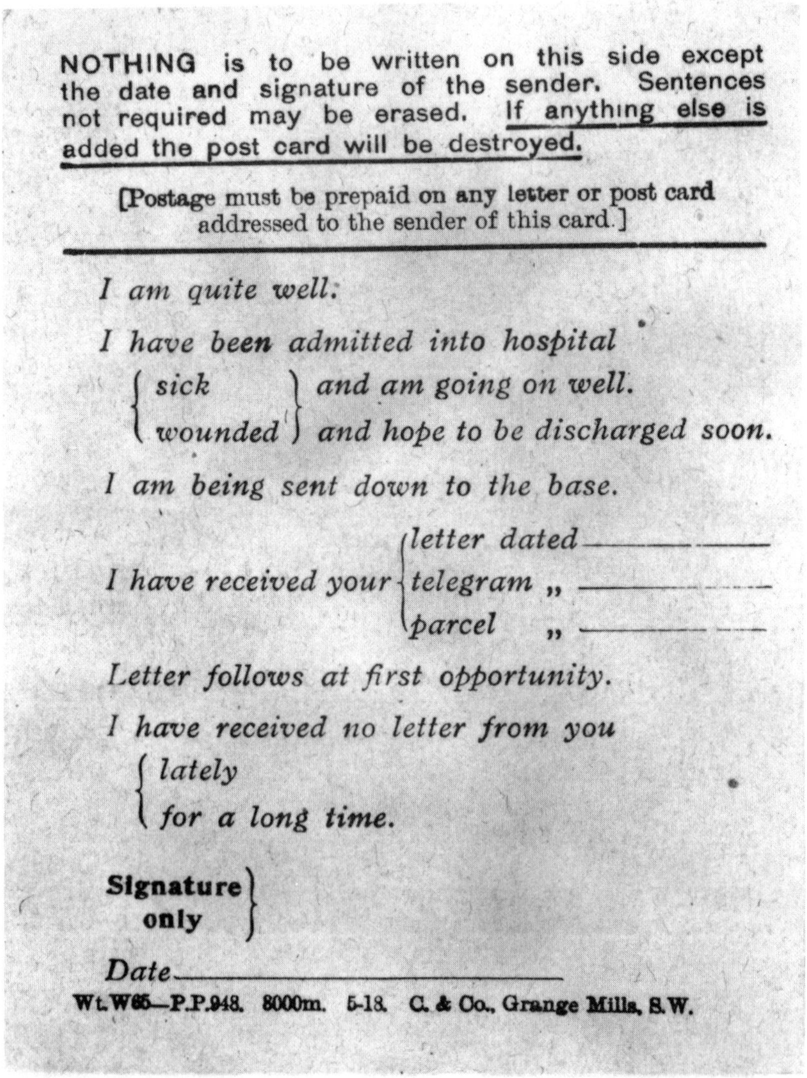

NOTHING is to be written on this side except the date and signature of the sender. Sentences not required may be erased. If anything else is added the post card will be destroyed.

[Postage must be prepaid on any letter or post card addressed to the sender of this card.]

I am quite well.

I have been admitted into hospital

{ sick } and am going on well.
{ wounded } and hope to be discharged soon.

I am being sent down to the base.

I have received your { letter dated _____
{ telegram „ _____
{ parcel „ _____

Letter follows at first opportunity.

I have received no letter from you

{ lately
{ for a long time.

Signature
only }

Date _____

Wt. W65—P.P.948. 8000m. 5-18. C. & Co., Grange Mills, S.W.

Figure 1. Field Service Post Card (*Imperial War Museum*).

ideas attached to the Field Service Post Card, the first wartime printing of which, in November, 1914, was one million copies" (186).

The Field Service Post Card constituted one way in which the British government tried to narrate the story of combat in advance, on behalf of, and over any possible objections of, the actual participants. The terms were stated clearly at the top of the card: "NOTHING is to be written on this side except the date and signature of the sender. Sentences not required may be erased. If anything else is added the post card will be destroyed." Beginning with the statement "I am quite well," the card consisted of a series of sentences that a soldier could let stand or cross out; the only writing involved in the transmission of such a message consisted of adding the date and one's signature to the form.

Certain of the Field Service Card's statements were acknowledged as mutually exclusive: one could not be both in the hospital and on one's way to the base; one could not both *have* received and *not* have received a letter recently from any one individual. To "erase" (cross out) some of the "sentences not required" was thus permissible. Multiple-choice logic governed the allowable editing of these postcards: one could choose between options A, B, or C, but there was no "D—Other," no blank space inviting descriptions of any experience outside the defined version. The real act of erasure, then, was not the crossing out of sentences but the prohibition against using the margins of the card to delineate anything that happened beyond its margins. Thin formulations of official communication constituted the representational limits of the Field Service Card, protecting the imaginative limits of civilians to whom thousands of them were mailed.

The postcard thus dictated that, for many civilians, one familiar verbal shape of combat would be constituted as a series of matter-of-fact sentences covering the whereabouts of the soldier and the mail he exchanged with those at home. The first three statements sketch out the spaces of war—trench, hospital, base. However, while hospital and base are named explicitly ("I have been admitted into hospital," "I am being sent down to the base"), the space of the trenches is designated only by the first sentence: "I am quite well." This assertion of health and good spirits, in essence, erases the trenches: the front line (already a metaphor for what is really a ditch) was not one of the options a soldier had to draw on in his description of where he found himself. Perhaps the combatants' slang for the Field Service Post Card—"whizz bang" (Fussell 183)—constituted an attempt to mail home a more accurate sense of front-line experience: "whizz-bang" was also a "light shell fired from one of the smaller field-artillery guns" (Brophy and Partridge 178), so that to send home a bland postcard was also, in a sense, to send home a letter bomb.

Wallace Stevens wrote modernist poems in Hartford, Connecticut, well cushioned from World War I. Yet his alertness to the ways in which language shapes the world we inhabit cuts to the central premise of this book. If the postcards that Great War soldiers mailed home display the enforcement of official mufflings of the war, Stevens's poem "A Postcard from the Volcano" (published in *Ideas of Order*, 1935) suggests the radical potential of words to register war's dislocations.

At a bare minimum, Field Service Post Cards communicated the information that a particular individual was alive; "A Postcard from the Volcano" undermines that minimal premise. Here are no individual signatures but a chorus of voices; here are writers not alive but dead. The "volcano" from which Stevens's card is posted does delineate a space appropriate both to the experience of soldiers (facing violent fire; emotionally petrified) and to the experience of dead volcano victims (remembering violent fire; physically petrified). But the postcards of Great War soldiers were mailed from one physical space to another (from the volcano of the war to the safety of home), whereas in Stevens's poem, speakers mail their postcards from one imaginative space to another: the dead mail this postcard from the live volcano of the past to living readers who inhabit the dead volcano of the present.

In Stevens's poem, the spaces of the dead and the living overlap; the world of the dead speakers is temporally rather than spatially distant—inaccessible not because of miles between or censored description, but because its inhabitants are long gone, far in the past. They have become bones scattered on a hill, collected by children all unaware "that these were once / As quick as foxes on the hill . . ." (*Collected Poems* 158–59). The voices explain that, despite the restrictions of textual space imposed by a postcard and of imaginative space imposed by the passage of years, they are able to express their lost world because their experience was embedded in their language: they have imprinted themselves on the landscape in ways that may be less discernible than bones but that are ultimately more profound. Though children cannot imagine that the bones of these dead ever articulated skeletons like their own, ever hung muscles and walked shoes just as their own bones do, they nevertheless speak the speech of the dead. The experience of the dead has been preserved in their idioms—their vernacular of perception.

The poem is riddled with gaps: pauses, ellipses, and, most conspicuously, the blank spaces separating its three-line stanzas. These blanks feel significant:

> And least will guess that with our bones
> We left much more, left what still is
> The look of things, left what we felt
>
> At what we saw.

Into the space between the feelings of the speakers and their reference to what they saw fall the images no longer available to us, the unrecoverable experience of the speakers. Despite the inaccessibility figured by the blank space separating "what we felt" and "what we saw," however, the voices don't give up on communication entirely. The mansion that still presides

over the landscape of the poem is one with which they were familiar and
which is described as having soaked up their words:

> We knew for long the mansion's look
> And what we said of it became
>
> A part of what it is . . .

Once again, the typographical blank space between stanzas reminds us of
the distance between "what we said" and "what it is"—the space between past and present, the time during which all the poem's speakers not
only died but were reduced to bones. In addition, the ellipses trailing off
after the assertion that words from the past help constitute a building in
the present point toward the simultaneous absence and presence of the
speakers' experience. That experience is lost, yet it leaves an identifiable
trace still discernible in the architecture of the mansion, now constituted,
at least in part, by "what we said of it." The children who at the beginning of the poem are pictured as collecting the bones of the dead speakers

> Will speak our speech and never know,
>
> Will say of the mansion that it seems
> As if he that lived there left behind
> A spirit storming in blank walls,
>
> A dirty house in a gutted world.

Now, more than seventy-five years after the end of the Great War, we
find ourselves in the position of the children that Stevens's poem
describes—inheritors of a literary and cultural past of which we are im-
perfectly conscious. Like the children who pick up bones without stopping to consider that they once strung nerves and housed passions, we
read modernism without fully realizing the extent to which it handles the
bones of the war dead. And like the children who unwittingly speak the
speech of the dead, those of us conversant in the idioms of modernism
are, I would argue, only dimly aware of some of their important origins in
the trenches of the Great War.

Stevens's empty mansion, with its "spirit storming in blank walls,"
provides an appropriate image of our erasure of the war from the structures of modernism. Our only access to that spirit, our only method of
filling in the blanks of those walls, is by returning to the language left
behind—the verbal legacy bequeathed to us by the dead:

> And what we said of it became
>
> A part of what it is . . .

This book attempts to trace how what the dead said of it became part of
what the mansion is—how what soldiers said of the Great War has become part of what modernism is.

THE SHAPES OF BODIES

ONE

CORPSELESSNESS

[handwritten marginal note, top right: "Also as well as"]

[handwritten note above paragraph: "Why War Memorials have become so important."]

[handwritten marginal note, right side: "Civilians distanced from death; never seeing bodies"]

The extremely restricted space within which trench warfare was fought simultaneously ensured that Great War soldiers would live with the corpses of their friends and that British civilians would not see dead soldiers. Soldiers buried their dead and then encountered them again ("Shells disinter the bodies, then reinter them . . ." [Vansittart 95]), but British policy dictated that the civilian bereaved would never have anything to bury. Soldiers inhabited a world of corpses; British civilians experienced the death of their soldiers as corpselessness. In England, then, World War I created two markedly different categories of experience, a discrepancy that complicated the gap that always separates language from experience. While verbal descriptions of war can never wholly convey the physical experience of war, the discontinuity between the experience of soldiers and of civilians—between death experienced as corpses and death experienced as corpselessness—meant that civilians were in a position to speak about death and to speak about soldiers without ever seeing dead soldiers.

Samuel Hynes has pointed out that the First World War marked a technological turning point in what it meant to be a civilian during war: "[F]or the first time in history non-combatants at home could *see* the war. The invention of the half-tone block had made it possible to print photographs in newspapers, and so to bring realistic-looking images into every house in England" (120). But, as he goes on to explain, it was forbidden to photograph corpses or scenes of actual combat and, beginning in 1916, amendments to the Defence of the Realm Act had the effect of making "any expression of opposition to, or criticism of, the war in any art form . . . a criminal offence" (80). Hynes gives a fascinating account of a documentary film produced by the Committee on War Films called *Battle of the Somme*. In this wildly popular movie, the most famous scene (and the only representation of death) involves one soldier sliding back down into a trench while his companions continue "over the top" and into no man's land. This "death," however, is the one scene in the film that is not authentic. Filmmakers staged it—a staging that speaks tellingly of exactly how much civilians were allowed to see. There is no blood here, no wound—just a silent, downward slide. This piece of theater constituted for civilians, according to Hynes, one of the most widespread and deeply memorable images of a war "corpse."

A civilian population whose ideas of war were shaped by such a corpse provides the context in which combatant fantasies of shoving dead bodies in the faces of bewildered civilians must be understood, since for many soldiers, it was the actuality of dead bodies that rendered the abstract vocabulary of patriotism ludicrous and infuriating. Reeking corpses at Gallipoli "haunted" a young subaltern who later testified that "henceforward I was proof against all the clichés about 'sacrifice,' 'glory,' and 'never sheathing the sword.' All such expressions were for me now permanently tainted by the thought of those vigorous young bodies, turned into objects of horror" (De Sola Pinto 73). Similarly, the ambulance driver in Helen Zenna Smith's *Not So Quiet . . .* insists (but only in her imagination) that her patriotic mother come with her: "Let me show you the exhibits straight from the battlefield. This will be something to tell your committees." She then begins to describe the men on stretchers in her ambulance, drawing nearer and nearer to the wounds and becoming more and more graphic in her descriptions. Finally, describing what she sees on the last stretcher, she tells of a "gibbering, unbelievable, unbandaged thing, a wagging lump of raw flesh on a neck that was a face a short time ago" (95).

I will argue in this chapter that when the British government used regulations to wipe the home front clean of corpses, they unwittingly wiped away something else: the British soldier's sense of home. The fracture between combatant experience and civilian perception of the war ensured a combatant alienation so profound that the idea of a homecoming became impossible. Eventually, in the delayed outpouring of combatant accounts of the war, soldiers brought back those corpses by naming them in their disturbingly explicit descriptions of combat. By recreating the experience of the war as accurately as they could, soldiers began to mend the representational gap between front and home front by articulating that gap. Once civilians could begin to realize the space that separated them from soldiers, soldiers could begin to feel at home again. In other words, veterans' accounts of the war may be understood as effecting a reclamation of home.

The geographical positioning that separated British civilians from the war was not just a matter of concern to individual alienated soldiers. In fact, the proper place of civilians in war may be understood as one of the fundamental issues that prompted Britain's entry into the war. Germany's position on the matter was articulated in the policy known as *Kriegsver-rat*, which held that "disruption of the war by civilians in occupied terri-tory is as treasonous as disruption by one's own nationals" (Eksteins 158). *Kriegsverrat* insisted that when Belgian civilians resisted an invad-ing army, they were tampering in politics in the same way that a traitor does and playing according to the same high stakes. Germany used this policy to justify the killing of hundreds of Belgian civilians during its invasion, arguing that the civilians were, in essence, fair game. Britain, on the other hand, interpreted Germany's treatment of Belgian civilians as "incontrovertible evidence . . . of German inhumanity." As a result, "'[P]oor little Belgium' and 'crucified Belgium' were the principal rallying cries in the mobilization of British prowar sentiment" (Eksteins 158).

England's outrage was premised on an idea that war should adhere to a rigid spatial logic: guns should be restricted to the territory of the battlefield; civilians should not be victimized by the violence of combat. Germany, however, had no such spatial logic, as *Kriegsverrat* demon-strated. To the degree that Germany's refusal to respect the distinction between soldier and civilian fueled British support for the war, England may be understood as fighting to ratify a structure of war, to confirm an interrelated set of conceptual and geographical rules. Although German combatants felt as alienated from civilians at home as British combatants did, Germany's political policy was designed to *blend* soldiers and civil-ians in the project of total war, while England's was designed to keep soldiers and civilians separate.

According to Trevor Wilson, the English response to German air raids on Britain demonstrates this same insistence on the separation of soldiers and civilians. In *The Myriad Faces of War,* Wilson painstakingly documents the German zeppelin and aeroplane raids on English targets: 700 casualties in December 1914 when three east coast towns were shelled; 7 killed and 35 injured in London, April 1915 (156–57); and so on. The most casualties inflicted by a single air raid occurred when Gotha aeroplanes and Riesen aircraft bombed London in 1917: 162 civilians were killed and 432 were injured (509). By November of that year, air raids had "seriously disrupted the lives of many Londoners" (509). Some families began to spend their nights in tube stations; many who could afford to left the city altogether. Wilson sums up his careful description of the air raids this way: "For all the attention they aroused, the large majority of Britons were not in danger from them. Punch felt called upon to remark in October [1917]: 'the space which our Press allots to Air Raids moves Mr. Punch to wonder and scorn. Our casualties from that source are never one-tenth so heavy as those in France on days when G.H.Q. reports "everything quiet on the Western front"'" (510). Wilson concurs with Punch: "The stress on air raids in the Press reflected a deeply held conviction among the public that a clear divide ought to exist between the warrior and the civilian—especially the civilian as woman and child. The fighting man was equipped for battle and so was eligible for death therein. The civilian had no place in combat and therefore should be exempt from its slaughter" (510).

For many civilians, the distinction between soldiers and civilians extended beyond political or rhetorical formulations, insinuating itself into the actual experience of war casualties. Particularly in England, where official policy dictated that soldiers be buried at the front and where guns, though often audible, were not generally a threat to the civilian population, the confrontation of war corpses was limited almost exclusively to soldiers. While the shock of war in 1914 galvanized the entire British culture, then, a combination of geography and reticence drew a circle around the shock of dead bodies, protecting civilians from their impact.

Civilian modernists were, of course, not in a position to recreate the experience of war. Instead, they handled the problem of the absent corpse by inventing architectural shapes to stand in the place of those absent bodies. I see these modernist houses as a gesture of provision—an offer of imaginative shelter to veterans tortured by a sense of homelessness. In *Jacob's Room*, Virginia Woolf returns again and again to architectural space as a visual strategy for displaying absence. This novel stands as the central example of the representational impulse I attempt to locate across an array of writers, but, as I try to show by a brief survey of other instances, architecture supplied many modernist writers with a vocabulary for articulating loss.

In 1916, the British government decided that soldiers would be buried where they died; families would not have the right to demand the return of combatants' bodies for burial (Curl 319). Around the same time, the introduction of conscription changed the group that constituted military families. In its War Graves issue commemorating the tenth anniversary of the armistice, the *Times* of London described how, suddenly, "British soldiers were men whose parents or wives had not accepted, as one of the conditions of a professional soldier's career, the possibility of an unknown grave in a foreign country; [and] their relatives poignantly and insistently demanded, and it was the desire of a sympathetic Adjutant-General in the Field to supply them with, the fullest information as to the location of the graves of those who fell" ("Imperial" vi).

A succession of organizations were responsible for supplying this information. In October 1914, Lord Kitchener requested that a mobile unit of the British Red Cross conduct a search for the missing; that request led eventually to the establishment of the Graves Registration Commission. The Commission, which had a nebulous military status, was soon replaced by the Directorate of Graves Registration and

[handwritten in left margin: Importance of War Memorial.]

Enquiries—an official branch of the Army. Finally, in 1917, the Prince of Wales granted a Royal Charter to an organization that continued the work of commemoration for years after the war—the Imperial War Graves Commission ("Imperial" vi). That the *Times* ran a War Graves Number on the tenth anniversary of the armistice speaks to the continuing British concern for marking, scrupulously and reverently, places all over the world where the bodies of British Great War soldiers lay.

During the war, information about graves was always delayed and frequently difficult to come by at all. The dead on the western front were buried on battlefields or in cemetery plots acquired from France and Belgium—near trenches or behind the lines. In the violent confusion of an active front line or in the chaos of an understaffed casualty clearing station, soldiers and nurses, comrades and hospital staffers rapidly became familiar with the project of burying corpses. According to the *Times*, the Canadian attack on Vimy Ridge established the pattern for burial of the dead. Before the attack, "[O]f their own initiative and with the assistance of the Directorate [of Graves Registration and Enquiries,] . . . [the Canadians] had marked out land, dug trenches, and made all arrangements for the burial of the killed in the forthcoming action. Within twenty-four hours of that brilliant and successful feat of arms the graves were each marked and recorded. . . . Thence onwards throughout the War a similar system was adopted on most sectors of the Front as part of the normal preparation for any attack. . . . [O]ne saw no more scenes such as that on the Somme battlefields, where 50,000 scattered white crosses, placed on the graves by the *personnel* of the Directorate following up the slow advance, stood broadcast among the shell holes and the poppies and the dishevelled earth" ("Imperial" vi).

Erich Maria Remarque's *All Quiet on the Western Front* mentions this practice of preparing for an offensive with coffins: "There are rumours of an offensive. We go up to the front two days earlier than usual. On the way, we pass a shelled school-house. Stacked up against its longer side is a high double wall of yellow, unpolished, brand-new coffins. There are at least a hundred. 'That's a good preparation for the offensive,' says Müller, astonished" (99). In *Not So Quiet . . .* , Helen Zenna Smith talks about funeral duty: "I have been conveying these flag-covered boxes for months now to the ugly little cemetery that scars the valley. . . . I have lost count of the number of times I have been a supernumerary in the last scene of the great war drama that opens daily in a recruiting office and drops its final curtain amid no applause on a plain deal coffin draped with a Union Jack, to the tune of 'The Last Post' from an orchestra of two" (116).

For the families of soldiers killed at the front, however, death was not a corpse at all but a series of verbal descriptions. Next of kin were informed of a casualty by a telegram, the terse language of which gave merely the date and location of death: "Regret to inform you Captain

E. H. Brittain M.C. killed in action Italy June 15th" (Brittain 438). The telegram was frequently followed by letters from friends and/or commanding officers, who gave more precise details about the location and circumstances of death. Certainly whenever possible, but sometimes in spite of actual circumstances, these letters included assurances that bereaved parents and widows ought to rest safe in the knowledge that their sons or husbands had died honorably, even heroically.

Combatants were surprisingly conscientious about composing such condolences, though apparently somewhat less conscientious about conforming their descriptions to the actual circumstances of death, as "The Leveller" by Robert Graves testifies. In this poem, a baby-faced eighteen-year-old and a whiskered world rover are fatally wounded by the same shell. The elder man "had known death and hell before / In Mexico and Ecuador."

> Yet in his death this cut-throat wild
> Groaned "Mother! Mother!" like a child,
> While that poor innocent in man's clothes
> Died cursing God with brutal oaths.
>
> Old Sergeant Smith, kindest of men,
> Wrote out two copies there and then
> Of his accustomed funeral speech
> To cheer the womenfolk of each:—
>
> *"He died a hero's death: and we*
> *His comrades of 'A' Company*
> *Deeply regret his death: we shall*
> *All deeply miss so true a pal."*
>
> (reprinted in Gardner 93–94)

The speaker does not qualify his report of Sergeant Smith's account with criticism for the way it collapses the differences between the two deaths. It is taken as a given that surviving comrades send off opaque missives, indeed "leveling" all deaths at the front.

Both fictional and nonfictional accounts of the war document the pressure to produce narratives of heroism, as well as the importance of these letters from the front to civilians. In her autobiographical *Testament of Youth*, Vera Brittain describes the way she pored over the letters from comrades describing the death of her fiancé, desperately wishing to place him, too, in the ranks of the heroic and searching for any scrap of evidence that he had thought of her in the last moments of his life. Unfortunately, Roland had died in the course of mundane duty as a member of a wire-cutting party, and neither her visits to chums of his in the hospital nor written requests to men who had fought beside him produced any indication that he had been aware of anything at his death, other than his own excruciating pain.

In *All Quiet on the Western Front,* Paul Bäumer accepts the obligation of letter-writing that the death of a childhood friend requires. He knows Kemmerich's mother and witnesses her son's death; writing a letter to her is therefore understood as inevitable. Corpse, mother, and letter stand side by side in his mind: "This forehead with its hollow temples, this mouth that now seems all teeth, this sharp nose! And the fat, weeping woman at home to whom I must write. If only the letter were sent off already!" (30). Later, while on leave, Bäumer refuses to admit to Mrs. Kemmerich that her son did not die instantly and painlessly. Though the old woman insists that she wants to know the truth, he insists that "I will never tell her, she can make mincemeat out of me first. I pity her, but she strikes me as rather stupid all the same. Why doesn't she stop worrying? Kemmerich will stay dead whether she knows about it or not" (181).[1]

But civilians did want—or thought they wanted—to know about it. Mrs. Wheeler in Willa Cather's *One of Ours* clings to the letters of her son and his comrades, which describe Claude's courage in battle. During the "dark months" following his death, "[W]hen human nature looked to her uglier than it had ever done before, those letters were Mrs. Wheeler's comfort. . . . When she can see nothing that has come of it all but evil, she reads Claude's letters over again and reassures herself; for him the call was clear, the cause was glorious. Never a doubt stained his bright faith" (389–90). Vera Brittain similarly agonized over the details of her fiancé's death, even though his was an ordinary casualty, not a heroic one. That her fiancé was killed during the course of routine duty made it more difficult for Brittain to make sense of his death, though she makes a valiant attempt: "'All heroism,' I argued desperately in my diary, 'is to a certain extent unnecessary from a purely utilitarian point of view'" (243).

Such scrupulous attention to the way in which an incident was articulated and then interpreted was a common preoccupation among civilians agonizing over written accounts of front-line casualties, as they struggled to draw some meaning from the deaths of men they cared for. Because no corpse ever arrived for memorial service and burial, because—during the war, at least—no grave was accessible to receive flowers or epitaph, the days immediately following news of a death were days spent reading about and interpreting death, instead of confronting and commemorating physical evidence of it. And since making sense of death was a matter of textual interpretation, the vocabulary that had traditionally bestowed meaning upon war deaths—words like "heroism" and "honor"—became extremely important.

For civilians who did not have loved ones in the war, casualty lists, rather than telegrams and letters, constituted their home-front experience of war deaths. Posted on buildings and printed on the front page of the *Times,* names of the dead, listed in small type, were the perpetual front-page story. Casualty lists were thus, to civilians, the daily representation of war's physical consequences. The distance between this representation and the reality of corpses in no man's land is illustrated by Brittain's comment on the Battle of Loos. Brittain, a V.A.D. (Voluntary Aid Detachment) nurse, would have had no illusions about the physical details "Wounded in Action" or "Recovering from Wounds" represented. Her comment on Loos, however, is that "[t]he country, though growing accustomed to horror, staggered at the devastating magnitude of the cost of Loos. Even now, eighteen years afterwards, September 25th remains with July 1st and March 21st, one of the three dates on which the '*In Memoriam*' notices in *The Times* fill the whole of one column and run onto the next" (200).

Clearly, Brittain is not attempting to downplay the devastating number of Loos casualties; on the contrary, she indicates that civilians are stunned by the dimensions of the typeset columns. That she chooses to illustrate public dismay at the physical cost of Loos by describing how much space names take up on a page of newsprint reminds us, however, of the ease with which we learn to glide over gaps between material reality and verbal representations of that reality. She could easily have conjured up grisly images of what two columns of ink pointed to across the Channel, as she does elsewhere in her descriptions of nursing: "After the Somme I had seen men without faces, without eyes, without limbs, men almost disembowelled, men with hideous truncated stumps of bodies" (339). Instead, however, she chooses to speak of front-line death as English civilians actually experienced it during the war: not as shells, blood, and wounds but as ink, paper, and words—not as corpses but as corpselessness.

Given the unselfconsciousness with which civilians occupied a territory free of dead soldiers, their quests for information about specific deaths at the front and distress over the government's decision not to return bodies to England for burial seem slightly incongruous. For, perhaps unwittingly but nonetheless insistently, civilians took pains to ensure that their home-front landscape remained free of corpses, populated only by bright images of glory, which propaganda certainly supplied and encouraged but which families took up with enthusiasm. In Brittain's *Testament,* a bereaved mother displays just such a preference for the shining symbols rather than the bloody relics of war when she receives in the mail a package containing the clothes and army kit of her dead son and orders her husband to get rid of them: "[D]on't let me see them again: I must either burn or bury them. They smell of death; they are not Roland; they even seem to detract from his memory and spoil his glamour. I won't have anything more to do with them!" (252).

Not wishing to keep the clothes a son was killed in is understandable. But, in her fastidious disposal of evidence, Roland's mother suggests the zealousness with which the British public ignored and suppressed the physical details of an unbelievably gruesome war. Eventually, representations of death stray so far from the reality of trench warfare that they begin to seem—as they seemed to many soldiers at the time—like a civilian conspiracy of incomprehension.

Such incomprehension is camouflaged by language that allows civilians to sound as if they are speaking about the war as actually fought without accepting any obligation to make their words fit the avowed subject. Siegfried Sassoon fantasizes avenging such verbal irresponsibility in "'Blighters,'" a trenchant poem that puns on "show," a word meaning "attack" in military slang. Here, the flippant "audience" chortles over tanks—gleefully watching the "show" without, of course, having to confront the physical consequences of military technology. In other words, they celebrate corpses while keeping them at bay:

> The House is crammed: tier beyond tier they grin
> And cackle at the Show, while prancing ranks
> Of harlots shrill the chorus, drunk with din;
> "We're sure the Kaiser loves our dear old Tanks!"

Having set up this biting picture of war hysteria, the combatant speaker steps into the poem himself, fiercely swearing that

> I'd like to see a Tank come down the stalls,
> Lurching to rag-time tunes, or "Home, sweet Home,"
> And there'd be no more jokes in Music-halls
> To mock the riddled corpses round Bapaume.

(reprinted in Gardner 115)

This poem illustrates how language colludes in the civilian habit of replacing war with a set of relatively innocuous words and images. While soldiers, not civilians, were undoubtedly responsible for the invention of the pun "show" in the first place, and while their intentions may well have been euphemistic or at least grimly humorous, it is the flippancy with which civilians ignore the gap between language and experience that infuriates the poet. Again, like the mother erasing evidence of war's filth, the political irresponsibility lies not in the occupation of the safe side of the pun (a civilian show), but in blindness to its dark and dangerous side (a military show).

A further complication of civilians' experience of disembodied death arose from the fact that huge numbers of soldiers simply disappeared on the battlefields of World War I. In a conflict where shell explosions could create, as Modris Eksteins has pointed out, craters the size of swimming pools, such unaccounted-for bodies are not hard to understand. The large number of missing men, however, widened the gap between combatant and civilian experiences of death even further than the discrepancy between corpses and corpselessness did. "Missing" would have one meaning to the medical officer of the 2nd Royal Welch Fusiliers who wrote that "[a] signaller had just stepped out, when a shell burst on him, leaving not a vestige that could be seen anywhere near" (qtd. in Keegan 264) and quite another meaning to a frantic mother clinging to the ordinary verbal distinction between "missing" and "dead." As often as civilians might tell themselves that "[m]issing *always* means dead" (Kipling, "The Gardener" 344), the equation for them could never be anything but a verbal one. They could hardly be blamed for consulting their own experience on this matter, which would have told them that there *is* a difference between missing and dead and that to be labeled "missing" *rather* than "dead" justifies a certain amount of hope.

At the front, however, two soldiers who have a conversation about how a trench mortar will blow a man out of his clothes would understand that "missing" is not a euphemism for "dead" but rather a way of dying. "I search around," one of them says. "And so it is. Here hang bits of uniform, and somewhere else is plastered a bloody mess that was once a human limb. Over there lies a body with nothing but a piece of the underpants on one leg and the collar of the tunic around its neck. Otherwise it is naked and the clothes are hanging up in the tree. Both arms are missing as though they had been pulled out. I discover one of them twenty yards off in a shrub" (Remarque 208). Such a corpse might well be listed in the newspaper as "Missing." The distance separating a civilian's from this speaker's comprehension of what it means to be missing, though, illustrates the distance separating front from home front, soldier from civilian, the territory of corpses from the territory of corpselessness.

For soldiers, the erasure of corpses from the home front constituted a painful erasure of home itself. In their chatty dictionary of Great War slang (1930), John Brophy and Eric Partridge discuss soldiers' vocabulary of home in their entry on the word "Blighty." For British soldiers, "Blighty" meant "England, in the sense of home. In this one word was gathered all the soldier's homesickness and affection and war-weariness. . . . *Blighty* to the soldier was a sort of faerie, a paradise which he could faintly remember, a never-never land. The word was also used as an adjective, not merely for things English and homelike, but as a general expression of approval" (99–100). As contemporary readers, we may wince at the credulous tone of this entry. Our intuitive comprehension of what the safety and familiarity of civilian life must mean to any soldier in any war, though, confirms the poignancy with which this definition describes a Tommy's ache for home, so we tolerantly chalk up phrases like "never-never land" to the innocence of another age.

Robert Graves, also a veteran of World War I, discusses "Blighty" in *Good-bye to All That.* With typical gruffness, he suggests that an English soldier's relationship to Britain was as likely to be tense and complicated as it was to be sentimental. The proverbial ache for home may even have been laced with hostility:

As Blighty, Great Britain was a quiet, easy place to get back to out of the present foreign misery, but as a nation it was nothing. The nation included not only the trench-soldiers themselves and those who had gone home wounded, but the staff, Army Service Corps, lines of communication troops, base units, home-service units, and then civilians down to the detested grades of journalists, profiteers, "starred" men exempted from enlistment, conscientious objectors, members of the Government. (230)

From Graves's description of this "carefully graded caste-system of honour" (230) begins to emerge the complexity of what Brophy and Partridge call a soldier's "homesickness and affection and war-weariness": men exempted from enlistment are deemed slightly better than conscientious objectors but somewhat worse than the detested journalists, and so on.

It is not the specifics of hierarchy that are striking in the Graves passage so much as the intense ambivalence upon which they are premised. He takes as a given that patriotism is far from monolithic and that antagonism is not reserved for belligerents of the opposing country. Combatants distribute their loyalties to the noncombatant population across a range of detailed judgments regarding what does and does not constitute acceptable involvement in the war.

"Enemies?" a female ambulance driver in Not So Quiet . . . asks facetiously. "Our enemies aren't the Germans. Our enemies are the politicians we pay to keep us out of war and who are too damned inefficient to do their jobs properly" (Smith 55). National hostilities—the "us" versus "them" dualism inherent to war's structure—are both fractured and repeated in the mixture of affection and animosity soldiers feel for their own country. That "blighty" was also slang for "a wound which would send you back to 'Blighty,' the soldier slang word for England" (De Sola Pinto 76) speaks to the fierce pain such ambivalence engenders: England itself becomes the wound that war inflicts on its participants.

Graves is critical of home while Brophy and Partridge are sentimental about it, yet the difference between their attitudes may seem more a matter of temperament than loyalty. The diaries, memoirs, and novels of many veterans suggest, however, that—regardless of temperament or loyalty—one of the most devastating consequences of fighting the war was combatants' discovery that the concept of "home" no longer existed as a geographical site. Instead, "home" merely registered a set of collapsing imaginative expectations. Eric Leed has observed how in "the experience of war the 'home' became more alien than any enemy" (213). In All Quiet on the Western Front, Paul Bäumer describes sitting by his mother's bed: "I breathe deeply and say over to myself:—'You are at home, you are at home.' But a sense of strangeness will not leave me" (Remarque 160). Such comments make clear the way in which the houses and neighborhoods of a combatant's civilian past ceased to provide the understandable context within which a soldier felt "at home."

One of the most dramatic symptoms of this slippage between the emotional and physical locations of home is soldiers' descriptions of Britain as a foreign place. English combatants spent much of the Great War living among speakers of French and fighting against speakers of German. Decidedly unbilingual, they achieved a certain notoriety for their verbal corruptions—turning "Ypres," for example, into "Wipers" and "*ça ne fait rien*" into "san fairy ann" (Brophy and Partridge 180–81, 158). Yet when veterans returned to England, the language of civilians there seems to have become as inaccessible as the language of the French or the Germans must have been at the front. Graves tells how "England was strange to the returned soldier. He could not understand the war-madness that ran about everywhere looking for a pseudo-military outlet. Everyone talked a foreign language; it was newspaper language" (271). Bäumer's conclusion that "I do not belong here any more, it is a foreign world" (Remarque 168) testifies to the fact that German soldiers experienced the same disturbing alienation. Rabid civilian militarism and home-front incomprehension of trench warfare's physical realities helped, along with the array of complicating factors that Graves lists, to ensure that soldiers would feel alienated enough by the civilian population to alter their conceptions of home accordingly. That a territory filled with just such a collection of civilians should still be called "home" became inconceivable.

Even if home no longer existed as a fixed place on the map to which soldiers could with confidence return, they still clung to the psychological stability the concept represented. Bäumer demonstrates the flexibility displayed by combatants who, disillusioned with the war mania of civilians, lifted their emotional attachment to home away from its previous moorings and resituated it within a military context. For them, home was no longer the hills of childhood, the playing fields of school, or the addresses of relatives; it became instead a place behind the line, a group of comrades, the sound of familiar voices within earshot of a foxhole. When one of Bäumer's friends, for instance, nervously confesses that he wishes he were home, Bäumer explains, for the reader's benefit, that by "[h]ome— he means the huts" (65). And when Bäumer himself is trapped in no man's land and feels panic rising, he calms himself by concentrating on the voices of the men he can hear in his own trenches not far from where he lies. Like a child listening to the voices of his parents at night, the soldier asserts that "[t]hey are more to me than life, these voices, they are more than motherliness and more than fear; they are the strongest, most comforting thing there is anywhere: they are the voices of my comrades" (212).

Graves's nonfiction and Remarque's fiction, taken together, suggest how combatants (both English and German) abandoned geography as the delineator of loyalty, replacing it with shared experience. Prewar definitions of home disappeared into the space that separated the radically different experiences of soldiers and civilians. But if the notion of home lost a world of materiality in the imaginative maneuver that allowed a soldier to call his hut at the front "home," it at least retained a modicum of emotional legitimacy.

Civilians experienced corpselessness, as I have described it, through two categories of artifacts, each with a different relation to the absent corpse. The first category included official representations of war—government letters, postcards, telegrams, and casualty lists, all of which to differing degrees evaded the inaccessible corpse, protecting civilians from gruesome physical facts by allowing them to verbalize a disembodied death. The second category of artifacts generated by corpselessness were those invented by artists and architects—the modernist fiction and the war memorials that pointed toward corpses buried elsewhere, providing proxies for those bodies that were simultaneously absent and present, physically gone but stunningly felt in psychological and emotional terms. By constructing substitutes for absent corpses, these artifacts moved toward closing one of the most important gaps separating the experience of soldiers and civilians.

When Lloyd George approached Sir Edwin Lutyens about the project of designing a temporary memorial to be erected in Whitehall for the July 1919 Peace Celebrations, he suggested building a "catafalque." Lutyens, however, immediately responded that a "cenotaph" would be a more appropriate monument. Presence or absence of a corpse constitutes the essential distinction between catafalque and cenotaph: a catafalque is a platform made to hold a coffin, while a cenotaph is a memorial to someone whose corpse lies elsewhere. Lutyens's suggestion accurately reflects British concern for inventing forms capable of memorializing the specific trauma of national bereavement: a million young men, vanished.

At quarter to twelve on the day of the July 19, 1919, Peace Celebrations, four soldiers, the *Times* reported, took their positions at the corners of the Cenotaph (figure 1.1). With "the elaborate movements of ceremonial drill, [they] reversed their rifles, crossed their hands on the butts, and stood with lowered heads. So they stayed, like images of military mourning, until at noon they were relieved with similar ceremony by four others, who maintained their attitude of respect without the visible tremor of a nerve until by 2 o'clock the procession had passed by" ("At the Cenotaph" 15). That these guardsmen were integral to the design of the memorial as Lutyens envisioned it becomes clear from his comments on suggestions that it be altered prior to the monument's permanent installation in Whitehall. "Many have suggested to me," he writes, "to place bronze figures, representing sentries, round it. This I would greatly regret: it would prevent living sentries being posted on days of ceremony" (qtd. in Hussey 394). Lutyens's wish to incorporate live yet tremorless soldiers into the design of the Cenotaph suggests that his notion of com-

Figure 1.1. The Cenotaph, Whitehall, London, designed by Sir Edwin Lutyens (British Architectural Library, RIBA, London).

memoration blends concepts we ordinarily think of as mutually exclu-sive: the guards must mimic the stony inaccessibility of the dead but not permanently, as sculptures would. They must fluctuate, ceremonially, between life and death.

The inscription on the Cenotaph is "The Glorious Dead," but by definition a cenotaph is about absence as well as death: it points toward a corpse, not here but elsewhere. By incorporating soldiers rather than statues into the design of the Cenotaph, Lutyens also affirms the comrade-ship between the dead, the living, and the missing. Corpses of soldiers are not merely remembered, they are ceremonially joined by living soldiers. The missing are referred to not obliquely but by the very nature of the artifact, which implicitly refers to inaccessible bodies. And the incorporation of living soldiers into the memorial at certain times and on certain days means that there will be other times and other days when there will be no bodies. Thus all the combinations of memory are enacted: imaginative presence and physical absence; corpses and corpselessness.

Guided by the same logic, architects for the Imperial War Graves Commission decided to combine memorials to the missing with British battle memorials rather than keeping separate the two kinds of commemoration. Though not explicitly articulated as such, their decision ensures that the missing are represented as having actively participated in the battle: monuments to their efforts are as integrated into the design of the whole commemorative landscape as the cemeteries adjoining most battle sites.[2] Just as the commission leveled distinctions of rank or differences based on performance during the war, they made sure that the missing were memorialized along with the accounted-for dead by treating each grave equally. Thus, not only are the graves of privates and captains, men killed eating soup and men killed cutting wire, marked with identical headstones,[3] but men who left corpses behind are commemorated side by side with men who were shattered into invisibility. The dead and the missing are equally represented as crucial to the war effort.[4]

The Cenotaph stands in the middle of Whitehall. Though it was suggested when the memorial was made permanent that it should be moved out of the path of traffic, Lutyens expressed his hope that it would remain where it was: "The site has been qualified by the salutes of folk and allied armies. No other site would give this pertinence" (qtd. in Hussey 394). Interestingly, many other Great War memorials also occupy busy, public sites rather than being sequestered in quiet areas like gardens, parks, or cemeteries. Town councils after the war wanted their memorials to stand at town centers, but often the best, most central spots were already occupied by statues commemorating important people in the community's history or by monuments to Queen Victoria. So, as one art historian sadly notes, sometimes a "war memorial was put in the middle of a principal thoroughfare, or at an important junction of streets, or in a space in front of a public building. Such sites, busy with frequent traffic, are hardly conducive to quiet contemplation, and after a short time the memorial becomes another familiar object of the busy town centre, and is rarely looked at" (Whittick 44). This historian obviously regrets the placement of memorials in the thick of traffic. Yet for them to stand as objects in the midst of everyday community routine may be understood as a siting decision similar to the one that combines cemeteries and memorials to the missing or posts live soldiers at the corners of the Cenotaph. By claiming a place at the center of a town's business district, a memorial *does* become a "familiar object"—just as the soldiers being commemorated would have been, had they not served in the war. Instead of dedicating a removed site to the project of reflecting upon death (a place probably only those with leisure would frequent), instead of cordoning off a special area for thinking about the past, the incorporation of memorials into the center of town life gives the dead their own place at that center.

Another architectural historian has remarked that the architects of World War I memorials were "anxious to avoid sculpture as much as possible, so that the ghastly angels and sentimental figure of French memorials could be eschewed. Architectural elements were of paramount importance" (Curl 319). Certainly, the artistically literate members of the commission (Sir Frederick Kenyon, Director of the British Museum, served in an advisory capacity) would have been glad to preempt the sculptural sentimentality of ghastly angels and weeping ladies. It also seems significant, though, that quite a number of the memorials to the missing, instead of being designed to contain something, serve primarily as the architectural boundaries of empty space. Just as Fabian Ware, founder of the War Graves Commission, insisted that the missing not be memorialized with headstones, since "[w]e have always opposed anything that might lead relatives to imagine that a body was buried when it was not there" (qtd. in Longworth 82), so the arches and walls in these memorials delineate space within which absence is allowed to impose itself as the dominant feature.

At Thiepval, in France, Lutyens designed a triumphal arch inscribed with the names of 73,501 soldiers missing from the Battle of the Somme (figure 1.2). While this gigantic monument certainly has a looming sculptural presence, its structure is geometrically organized according to a sequence of stacked arches framing empty space. The walls of the memorial thus give the names to be remembered a material but not an anthropomorphic form: absence is rendered in a way that constitutes gigantic presence.

Other important memorials are structurally analogous to the arch at Thiepval in their use of architectural idioms delineating empty space as central features of design. At Ploegsteert, in Belgium, for example, H. Charlton Bradshaw created "a circular colonnade that encloses an open space" (Curl 321; figure 1.3); Sir Herbert Baker's Tyne Cot Memorial at Passchendaele, in Belgium, is dominated by a series of recesses: it consists of a "semi-circular panelled wall in which are colonnaded openings, each of which forms the entrance to an apse" (Whittick 36; figure 1.4). Arcades at the Arras, Loos, and Pozières memorials in France (figures 1.5, 1.6, 1.7) are articulated by a combination of colonnades and walls, each of which delineates a corridor. These memorials to the missing thus allow the dead to preside over architectural spaces to which the living may pay their respects. While the dead body occupies a grave to which the living may attend, the missing body is marked by unoccupied space through which the living may stroll. Of course, there are also Great War memorials that function primarily as objects or as frames for objects rather than as boundaries of space, but the memorials just mentioned are certainly some of the most famous. With the exception of Ploegsteert, they are five of the six largest, and their collective walls hold the names of well over half the total number of British missing.

Bands in the festival parades of July 19, 1919, stopped playing when they passed the Cenotaph. Just as a sudden silence may mark the place where the voice of an absent friend belongs, that series of ceremonial pauses marked the place where a million British voices belonged. The spaces described by memorials to the missing in France and Belgium are bounded by walls of names, denoting the missing associated with each battleground: 73,501 at Thiepval; 11,449 at Ploegsteert; 34,957 at Tyne Cot; 35,938 at Arras; 20,702 at Loos; 14,695 at Pozières on the Somme ("Imperial" xi). Language and architecture collaborate to mark spaces symbolic of the vanished bodies of over 300,000 men. Few in the crowd, the *Times* reported, could "fail to feel the silence, broken only by their own cheering, which fell as each band, on nearing the cenotaph, stopped

Figure 1.2. Memorial to the Missing of the Somme at Thiepval, designed by Sir Edwin Lutyens (British Architectural Library, RIBA, London).

Figure 1.3. Memorial to the Missing at Ploegsteert, designed by H. Charlton Bradshaw (British Architectural Library, RIBA, London).

Figure 1.4. Tyne Cot Memorial to the Missing at Passchendaele, designed by Sir Herbert Baker (British Architectural Library, RIBA, London).

Figure 1.5. Arras Memorial to the Missing in the Flying Services at the Faubourg d'Amiens Cemetery, designed by Sir Edwin Lutyens (British Architectural Library, RIBA, London).

Figure 1.6. Loos Memorial to the Missing at Dud Corner Military Cemetery, designed by Sir Herbert Baker (British Architectural Library, RIBA, London).

Figure 1.7. Pozières Memorial to the Missing, designed by W. H. Cowlinshaw (British Architectural Library, RIBA, London).

playing" ("At the Cenotaph" 15). Memorials to the missing operate as the architectural analogues of those silences.

Lutyens's Cenotaph has been criticized for being "negative." It "looks back, not forward; there is no indication of that for which these sacrifices of the fighting men and others were made. It is as if the greatness of the theme made us inarticulate" (Whittick 7). Intended as criticism, Whittick's remarks eloquently articulate the quality of the Cenotaph and of memorials to Great War missing that make them so compelling—a quality more akin to a gasp of inarticulateness than to any congratulatory sentiment about the good that was gotten or the future that was fought for. It is the magnitude of the sacrifice that is striking when one confronts seventy thousand names of the sacrificed, when one walks through a structure built of those names and occupies a space that could not even begin to contain that many bodies but that nonetheless represents a place where each is commemorated individually.

The burial of dead soldiers separately rather than in a common grave represented a departure from a long historical tradition, as did commemoration of the individual dead rather than the collective victory.[5] The *Times* War Graves Number narrated the history of a family whose son's body was missing. Though acutely personal, it also expressed what may be understood as a national fantasy about the possibilities of building memorials to the missing, articulating the deep need of an entire country to commemorate every single life given up to a war of attrition: "When the long search [for his body] was done and proven fruitless, the parents bought land for a memorial on the battlefield. In digging for its foundations men found him" ("The Silent World" v). The intimacy between corpse and war memorial suggested by this anecdote speaks for the imaginative relationship that civilians drew between missing bodies and artifacts designed to commemorate them. If rescuing a corpse from the category of "missing" proved impossible, then the construction of architectural memorials was the next best thing. The two projects were thus intimately linked in the minds of the bereaved.

The urgency with which the civilian public insisted upon the erection of war memorials to the dead and missing suggests that the commemoration of absence demands at least a representation of presence. A corpse can be understood as representing the conflation of absence and presence, embodying proof both that a person is here and will never be here again; so a war memorial can be understood as a civilian perception of war death, one that includes absence but stands in need of presence. By serving as proxy for missing corpses, war memorials reconstruct the inherently contradictory relationship between life and death as we intuitively apprehend it through corpses: death can only occur at the site of life.

Architects designing war memorials invented a set of artifacts capable at once of standing as substitutes for the body and of providing a vocabulary for investigating the complexity of loss. Civilian writers were bound by no such program yet frequently fit their discussions of war into architectural contexts, creating images of houses that bridge—imaginatively, at least—the space separating English home from western front. In a 1915 essay called "Within the Rim," for instance, Henry James describes how his "house of the spirit" has been transformed from a modest abode into "an extravagant, bristling, flag-flying structure" by events occurring *beyond* the horizon's rim. "[T]o and fro one kept going," he confesses, "on the old rampart, the town 'look-out,' to spend one's aching wonder again and again on the bright sky-line that at once held and mocked it. Just over that line were unutterable things, massacre and ravage and anguish" (20). From within the protective circumference of Britain's "rim," James emphasizes that imagination constitutes the civilian's only method of construing war's enormity. Thus, "[I]magination had doubtless at every turn . . . more to say to one's state of mind, and dealt more with the whole unfolding scene, than any other contributive force" (21). James stresses both the impossibility of spanning the distance that protects those "within the rim" from war and the necessity nonetheless of trying to make imaginative compensation for what occurs beyond one's immediate purview. Renovating his "house of the spirit" results, then, in "building on additions and upper storys, throwing out extensions and protrusions, indulging even, all recklessly, in gables and pinnacles and battlements—things that had presently transformed the unpretending place into I scarce know what to call it" (20).

Whereas James emphasizes the speculative nature of his architectural alterations ("which had quite as much to do with the air as with the earth" [20]), D. H. Lawrence, in a doleful letter of 1915, piles up images of house, history, leaves, and soldiers' corpses as he envisions the collapse of British historical structures under the weight of the war dead:

> So much beauty and pathos of old things passing away and no new things coming: this house of the Ottolines—It is England—my God, it breaks my soul—this England, these shafted windows, the elm-trees, the blue distance—the past, the great past, crumbling down, breaking down . . . under the weight of many exhausted, lovely yellow leaves, that drift over the lawn and over the pond, like the soldiers, passing away, into winter and the darkness of winter—no, I can't bear it. ("To Lady Cynthia Asquith")

In this rendering of war's registration on an image of home-front architecture, the overwhelming effect depends on an innumerability of corpses; otherwise, "the weight of . . . yellow leaves" to which the corpses are compared hardly seems sufficient to cave in the house. Perhaps even more striking is the way in which the combination of leaves and soldiers captures the simultaneous materiality *and* immateriality of those corpses so threatening to the structures of British culture. Hauntingly present yet oppressively absent, the "passing away" of soldiers' bodies rocks the physical and emotional foundations of England as gently as falling leaves and as wrenchingly as falling bodies.

Rudyard Kipling, using metaphorical techniques similar to Lawrence's in his story "Mary Postgate" (1915), conflates the collapse of architecture with the impact of a bomb. Mary hears an "explosion" and then discovers a child's body in the rubble of a stable. But, as Dr. Hennis points out, "You might have been misled by the beams snapping. I've been looking at 'em. They were dry-rotted through and through. Of course, as they broke, they would make a noise just like a gun" (394). A civilian child thus becomes a casualty of architectural destruction much as civilians might be presumed to be threatened by the crumbling architecture Lawrence describes. Ambiguity regarding the cause of the child's death lifts the physical threat of war away from the remote battlefield and resituates it in an otherwise serene civilian context, much as Siegfried

Sassoon envisioned in the poem "'Blighters'" quoted earlier. Architecture becomes the site at which war may be imaginatively transformed into a civilian experience. Kipling would have been unlikely to consent to the inclusion of his story in a survey of modernist metaphorical techniques. But the striking preoccupation with ways in which architecture supplies a vocabulary and a set of images through which civilians can begin to articulate war is one that cuts across other distinctions separating the more experimental modernist works by authors such as Lawrence and Woolf from the more conventionally realist works by authors such as Kipling. This intersection of metaphorical strategy, I would argue, has less to do with the formal concerns of writers than with their status as civilians during the war years—a status that at times unites writers who differ stylistically in what I would argue is a modernist project.

This array of examples is by no means exhaustive. Ezra Pound's *Canto VII*, Virginia Woolf's *To the Lighthouse*, Edith Wharton's *Book of the Homeless*, George Bernard Shaw's *Heartbreak House*, and E. M. Forster's "Dr. Woolacott" each either express civilians' relation to the war in terms of architecture or actually situate the home-front experience of war at a specific architectural site. Taken together, these works begin to suggest the surprising persistence with which writers turned to architectural images as a way of articulating a civilian conception of war and its casualties. Given the rich texture of the literary associations between architecture and war, then, fictional houses become a logical and productive site at which authors may proceed to investigate further the issue of corpselessness. In *Jacob's Room* (1922), Virginia Woolf conducts what is undoubtedly the most scrupulous inquiry into the possibilities of relationship between architecture and the absent corpse, but *The Professor's House* (1925) by American Willa Cather is also loosely organized around the idea of how architecture can participate in commemoration. Both works uncover the same interdependence of presence and absence, life and death that I view as a central attribute of war memorials.

Cather's Tom Outland is killed at Flanders. Like thousands of other Great War casualties, he becomes an elusive verbal concept, "not very real to me any more," as one of his former classmates confesses. "Sometimes I think he was just a—a glittering idea" (111). Although this remark reminds us how absent corpses are experienced by survivors as radically dematerialized, Tom himself had invented a device that emblematizes the pressure absence may exert. The principle of the Outland vacuum, a principle Tom discovered as an undergraduate, "is revolutionizing aviation" (40). Thus, the invention that posthumously establishes Tom's name and fortune is based on the pressure of absence, much like Tom's influence in the novel is.

The oppressive absence of inaccessible corpses prompted British civilians to concentrate on the construction of war memorials. In the same way, Tom's death prompts two projects of architectural commemoration.

His fiancée, Rosamond, actually builds a house named Outland that memorializes Tom as an inventor (it will contain all the equipment he used in his scientific work). But Professor St. Peter (Rosamond's father and Tom's friend and mentor) imaginatively transforms his attic workroom, a "shadowy crypt at the top of the house" (112), into a coffin without a corpse. Thus, the professor's house of the title both frames the space where Tom's body belongs and becomes the site at which the interrelationship of life and death emerges.

Professor St. Peter nearly dies in his ill-ventilated, gas-heated "crypt" of an attic when the wind slams a window shut. As if prepared to substitute his own corpse for Tom's inaccessible one, the depressed St. Peter seems passively to accept asphyxiation but, at the last moment, thinks of his old friend Augusta and tries to get up to open the window. Though he has waited too long and collapses, the sound of his body hitting the floor sends Augusta hurrying to his aid. "If he had thought of Augusta sooner, he would have got up from the couch sooner. Her image would have at once suggested the proper action" (279–80). Thus, Augusta not only saves St. Peter's life but helps him recover the impulse to live. Paradoxically, Augusta not only represents to St. Peter the instinct for survival but also the willingness to accept death. With her matter-of-fact "manner of speaking about it," Augusta "made death seem less uncomfortable. She hadn't any of the sentimentality that comes from a fear of dying" (281).

The Professor's House takes place after the end of the war, so that Tom—already dead at the beginning of the novel—only "lives" for us in the middle of it, when we hear his story in his own voice. Absence in Cather's novel is an old hurt; characters preoccupied by it have, for the most part, moved beyond grief into more egotistical meditations on the repercussions of Tom's life and Tom's death. Rosamond adopts the pose of historical preservationist, building a house to commemorate her fiancé, but she only has the funds and leisure to indulge in such a project because the man she eventually married had the business savvy necessary to take Tom's raw idea and turn it into a money-making venture. And though St. Peter is far more generous and less materialistic than his daughter, his sense of loss has also modulated into something more self-centered than his initial sorrow at Tom's death must have been. Now in his middle years, St. Peter reflects back on the life he has already lived and forward to the death that seems suddenly imminent, thinking of Tom primarily because Tom embodies that movement in both directions. St. Peter thinks back to his boyhood and Tom is relevant because he was young; St. Peter projects himself into old age and Tom is relevant because he is already dead.

Woolf's *Jacob's Room*, on the other hand, commences before the war. We know Jacob from his boyhood and do not realize he is dead until the last page of the book, when his mother and a friend are clearing his belongings out of his apartment. Absence in Woolf's novel is stunningly fresh; the narrator has positioned readers in a way that makes ducking the shock of his death impossible. Her detailed rendering of a character we cannot but think of as alive, then, climaxes with what may be understood as a magnification of the moment in which, for survivors, presence and absence are counterpoised most vividly: when the blow of death is fresh yet incomprehensible, when the sense of life is fresh but fatally shaken. It is only in retrospect that we recognize the thoroughness with which the narrator of *Jacob's Room* has prepared for the commemoration of his absence. By systematically altering the material details of graves, she disappoints—and thus exposes—a gamut of expectations not only about how memorials to the dead operate but also regarding the premises upon which those expectations are based.

Our assumptions about the stable relationship between tombstones and a grave site, for example, are subverted when the narrator notices that the tombstones she sees in a van on London's Waterloo Bridge are actually meant for corpses buried in Putney: "[A] mason's van with newly lettered tombstones record[s] how some one loved some one who is buried at Putney. Then the motor car in front jerks forward, and the tombstones pass too quick for you to read more" (112). We think of tombstones as planted features in the landscape, visible markers of the buried invisibility of corpses. Woolf, however, presents us with mobile stones that point to a corpse in Putney without actually marking it. Subverting our implicit trust in the durability of the materials marking graves and their ability to ensure permanence of epitaph, Woolf evokes smoke rather than granite to mark a grave, as we see when bits of the Cornish coastline prompt the narrator to think of buried corpses: "[I]mperceptibly the cottage smoke droops, has the look of a mourning emblem, a flag floating its caress over a grave. The gulls, making their broad flight and then riding at peace, seem to mark the grave" (49). In other words, the painstaking effort of the War Graves Commission accurately and permanently to mark the graves of as many dead soldiers as possible (Churchill declared that Lutyens's Stones of Remembrance would last two thousand years [Longworth 54]) are disregarded by a narrator who imagines a grave in the sea (indicated only by the swoop of a gull), a gravestone on a truck (in London, with its fleeting salute to a corpse buried in Putney).

These shifting, vanishing images betray the narrator's skepticism about the ability of conventional cemetery artifacts adequately to mark absence at all. Jacob's room, her own image of the young man's absence, is neither durable (though we become familiar with a few of the items there—his books, a black trunk, a wicker chair) nor confined to a single site—he grows up in Scarborough, lives in Trinity College, and finally moves to Covent Garden. Jacob himself seems to be the only feature of his room that remains constant over locations and years.

But Jacob is, of course, far from consistent, as the narrator admits when she despairs of ever pinning him down. For there always "remains over something which can never be conveyed to a second person save by Jacob himself. Moreover, part of this is not Jacob but [his friend] Richard Bonamy—the room; the market carts; the hour; the very moment of history" (72–73). That which can never be conveyed is the part of Jacob's identity that is responsive to the world around him and that thus remains in a state of perpetual flux. The unsettled character of his room corresponds both to the permeability of identity's boundaries and to the flickering self that is only accessible in Jacob's presence.

Apprehension of his death, of his room as the artifactual registration of his absence, and of the dismantling of his room occur simultaneously as the last stroke of the novel. While the volatility of the image may be disturbing, the honesty with which it confronts the volatility of Jacob himself ratifies its starkness. Conventional cemetery artifacts offer stable shapes of absence premised on a belief in the former stability of presence. Once that stability is questioned, however, the old shapes no longer answer their purpose. Permanence dissolves into mutability.

Jacob's room operates imagistically as an empty coffin—describing, at the end of the novel, not merely an approximation of his presence but also a silhouette of his absence. Women who love but have already been discarded by Jacob begin impulsively to invent substitutions for his presence even before he leaves for the front: Clara Durrant acknowledges Mr. Lionel Parry in the park, thinking him Jacob (167); Florinda notes that a man in the restaurant stares in a way that reminds her of Jacob (169); Sandra Wentworth Williams decides that he is like a character in Molière (169); and Fanny Elmer visits the British Museum because the statue of Ulysses gives her a "fresh shock of Jacob's presence, enough to last her half a day. But this was wearing thin" (170). These miniature gestures of imaginative remedy clearly anticipate the women's personal loss and demonstrate their impulse to create proxies for Jacob when confronted with his absence. But the imaginative maneuvers of the narrator refuse to provide analogues of the body to fill the space Jacob leaves behind. She puts before us objects, but the room remains uninhabited: "Listless is the air in an empty room, just swelling the curtain; the flowers in the jar shift. One fibre in the wicker arm-chair creaks, though no one sits there" (176). In *Jacob's Room*, architecture refers to absence by housing the relics that formerly surrounded presence.

Not until the final page of *Jacob's Room* do we realize that Jacob has become another World War I casualty. This page contains an unusual number of sentences lifted verbatim from elsewhere in the novel; if we trace the language on that final page to its sources, we find that the collation of original and repeated sentences begins to establish a metaphorical relationship between Jacob's body, his father's (Seabrook's) body, and Jacob's room, as shown in the following examples (emphasis added throughout):

The eighteenth century has its *distinction*. These *houses* were built, say, a hundred and fifty years ago. The *rooms* are *shapely*, the ceilings high. (last page of the book, 176)

"*Distinction*"—Mrs. Durrant said that *Jacob* Flanders was "*distinguished-looking.*" "Extremely awkward," she said, "but so *distinguished-looking.*" (70)

[H]ad earth and wood been glass, doubtless [*Seabrook* Flanders's] very face lay visible beneath, the face of a young man whiskered, *shapely*, who had gone out duck-shooting and refused to change his boots. (16)

The *rooms* are *shapely*, the ceilings high. (70)

"That young man, *Jacob* Flanders," they would say, "so *distinguished looking*—and yet so awkward." (155)

These *houses* (Mrs. Garfit's daughter, Mrs. Whitehorn, was the landlady of this one) were built, say, a hundred and fifty years ago. . . . The eighteenth century has its *distinction*. (70)

"But he [*Jacob*] is very *distinguished looking*," Sandra decided. (145)

Jacob and the rooms share distinction; Seabrook and the rooms are both shapely. From the observation that the bodies of both Jacob and Seabrook are metaphorically allied with these rooms, then, arises two representational consequences. One is political cynicism laid bare by the juxtaposed explanations for the father's death and the son's death: both are ridiculous, the narrator implies. Jacob went off to fight for his country and died in the execution of that project; Seabrook refused to change his boots and died of whatever malady strikes down such imprudence. By pairing the son's death with the father's, Woolf effects a juxtaposition bitterly irreverent of the glory of dying in the Great War. One suspects that averting Jacob's death would (or ought to) have been as simple as averting Seabrook's death.

The other consequence of the connection between Seabrook, Jacob, and Jacob's room is the apprehension of Jacob's room as an empty coffin. To trace the metaphorical path that arrives at the conflation of Jacob's room and a coffin, though, it is necessary to begin with the narrator's musings on the coffin of his father. Seabrook Flanders had been "dead these many years; enclosed in three shells; the crevices sealed with lead, so that, had earth and wood been glass, doubtless his very face lay visible beneath" (16). Here, then, earth and wood become windows for the narrator, establishing imaginative access to the dead Seabrook.

Because the novel's female narrator frequently finds herself excluded from the private quarters of young men and is therefore often reduced to loitering about the vicinity of Jacob's quarters in order to get a look at him, our glimpses of him, like hers, are not infrequently glimpses through windows: "Was it to receive this gift from the past that the young man came to the window and stood there, looking out across the court? It was

Jacob" (45). "'I rather think,' said Jacob, taking his pipe from his mouth, 'it's in Virgil,' and pushing back his chair, he went to the window" (64). "Now Jacob walked over to the window and stood with his hands in his pockets. . . . Pickford's van swung down the street" (116).

The narrator's imaginative rendering of Seabrook's coffin as fitted with windows which would allow her to look at the dead man corresponds to the windows before which Jacob stands, allowing her to look at Jacob. If Seabrook is imaginatively apprehended through windows in his coffin and Jacob is literally apprehended through windows in his room, then Jacob's room, by extrapolation, may be understood as housing his body in the same way that a coffin houses his father's corpse. Jacob's room becomes Jacob's coffin.

Coffins protect corpses from dirt and weather—inserting themselves between raw earth and fragile corpse, indulging the urge to protect a human body (even a dead one) from the natural process of decomposition and disintegration. For both Seabrook and Jacob, coffins repair failures of boundary between the body and the material world—different failures, but both of which result in death. Seabrook, who went "out duck-shooting and refused to change his boots" now lies "enclosed in three shells; the crevices sealed with lead" (16). Not having changed his boots is the only explanation we are ever given of Seabrook's death: we can therefore only presume that a chill led to disease, which led to his death, and that it all began with mud and water seeping through the inadequate boundary between his feet and the earth. Now, however, the wet boots have been replaced by a triple layer of protection that separates his entire body from the earth.

As if sentenced to death by puns inherited from his father, the body of Jacob *Flanders* (critics routinely point out the deadly significance his surname had acquired by 1922, the year the novel was published) is not *enclosed* by "shells; the crevices sealed with lead" but rather *penetrated* by shells and lead. Jacob's last name conflates his body with one of the war's most notorious landscapes, and, for him, "shells" and "lead" modulate from that which shatters the body's boundaries to that which reproduces the body's boundaries in the more durable, less permeable form of a coffin. The "shell," in other words, names both the agent of death and the shape of death—both weapon and coffin.

That different artifacts named by a single word should produce completely opposite effects demonstrates both the ease with which oppositions can collude and one way in which war can make that collusion explicit. Just as "blighty" describes both home and wound, a place at once accessible (newspapers from London reached the trenches within twenty-four hours) and inaccessible ("I breathe deeply and say over to myself:—'You are at home, you are at home.' But a sense of strangeness will not leave me, I cannot feel at home" [Remarque 160]), "shell" names that which Jacob desperately needs to live and that which ensures his death. Just as the word "show" signifies both a vaudeville entertainment and a bloody attack, language simultaneously "shows" experience by describing it and conceals experience by replacing it with a verbal representation. Just as corpses embody a paradox of presence and absence, words simultaneously figure presence and absence—the presence and absence of experience.

That language both conceals and exposes is a common observation, given a contemporary theoretical context sensitive to the fact that our only access to the past—or to anything outside the perimeter of our direct experience—is through representations. As Linda Hutcheon, in her consideration of the postmodern novel, has pointed out: "Historiographic metafiction . . . implies that, like fiction, history constructs its object, that events named become facts and thus both do and do not retain their status outside language. This is the paradox of postmodernism. The past really did exist, but we can only know it today through its textual traces, its often complex and indirect representations in the present" (78). While I agree that any sense we make of the past is actually a sense of having interpreted certain of its texts, my reading of modernism suggests that the geographic, imaginative, and political imperatives of World War I prompted both modernists and soldiers to confront the very issues Hutcheon names as postmodern several generations prior to the texts that we think of as postmodern.

Combatants' disintegrated concepts of home are at once confirmed and mended by Woolf's rendering of Jacob's room, for in her stark combination of home with coffin, absence becomes visible in two directions—the inaccessibility of corpses to civilians and the inaccessibility of home to soldiers. Further, her decision to articulate space that *surrounds* absence rather than words that could too easily be understood as attempting to *replace* absence suggests a strikingly "postmodern" reluctance to glide over the gap between language and experience, between the past and the present. I would argue that the self-consciousness for which Hutcheon gives the postmodern novel credit—an announced awareness that any text, historical or fictional, "operates within (and does not deny) its unavoidably discursive context" (81)—informs Woolf's treatment of war in 1922. For what the architectural rendering of Jacob's death finally acknowledges is that perhaps the only honest representation of absence is silence.

TWO

CORPSES

Trench soldiers in the Great War inhabited worlds constructed, literally, of corpses. Dead men at the front blended with the mud and duckboard landscape, emerging through the surface of the ground and through the dirt floors of dugouts: "In the ground here there are several strata of dead, and in many places the delving of the shells has brought out the oldest and set them out in display on the top of the new ones" (Barbusse 278). Live soldiers found themselves buried in falling dirt while shells disinterred their dead companions from shallow graves. Casualty lists that wound around buildings or spilled into extra newspaper columns shocked a civilian population confronted with statistics documenting the erasure of a generation; the corpsescapes of trench warfare embodied that erasure. As one witness described it: "You walk on the ground of Verdun as though on the face of the Country" (Henry de Montherlant qtd. in Meyer 64).

Elaine Scarry has pointed out that injured bodies bear no relation to the issues that are being contested in war: "Does this dead boy's body 'belong' to his side, the side 'for which' he died, or does it 'belong' to the side 'for which' someone killed him, the side that 'took' him? That it belongs to both or neither makes manifest the nonreferential character of the dead body" (119). Intuitive responses of soldiers to enemy corpses confirm this nonreferentiality: the "belligerence" that we describe as characterizing the relationship between nations at war collapses when a French soldier comes across a German corpse or when a German soldier happens upon a British one. And though "hostilities" may be reported as erupting between political entities, Great War soldiers found themselves exposing discrepancies between the affect implied by official definitions and the affect experienced by one individual responding to another.

Corpses collapse the distinction between ally and enemy and confuse the boundary between life and death. This pair of attributes, articulated both by combatants in their accounts of the war (fictional and nonfictional) and by noncombatants in novels and poems (written during or after but not about the war) subvert the very structure of war. First, the inability to distinguish between allies and enemies means that war's verbal dualism devolves into nonsense: the whole vocabulary of winners and losers trails away into triviality when the categories of language upon which we depend to distinguish between them are no longer able to do their jobs. Second, if one cannot establish death as an unequivocal concept easily distinguishable from life, it becomes impossible to compile the body counts upon which the substantiation of war's issues depends.

The parsing out of individuals, political parties, nations, or other coalitions into "sides" of a conflict frequently implies that there are only two possible positions to be taken in relation to an issue. Certainly, during World War I, governmental and public pressure leaned toward the elimination of any more than two possible ways of responding to the problem. Allied propaganda encouraged the public to imagine their enemies as monstrously wicked (one poster shows a lizard in German helmet clinging to a globe) and of their allies as scrubbed and virtuous (winged women lead them to victory in the posters). German recruiting posters were similar. As often happens during crises, at least in official public discourse, a spectrum of thoughtful responses was too often reduced to opposing extremes.

Most soldiers set off to fight, then, equipped with a set of binary categories. They soon learned, however, that war can not only confound such categories but also eliminate them; that injuries can not only render inaccessible the patriotic motives of fighting for one's country but also erase the name of one's country from consciousness. A character in Henri Barbusse's *Under Fire* notices, for example, "that some mounds of earth aligned along the ruined ramparts of this deep-drowned ditch are human" and naturally wonders whether they are German or French. "One of them has opened his eyes, and looks at us with swaying head. We say to him, 'French?'—and then, '*Deutsch?*' He makes no reply, but shuts his eyes again and relapses into oblivion. We never knew what he was" (335). That the speaker poses only those two questions to the wounded man—French? German?—reminds us of the fundamental dualism that structures war: membership in one of the dueling parties (rather than one's name, for example) constitutes the basis of identity.

That the speaker never finds out to which side the wounded man belongs demonstrates, however, the destabilization of categories that function perfectly well in theory and from a distance but that come unstuck when exposed to the actual business of fighting. In other words, war may be understood as organizing itself not only according to *our side vs. their side* but also according to *inside vs. outside,* with each metaphorical formulation disrupting the other. From a civilian perspective, the world constitutes itself into either the one side or the other. From a battlefront perspective, the space implied by inside and outside may trivialize a soldier's separation from a soldier of a different nationality. The crucial point is not that one metaphor is more accurate than the other but that combatants were forced to negotiate between the two while it was possible for civilians, by virtue of their distance from the front, to maintain a single, unambivalent view. The soldier who "never knew what he was" must accommodate that lack of knowledge, unlike the civilians for whom national loyalties were so clear that a dachshund was liable to be "stoned in the High Street" for his blatant display of Germanness (Greene 66). Corpses thus taught soldiers an uncomfortable lesson in the difficulties of articulating war.

Paul Fussell has argued that the alleged "inadequacy" of language in the face of war was actually a problem of an unreceptive audience: the problem, to his mind, "was less one of 'language' than of gentility and optimism." He quotes Louis Simpson: "To a foot-soldier, war is almost entirely physical. That is why some men, when they think about war, fall silent. Language seems to falsify physical life and to betray those who have experienced it absolutely—the dead" (170). Simpson here describes the dead as "those who have experienced [physical life] absolutely"— testifying to the way in which life and death seem to blend for soldiers at war and linking this blend explicitly to the difficulty of articulating war.

E. M. Forster's "Our Graves in Gallipoli" (1922) illustrates the way in which corpses render irrelevant those distinctions of nationality that prompt war in the first place. In this essay, two graves have a conversation about the absurdity of British economic priorities: "Nothing for schools, nothing for houses, nothing for the life of the body, nothing for the spirit. England cannot spare a penny for anything except for her heroes' graves" (33). In the course of conversation, the two graves suddenly realize that they belong to belligerent nations—one to England, the other to Turkey. But "All graves are one," they agree. "It is their unity that sanctifies them, and some day even the living will learn this" (35).

Forster's essay dismisses an argument that was being put forth at the time, which held that the men who had already died at Gallipoli justified sending more men to die there. In the following quote, the degeneration of a proper noun into nonsensical syllables—"Gallipoli" into "Gally Polly"—symbolizes the corpses' resistance to the projects of either substantiating political issues or condoning the continuation of military campaigns: "English young men must be persuaded [to fight]. . . . A phrase must be thought of, and 'the Gallipoli graves' is the handiest. The clergy must wave their Bibles, the old men their newspapers, the old women their knitting, the unmarried girls must wave white feathers, and all must shout, 'Gallipoli graves, Gallipoli graves, Gallipoli, Gally Polly, Gally Polly,' until the young men are ashamed and think, What sound can that be but my country's call?" (34). In *A Passage to India*, Forster uses repetition in a similar way to expose both the arbitrariness of language and its tendency to lapse into nonsense. At the trial of Aziz, "Mrs. Moore, Mrs. Moore" is transformed by the chanting crowd into "Esmiss Esmoor, Esmiss Esmoor" after her death. At first invoked by an attorney as the name of someone who had been a sympathetic English ear, a friend to Aziz, and present at the infamous Marabar picnic, it is soon caught up and chanted by numbers of Indians within and without the courtroom. The slide of language into pure sound represents the futility of the attorney's appeal, of rapprochement between the native and colonialist communities, of trying to use even the most well-intentioned language to bridge profound cultural gaps. At the same time, the meaningless syllables become the script of an announced solidarity among Indians—a solidarity that is deeply disturbing to the English aristocracy, disturbing particularly for the ease with which it embraces a nonsensical slogan as rallying cry.

In the same way, the lapsing of "Gallipoli" into "Gally Polly" suggests both the ease with which language can be twisted to support petty causes and the resistance of the dead to *any* cause. Corpses of the Gallipoli soldiers and of Mrs. Moore elude all efforts to enlist their materiality in the endorsement of causes—for or against Churchill's Gallipoli campaign, for or against the acquittal or conviction of Dr. Aziz. And as the language describing corpses tends to slip away into meaninglessness— "Gally Polly," "Esmiss Esmoor"—the enlistment itself is foiled; the squaring off of nations into war emerges (literally) as nonsense.

In modernist writing by both combatants and civilians, life and death are not perceived as linear, sequential experiences; the latter does not usurp the former. Rather, the two states exist in an unpredictable relation to each other, sometimes fluctuating back and forth, sometimes holding each other in tense balance. Only rarely does either life or death appear fully in control, its opposite fully repressed, enough under wraps to be safely ignored. Most of the time, each looms over the other.

Soldiers' descriptions of corpses make clear that dead bodies at the front were simultaneously understood as both animate subjects and inanimate objects. The disturbing susceptibility of bodies to become indistinguishable from the landscape of mud and objects through which they moved is documented over and over in accounts of the war. Henri Barbusse's description cited earlier tells about a human "moun[d] of earth"—the barely flickering consciousness of a soldier incapable any longer of aligning the body it inhabits with anything beyond "the ruined ramparts of this deep-drowned ditch." Later, he mixes vocabularies of life and death, men and earth: "All these men of corpse-like faces who are

before us and behind us, at the limit of their strength, void of speech as of
will, all these earth-charged men who you would say were carrying their
own winding-sheets, are as much alike as if they were naked" (335).
Though these men are alive, every adjective suggests otherwise: they are
"corpse-like," silent, lacking will, and "earth-charged." They seem to be
"carrying their own winding sheets." Edwin Campion Vaughan writes in
his diary how "[i]n the faint light that still remained we saw the sandbags
and pieces of timber half buried in the mud. Holmes stooped to raise one
of these short beams, then let it go, with a shuddering exclamation, for he
had bent back an arm with Sergeant's stripes" (45). The Sergeant's arm
has been mistaken for part of a dug-out. In a similar scene, Paul Bäumer's
comment at the end of All Quiet on the Western Front describes the
soldiers' collective inability to distinguish themselves from the wet,
muddy landscape in which they are stuck: "Our hands are earth, or
bodies clay and our eyes pools of rain. We do not know whether we still
live" (Remarque 287).

These weird blends of life and death are prompted by the soldier's
recognition of the ease with which his body could become a corpse. In
Good-bye to All That, Robert Graves estimates that the average life
expectancy of a soldier at the front was three months (59), while Modris
Eksteins quotes the letter of the "anguished American ambassador" in
London who says that "[w]hen there's 'nothing to report' from France,
that means the regular 5,000 casualties that happen every day" (155).
Those at home were subject to their own idiosyncratic casualty rates,
which were often devastating. Vera Brittain lost her fiancé, her brother,
and her brother's two best friends. Of Katherine Mansfield, who also lost
a brother, John Middleton Murry observed that "no single one of Katherine Mansfield's friends who went to the war returned alive from it"
(Murry 58). And E. M. Forster made the plaintive remark that "insensibly
one has dropped into the habit of thinking that a person who so much as
goes out of the room in these days may not come back into it again" ("To
Forrest Reid"). Clearly, whatever the actual statistics of life expectancy at
the front, fatality rates were understood by both soldiers and civilians as
collapsing the distance between life and death for combatants, bringing
the living into closer and closer intimacy with the dead.

The perpetual likelihood of a soldier's joining the ranks of the dead
may provide one explanation for the surprising and elaborate responses
corpses elicited from the men around them. While civilians surrounded
the dead with rituals of grief and commemoration, soldiers' reactions
betray instead a sense of corpses as still harboring some sort of life and
therefore as demanding that one respond to them. Sometimes, as numerous anecdotes testify, the "aliveness" of a corpse prompted clowning.
One soldier, who helped bury soldiers at Gallipoli, admits that "[h]ands
were the worst; they would escape from the sand, pointing, begging—

even waving!" but then exposes the funny side of horror when he tells how "[t]here was one which we all shook when we passed, saying, 'Good morning', in a posh voice. Everybody did it" (Thompson qtd. in Vansittart 71). Another combatant describes the niceties of etiquette due to a corpse: "This morning, carrying out a few improvements to our dugout, we started to level up the ground under our table which is very rickety. The earth was spongy, and we started digging with entrenching tools, but we struck an old blue tunic, and when we gave it a tug, the resistance— and an unpleasant smell—warned us that we had a guest, so we apologized and patted the earth back" (Vaughan 34). "There has been a dead man lying on the fire-step waiting to be taken down to the cemetery tonight," Graves reports. His arm, stiffened in death, is stretched out across the trench and his "comrades joke as they push it out of the way to get by. 'Out of the light, you old bastard. Do you own this bloody trench?'" (*Good-bye* 142–43).

For nurses, the bodies of men who had been fatally wounded but were not yet dead constituted a similarly ambiguous territory, except that because dead patients could be moved out of beds, out of hospitals, and into the ground, death could achieve finality for them in a way that it frequently could not for soldiers: "There are three dying in the ward today," a nurse says in Ellen LaMotte's *The Backwash of War*. "It will be better when they die. The German shells have made them ludicrous, repulsive. We see them in this awful interval, between life and death. This interval when they are gross, absurd, fantastic" (94). This nurse knows that once the three are dead, they will also be *gone*. For soldiers, however, the dead tend not only to stay but to wait: "Along the hazy, filthy, and unwholesome space, where withered grass is embedded in black mud, there are rows of dead. They are carried there when the trenches or the plain are cleared during the night. They are waiting—some of them have waited long—to be taken back to the cemeteries after dark" (Barbusse 152–53). Wilfred Owen cites the same disconcerting sense of the infinite patience of corpses that makes them inescapable. The "unburiable bodies" of the dead, he tells, "sit outside the dug-outs all day, all night. . . . [T]o sit with them all day, all night . . . and a week later to come back and find them still sitting there, in motionless groups, THAT is what saps the 'soldierly spirit'" (qtd. in Hynes 201).

When they found themselves confronting a corpse alone instead of in the company of friends, the responses to corpses tended to be more sober. The same soldier who apologized to his unexpected guest later describes happening upon a German corpse:

> Covered with snow, as with a sheet, lay the body of a Boche, looking calm and, I somehow felt, happy. Yet the sight of him made me feel icily lonely. It seemed such a terrible thing to lie alone, covered with snow throughout the night, with never a sound until we came along, and

tapped and clipped and never spoke, and then went away for ever. It seemed so unfriendly, and for a long time I sat wishing we could do something for him.

At length I passed down along the line again to Thatcher who decided it was time to withdraw; so we passed along the word to cease work and the troops fell in. As they lined up, I could not help thinking of my poor Boche up on the hill, and I imagined a piteous look on his face as he heard us marching away, leaving him once more to silence and solitude. (Vaughan 73–74)

In another soldier's description, the bodies lining a trench glide eerily between life and death, illustrating the disturbing degree of intimacy between soldiers and corpses: "[E]arthy bodies," the soldier tells, "are squatting with their chins on their knees or leaning against the wall as straight and silent as the rifles which wait beside them. Some of these standing dead turn their blood-bespattered faces towards the survivors; others exchange their looks with the sky's emptiness" (Barbusse 285–86). In contrast, captions in a collection of war photographs betray the glibness with which nonparticipants were capable of dismissing such intimacy: "No more parades," the caption attached to a photograph of corpses littering the ground affirms; and a grisly image of a shattered body is appended by the declaration that "[t]his was a man" (Stallings 98, 148). The tone of such captions is difficult to interpret. Is it frankly congratulatory or absurdly morbid? Offensive or just clumsy? In any case, the soldier's description of the "standing dead"—a miserable blending of corpses, rifles, and survivors—attends to the human cost of such a campaign in a way that the photographic captions miss completely. Only a commentator at the remove that photographs permit would be liable to strike such a peculiar attitude, while the soldier's description of the "standing dead" mixes horror and sympathy in a way that suggests sad familiarity with such a landscape.

At other times, a soldier's response is agonized, as in Bäumer's famous shell-hole speech to the French soldier he has killed in *All Quiet on the Western Front* demonstrates. Bäumer realizes that the Frenchman is dead but still feels an irrepressible urge to explain his act to himself—a self suddenly shattered by the need to take responsibility for killing another human being. Bäumer's first confused impulse is that he ought, somehow, to substitute himself for his slain enemy: "My state is getting worse," he confesses, "I can no longer control my thoughts. What would his wife look like? . . . Does she belong to me now? Perhaps by this act she becomes mine" (222). Just as mourning relatives may attempt to create an alternative presence when faced with fatal absence, so Bäumer attempts to fill the blank space he has created in the family of the French soldier. But by inserting himself into the space, he is paralyzed with guilt: "I have killed the printer, Gérard Duval. I must be a printer, I think confusedly, be a printer, printer—" (225).

The logic of Bäumer's response may be seen in his panicked resolution somehow to make amends to the survivors of Gérard Duval: "This dead man is bound up with my life, therefore I must do everything, promise everything in order to save myself; I swear blindly that I mean to live only for his sake and his family, with wet lips I try to placate him" (225). What Bäumer articulates here is an awareness of the interrelationship between himself and a stranger, between his life and the stranger's death. As seen in his skittish decisions to mimic Duval (by becoming a printer) or posture as him (by claiming his wife), life reverberates with death and death reverberates with life. Or, as Vicki Mahaffey has elegantly put it, "[T]he interpersonal awareness that comes with maturity is not only a celebration of relationship, but also an exodus, a choral preparation for the isolation of death" (13).

Civilian modernist writers reproduced the combatant tendency to understand life and death as experiences between which one fluctuates. While for modernist precursors, the past often insinuated itself into the present in the form of ghosts (as in Henrik Ibsen's *Ghosts*, 1881; or Henry James's "The Jolly Corner," 1909), later modernists often embodied the persistence of the past within corpses, which were experienced as threats to the ability of survivors to construct stable senses of their own identities.

In James Joyce's "The Sisters," the young speaker's encounter with the corpse of the dead priest repeats a pattern of distraction that, according to Father Flynn's sisters, was the beginning of his death. A chalice is broken. Was it the boy's fault? The sisters seem to think so, suggesting the degree to which the priest and the speaker have become intertwined. "After that," Eliza tells, "he began to mope by himself, talking to no one and wandering about by himself" (17). One night, she says, a clerk and another priest found Flynn: "And what do you think but there he was, sitting up by himself in the dark of his confession-box, wide-awake and laughing-like softly to himself?" (18). At his coffin, the boy demonstrates that, as Vicki Mahaffey has pointed out, he has learned this attitude toward them from his old friend: "I pretended to pray but I could not gather my thoughts because the old woman's mutterings distracted me. I noticed how clumsily her skirt was hooked at the back and how the heels of her cloth boots were trodden down all to one side. The fancy came to me that the old priest was smiling as he lay there in his coffin" (14). Just as the priest enacted his inability to focus on religion in the confession-box, the boy finds himself unable to pray at the coffin where he imagines the priest to be smiling. It is his own snobbery toward Nannie, the other sister, that holds the boy's attention—a snobbery that replicates the attitude that allowed Flynn to dominate his sisters' lives.[1]

The boy in Joyce's story, a mere bystander to the priest's domestic tyranny, gets the impression that the priest is smiling—a fairly innocuous suggestion of Flynn's achievement in having passed on his attitudes to the boy. In Katherine Mansfield's "The Daughters of the Late Colonel" (1922), another story about two women in the habit of circling around a selfish man recently dead, the daughters experience the persistence of their father with a gothic sense of fear: "Josephine had had a moment of absolute terror at the cemetery, while the coffin was lowered, to think that she and Constantia had done this thing [buried him] without asking his permission. What would father say when he found out? For he was bound to find out sooner or later. . . . She heard him absolutely roaring, 'And do you expect me to pay for this gimcrack excursion of yours?'" (268–69). Later, Josephine becomes convinced that her father is locked in a dresser drawer with his handkerchiefs or possibly shut up among the overcoats in the wardrobe. The Colonel's death in no way relaxes his tyrannical hold on his daughters. On the contrary, having insinuated himself into their lives and their visions of themselves, his psychological presence does not depend on his material presence at all. The modernist sensibility, attuned to psychological as well as physical realities, portrays psychological persistence with grim humor—smiling corpses and fathers among the overcoats.

Other works calibrate more precisely the tendency of corpses to move backward toward life, specifying how far back into life the dead have proceeded or attending to the responses that such a reversal evokes. In D. H. Lawrence's *Women in Love* (1920), Mrs. Crich delivers a terrible sermon to her children over the body of her dead husband, who "lay in repose, as if gently asleep, so gently, so peacefully, like a young man sleeping in purity." It is this apparent reversion of her husband back to life and to youth that at first captivates but then enrages Mrs. Crich: "She stood for some minutes in silence, looking down. 'Beautiful,' she asserted, 'beautiful as if life had never touched you—never touched you. God send I look different. I hope I shall look my years when I am dead. Beautiful, beautiful,' she crooned over him. . . . Then there was a tearing in her voice as she cried: 'None of you look like this when you are dead! Don't let it happen again'" (327). The mother even goes further in her pronouncements on the indecency of this old man's corpse sliding back to youth, declaring that "[i]f I thought that the children I bore would lie looking like that in death, I'd strangle them when they were infants" (327).

Her husband's corpse seems defiant not only of death but also of old age. It is precisely that ability of a corpse to glide backward along a time line along which the rest of us have no choice but to proceed forward, that horrifies and enrages her. His defection by death is compounded by his having left her grieving in old age for a man suddenly youthful again; she is forced not only to mourn the death of an old man but the loss of her own youth.

In the "Death by Water" section of T. S. Eliot's *The Waste Land* (1922), death is not only *by* water but *like* water—an element through which one swims and which possesses no shape, only principles of motion. Eliot undoes the whole metaphor of time as a vector ending in death not just by reversing the direction of time's arrow but by imagining death as a space into which time flushes, oceanlike. Instead of watching Phlebas the Phoenician move from time into death and then stop, we observe, in "Death by Water," the behavior of time immersed in death:

> Phlebas the Phoenician, a fortnight dead,
> Forgot the cry of gulls, and the deep sea swell
> And the profit and loss.
>   A current under sea
> Picked his bones in whispers. As he rose and fell
> He passed the stages of his age and youth
> Entering the whirlpool. (46)

Phlebas's corpse functions the way sand does in wind or water—as a medium providing visible registration of the movements and methods of death. We note the persistence of memory, which only dribbles away into forgetfulness two weeks after death: Phlebas is "a fortnight dead" before he forgets the site of his demise ("cry of gulls . . . deep sea swell") and his business preoccupations ("cry of gulls . . . profit and loss"). We watch the stages of life move up and down like surf and then swirl into a whirlpool. Death's processes here are kinetic ones that travel in all directions: currents, waves, tides, whirlpools.

The title of Joyce's *Finnegans Wake* (1939) speaks to the centrality that Joyce accorded the corpse in his conception of the book's structure, while the behavior of corpses in the book undermines preconceived notions about the finality of death. Although a wake is conventionally an occasion upon which one views a corpse and bids a definitive farewell, at Finnegan's wake, the corpse of Finnegan sits up at the sound of the word "*Usqueadbaugham*!" ("Anglo-Irish usquebaugh: whiskey; Latin usque ad necem: even unto death"), protesting "Anam muck an dhoul! Did ye drink me doornail?" ("dead as a doornail?") (annotations from McHugh 24). Meanwhile, the corpse of HCE, soon after being buried at the bottom of Lough Neagh in an escape-proof coffin, is seen at numerous sites around the battlefields of the wars that have sprung up in the chaos surrounding his death. Joseph Campbell explains the relationship between the book's structure and the corpses of Finnegan and HCE as reaching "down to the root of Joyce's intention": "The bier of Finnegan is the stage on which history enacts itself in the goings and comings of HCE. If Finnegan wakes, the stage is overturned and doomsday arrives. Thus Finnegan must lie quiet, whereas HCE, to perform his function as history itself, must circle endlessly" (95–96).

The ease with which characters such as Finnegan slip between life and death indicates, as John Bishop has pointed out, Joyce's interest in the connection between death and sleep—a connection embedded, as Joyce was aware, in the very language we use to describe the unconsciousness of sleep and the unconsciousness of death. "Our idiomatic custom of saying that people asleep are 'dead to the world,'" Bishop observes, "raises the troublesome question of how being 'dead to the world,' not awake, resting in peace 'in bed' differs from what one foresees happening to anyone 'dead to the world,' at his wake, resting in peace, and also 'in bed'—particularly if we dig a little more deeply into these terms" (66).

Bishop also points out not only how "[e]tymologically, the word 'bed' derives from the proto-Indo-European root *bhedh-, meaning 'to dig or bury,'" but also how "the word 'cemetery,' . . . derives from the Greek koimêtêrion ('sleeping room,' 'dormitory')—[which, in turn, derives] from the verb koimaô ('to put to bed')—and which customarily designates a place where people 'lie in peat' (. . . [but also 'in peace'])" (66–67). In other words, Joyce's problematizing of the status of corpses in the narrative line of Finnegans Wake recreates a contradiction between sleep and death that already exists within the very language we use to distinguish between the two. The project of separating bed (site of life/sleep) from cemetery (site of death) is revealed as futile, for their opposites inhabit each etymologically: "bed" (where we sleep) derives from *bhedh- (to bury); and "cemetery" (where we bury) derives from koimêtêrion (a place to sleep).

In the following examples, the sensibility that prompts soldiers at the front to describe their comrades as gliding between sleep and death may thus be understood as a remarkably modernist one. "There were dead men, sleeping men, wounded men, gassed men," according to Robert Graves, "all lying anyhow" (Good-bye 201). Henri Barbusse asks, "Are they dead—or asleep?" and then concludes gently that "[w]e do not know; in any case, they rest" (335). Elsewhere, Barbusse tells about taking away a handkerchief over a face that is "quite young, and seems to sleep, except that an eyeball has gone" (154). Finally, the comments of a Gallipoli veteran could almost be read as a combatant's gloss on Finnegans Wake: "We set to work to bury people. We pushed them into the sides of the trench but bits of them kept getting uncovered and sticking out, like people in a badly made bed. . . . The bottom of the trench was springy like a mattress because of all the bodies underneath" (Thompson 71). Corpses not only seem to be sleeping, but to be providing a mattress for the living as they enact that lapse into unconsciousness that death will merely extend.[2]

In The Waste Land, death seeps out of its container, disrupting verb tenses, the connection between the conscious self and the body it inhabits—even a speaker's ability to tell whether he or she is living or dead. In his notes to the poem, T. S. Eliot directs his readers to the vegetation myths treated by Sir James Frazer in The Golden Bough, and much of his poem may be understood as delineating a territory between life and death, a conception of the self and of the body that is neither animal nor mineral but rather vegetable—alive but unable to articulate itself. "I could not / Speak, and my eyes failed, I was neither / Living nor dead, and I knew nothing . . ." (38). This state of consciousness hovers somewhere between life and death. There is no speech, no vision, no knowledge, yet some fragile minimal consciousness allows the speaker to describe the experience in retrospect.

The paralysis in *The Waste Land* seems to be temporary, something into and out of which one may move. A soldier at the front describes corpses as in a similarly ambiguous state: "Lying flat on their backs, with marble faces rigid and calm, their khaki lightly covered with frost, some with no wound visible . . . they lay at attention, staring up into the heavens" (Vaughan 32). These soldiers may be understood to be (a) neither living nor dead; (b) both living and dead. They are immobile, but so are men at attention; their eyes are unseeing, yet they stare up at the sky; they're on their backs, but are "lying" as live men do rather than "laying" as dead men would.

During the Great War, the most common soldier's nightmare was of being buried alive "in a bunker by a heavy shell" (Leed 22). This fear expresses how profoundly disturbing combatants found the lack of a clear boundary between life and death to be, for to be buried alive means literally to occupy the positions of life and death simultaneously—to become a conscious corpse. At the front, land was treacherous; dirt was not a reliable surface across which one could move. Instead, it was liable to become mud or quicksand or water into which you could be sucked or trapped; it represented potential drowning, suffocation, immobilization. Nor did dirt remain underfoot. Shells made it explode, fly, or fall—turning it into precipitation, into a weapon, into a grave that could literally descend upon you at any moment.

Eric Leed's description of what happened at the front is that "death lost the perfect, abstract clarity that it normally enjoyed as the brief moment between life and not-life." Instead, it mutated into an experience "given not just to those who appeared in the mortality statistics but also to those who were forced to remain in the expanding moment between the extinction of all choice and the extinction of life" (23). This sudden stretchiness of the borders between life and death that is so pervasive, as I have tried to show, in accounts of war, renders narrative awkward. Robert Graves found himself in the position of having to write to his family after they had received inaccurate word of his death, while the *Times,* as Samuel Hynes has pointed out, "continued to print its Roll of Honour well into [1919], as men went on dying of old wounds, and men previously described as missing were declared dead" (257). Some dead are revealed as living, some missing turn up as dead, and the tendency of war's casualty lists to spill over war's temporal borders makes narrating the official conclusion of war difficult. Similarly, in *The Waste Land's*

"What the Thunder Said" (the noise of which, critics have speculated, may refer to the sound of artillery fire and the explosion of shells—"dry sterile thunder without rain" [47]), a chorus of voices complains that "He who was living is now dead / We who were living are now dying / With a little patience" (47). As the strange array of apparently contradictory verb tenses here displays, language itself relies on certain conceptions of death and its relation to the orderly progression of time in one direction; for death to constitute both a definitive conclusion ("He who was living is now dead") and a continuing process ("We who were living are now dying") disrupts the ability of language to chart sequential time.

Eliot populated *The Waste Land,* published four years after the end of the war, with victims of just such a lack of boundary—a poem whose opening speaker, as Michael Levenson has persuasively argued, addresses us from beneath the ground:

> April is the cruellest month, breeding
> Lilacs out of the dead land, mixing
> Memory and desire, stirring
> Dull roots with spring rain.
> Winter kept us warm, covering
> Earth in forgetful snow, feeding
> A little life with dried tubers. (37)

Levenson lucidly points out: "The eye here sees from the point of view of someone (or some thing) that is buried. In what other circumstances would snow act as cover?" He then concludes: "[T]he opening of *The Waste Land* looks at spring from the point of view of a corpse. . . . Only here is a corpse that has not died, that retains a little life. We recall that the title of this opening section is 'The Burial of the Dead' and already we have a fierce irony. These buried are not yet dead" (172).

Levenson draws a connection between *The Waste Land*'s potentially sprouting corpses ("'That corpse you planted last year in your garden, / 'Has it begun to sprout? Will it bloom this year?'" [39]) and a modernist sensibility that acknowledges the instability of the self. "If a corpse can sprout," he reasons, "then no boundaries are secure" and what we witness in the poem is evidence of the "dissolution of boundaries around the self" (175). It is just such dissolving boundaries, in fact, that other modernists cite as a feature distinguishing their own renderings of character from those of the generation preceding them. "Psychology has split and shattered the idea of a 'Person' . . ." E. M. Forster asserts in "What I Believe" (65); Katherine Mansfield imagines the self, according to one critic, "as multiple, shifting, non-consecutive, without essence, and perhaps unknowable" (Fullbrook 17); D. H. Lawrence warns his friend Edward Garnett, in a letter of 1914, not to "look for the development of the novel to follow the lines of certain characters: the characters fall into the form of some other rhythmic form, as when one draws a fiddle-bow across a fine tray delicately sanded, the sand takes lines unknown" ("To Edward Garnett"); Virginia Woolf, in "The Narrow Bridge of Art," theorizes a poetic novel concerned more with the individual consciousness than with social relationships, one that "will take the mould of that queer conglomeration of incongruous things—the modern mind" (226). The war undermined (quite literally) a soldier's confidence in the stability of death and a corpse's embodiment of death; the modernist imagination participates in that disturbing disinterment by investigating how the instability of death alters our concepts of the self.

Both at the front and in modernist works, corpses sprout, fluctuate in and out of consciousness, appear to sleep or to speak. They camouflage themselves as pieces of the material world but then emerge from that camouflage and pronounce themselves emphatically separate from the landscape. Corpses prompt multiple and elaborate responses, demand further interpretation, prove themselves infinitely susceptible to metaphor. In other words, in neither trench experience nor modernist language does death represent the possibility of closure. The past refuses to remain in the past.

In texts, a past that remains stubbornly present flummoxes the ability of characters to create new selves and the possibility for plot to move smoothly forward. Language repeatedly circles around what has gone before, caught by the self-reflective demands of psychological realism. Just as survivors find themselves replaying events in their minds, modernist texts juxtapose past and present in ways that make the distinction between the two unclear. Just as Clarissa, in Woolf's *Mrs. Dalloway*, moves from thoughts of Doris Kilman and her daughter Elizabeth to thoughts of Peter Walsh in the cabbage patch at Bourton twenty years previously, so corpses in modernist texts represent the persistent return of the past. The past stays with you, branching into new metaphors, reminding you and influencing you from the inside as surely as the present, with all its insistence and all its demands, does from the outside.

THE SHAPES OF COUNTRIES

THREE

PHYSICAL BORDERS

I have previously argued that both official British discourse and British popular sentiment articulated Germany's invasion of Belgium and its air raids on England as a violation of the proper spatial organization of war: civilians, according to this English view, were supposed to occupy safe havens, soldiers were supposed to occupy war zones, and the two kinds of space were not supposed to intersect. Thus Germany's invasion of a neutral country and its shelling of British civilian targets were both condemned as transgressions of this spatial organization, but it was the "rape of Belgium" (both figurative and literal) that became for England the most powerful symbol of German transgression. In this chapter, I examine ways in which charges of rape, along with the British attempt to substantiate those charges, raised the issue of factuality in a way similar to the way in which the same issue reverberates through modernism. The "rape of Belgium" provides a historical context in which the modernist mistrust of factuality may be more clearly understood.

Elaine Scarry has analyzed the disputes that lead to war in a way that reveals their imaginative underpinnings:

> In the dispute that leads to war, a belief on each side that has "cultural reality" for that side's population is exposed as a "cultural fiction": that is, by being continually called into question, it begins to become recognizable to its own population as an "invented structure" rather than existing as it did in peacetime as one that (though on reflection invented) could be unselfconsciously entered into as though it were a naturally occurring "given" of the world. . . . Whatever the particular descriptions that have collided, what has always collided is each population's

right to generate its own forms of self-description. Prior to World War I, for example, Germany may believe that the series of treaties between Britain, Belgium, France, and Russia are the "encirclement" of Germany, while these other countries may believe that it is the "encirclement" of France by Germany that is prevented by the treaties. . . . Thus in a dispute, each side reasserts that its own constructs are "real" and that only the other side's constructs are "creations" (and by extension, "fictions," "lies"). (128–29)

From the British point of view, in late July 1914, two of the naturally-occurring givens for understanding an invasion of Belgium might be formulated as: (1) war should confine itself exclusively to a battlefield occupied only by combatants; and (2) the national borders of Belgium should remain as they currently existed. These assumptions conflicted with certain of Germany's assumptions, in particular the beliefs that: (1) war might well extend into civilian spaces and involve civilians; and (2) the existing geography of European alliances already enacted that potential extension by constituting a threatening encirclement of Germany. These assumptions collided in August 1914: Germany insisted that its invasion of Belgium was justified by the threat of *encirclement,* while Britain insisted that the invasion was the *rape* of a neutral country. In other words, the beginning of World War I was articulated in metaphors of boundary that made claustrophobia the motivating German paranoia and penetration the motivating Allied one.

Barbara Tuchman has described how, at the beginning of the century, "Pan-German Societies and Navy Leagues multiplied and met in congresses to demand that other nations recognize their 'legitimate aims' toward expansion, . . . [how] other nations answered with alliances, . . . [and how] when they did, Germany screamed *Einkreisung!*—Encirclement! The refrain *Deutschland gänzlich einzukreisen* grated over the decade" (7). When Russia declared war on Germany, the Kaiser scribbled panic into the margins of telegrams: "The world will be engulfed in the most terrible of wars, the ultimate aim of which is the ruin of Germany. . . . The encirclement of Germany is at last an accomplished fact. We have run our heads into the noose" (qtd. in Tuchman 75).

Germany justified the invasion of Belgium by invoking a fear of shrinking boundaries; England justified its response to that invasion by invoking a horror of penetrated boundaries. Modris Eksteins has observed that despite the fact that "[t]he invasion of France was a much more serious strategic threat to the British than the invasion of Belgium . . . publicly, it was over 'poor little Belgium' that the British government declared war and mobilized sentiment" (132). Violated Belgium became one of the obligating sources of British indignation. "Remember Belgium," poster captions enjoined beneath images of German soldiers dragging off young girls by the hair, while atrocity stories that circulated in France and Britain "had a basic formula, involving the raping of nuns, impaling of babies on bayonets, mutilation of Belgian girls" (J. Williams 33). Peter Buitenhuis specifies the nature of Britain's outrage even more explicitly, writing that soon after the German army crossed into Belgian territory, its activity there "became in the popular mind a chronicle of murder, rapine, pillage, arson, and wanton destruction. The image used throughout is unmistakable. In poster and report and appeal, Belgium is the raped and mutilated maiden, left to die" (12).

Germany's rhetoric of encirclement reveals its leaders' assumptions about the arrangement of Europe, for the premise of encirclement is that the world is constructed on terms that are negotiable, that lines demarcating territory are susceptible to pressure, and that an individual nation would thus naturally attempt to exert pressure to its advantage. General Erich Ludendorff's postwar description of prewar Europe demonstrates that Germany's fear of encirclement contained within it both an impulse to expand and a suspicion that its neighbors harbored similarly expansive desires: "In our unfavourable military-political position in the centre of Europe, surrounded by enemies, we had to reckon with foes greatly superior in numbers and prepare ourselves accordingly, if we did not wish to allow ourselves to be crushed" (25). Based on this formulation, moving toward Belgium is a natural response: in order not to be crushed by surrounding enemies, it is necessary to push outward against the crush.

Encirclement is active behavior. Germany claimed that other countries were attempting it and that those movements preceded the invasion of Belgium and thus constituted the conflict's original impetus. War, according to Germany, began not with a crime of punctured borders but with a nightmare of shrinking ones. To preempt that perceived shrink, the Kaiser's army moved into Belgium, whose previous borders faded for Germany in the face of its decision to articulate the world differently. Ludendorff described the invasion of Belgium as being "based on the assumption that France would not respect Belgian neutrality or that Belgium would join France. On this assumption the advance of the German main forces through Belgium followed as a matter of course. . . . Nobody believed in Belgium's neutrality" (24–25).

By its decision to disbelieve in Belgian neutrality, Germany was retracting its consent from Europe's boundaries as they stood in 1914 and demanding that those national boundaries be seen as renegotiable. In essence, Germany was acknowledging the constructed, fictional nature of national boundaries, while England, by describing Germany as a rapist, resisted the idea that national boundaries are indeed what Scarry calls "cultural fictions." For the German general staff, preoccupied by the logistics of routing, Belgium became a path merely; its announced boundaries undoubtedly subsided in the face of a decision about how best to move an entire army from A to B.

Allied generals, on the other hand, clearly intended to respect the existing national borders as scrupulously as they would respect a woman's chastity. France, for one, wanted to leave no doubts "who was the attacked and who the attacker. The physical act and moral odium of aggression must be left squarely upon Germany. Germany was expected to do her part, but lest any overanxious French patrols or frontier troops stepped over the border, the French government took a daring and extraordinary step. On July 30 it ordered a ten-kilometer withdrawal along the entire frontier with Germany from Switzerland to Luxembourg" (Tuchman 84). In a sense, then, France, like an undercover police officer trying to lure a rapist into attacking, dared the Germans to violate an unprotected border.

In Britain, the penetration of national boundary was articulated as rape, both literally and figuratively. The literal charges of rape were just that: Britain accused German soldiers of raping Belgian civilians. Figuratively, the country of Belgium (personified as a woman) was described as having been raped by the country of Germany (personified as a psychopath) because of the way in which "her" boundaries had been involuntarily violated by "him." By describing the movements of an army *as* the rape of Belgium rather than *as accompanied by* the rapes of Belgian women, the understood factuality of a number of literal rapes was lifted away from those violated bodies and projected onto a metaphorical vision of a violated nation. Physical borders of many individual bodies were gathered together and superimposed onto the physical borders of a single nation, obscuring the difference between female boundaries, which are literally physical, and national boundaries, which occur in the physical world but derive their clout from imaginative consensus. In discussions of rape, men and women sometimes argue about what constitutes consent, but no one disputes the notion that the female body contains physical boundaries susceptible to violation. The physical boundaries that separate nations, however, can easily constitute the subject of a border dispute. One country cites one line on a map; another country cites a different line. Unlike a body's borders, a national border depends on consensus that it exists.

England's description of the invasion as a crime against the body reveals something about what kind of boundary it understood Germany to have violated: not a contractual agreement but a naturally occurring world organization. Though crossing a national border is a passage one makes through a physical landscape that has a number of material manifestations of boundary (border guards, forts, fences); and though it is true that many people were killed because the German army crossed a line that had been marked on maps and existed in the minds of thousands of people; it is also true that, despite the ways in which the crossing of a national border had physical consequences, the border itself was a contractual entity, not a physical one.[1] As suspect as Germany's invasion may have been, from a diplomatic point of view, the violation was a contractual one, not a physical one, and thus not what Britain tried to make it out to be when calling it "rape."

That nuns and virgins rather than wives and mothers should so frequently be portrayed as the victims of German rape suggests even more graphically the rigidity with which England viewed the geopolitical organization of Europe. No matter how entrenched or inevitable a national border may seem, it can never achieve the kind of nonnegotiability of a woman's virginity, which remains stubbornly either/or, a line that can only be crossed once. By charging Germany with the double crime for which no reparation is possible—raping not just a woman but a virgin—England managed to blend maximum moral opprobrium with a sense that such a violation could never really be repaired. This extreme rhetoric ensured that the fictional *metaphor* of rape (crossing a national border) disappeared behind the factual *literal* rapes (suffered by Belgian women during the invasion).

The literal rapes of which England accused Germany were considered part of a larger violation against civilized standards of behavior. According to Samuel Hynes, "Some of the most influential documents in the shaping of English war imaginations were those that recorded, in what seemed factual, documentary form, alleged atrocities committed by the German army in the invasion of Belgium and northern France" (52). The first of these documents to be published was a pamphlet by William Le Queux: *German Atrocities: A Record of Shameless Deeds*. "It was issued in September 1914, priced for a mass public at twopence, and purported to be based on Belgian government statements, interviews, and the reports of war correspondents" (52). "Official" reports such as *The Official Book of the German Atrocities* began to appear in 1915. As Hynes points out, the book was described as having been "'Published by Authority'—whose authority was not made clear" (52–53).

England went to war against Germany on the basis of such "facts." As Le Queux declares, "This fearful and disgraceful record of a Nation's shame and of an Emperor's complicity in atrocious crimes against God and man is no work of fiction, but a plain unvarnished statement of the grim and terrible work of the Kaiser's Huns of Attila" (5). Such stories fanned British outrage and galvanized British resolve to punish the "dirty Huns." Le Queux's pamphlet contains the following incident, listed under the heading "Fate of a 16-year-old Girl":

> [O]n Thursday, August 20, German soldiers fetched from their house a young girl, about sixteen years old, and her parents. They conducted them to a small deserted country house, and while some of them held back the father and mother, others entered the house, and, finding the cellar open, forced the girl to drink. They then brought her on to the lawn in front of the house and assaulted her. Finally they stabbed her in the breast with their bayonets. (35)

Another event is labeled "The Maiden Tribute" and describes a group of German soldiers terrorizing a family. After having shot and killed the father,

> They were going to shoot the grandfather when the mother and daughter fell on their knees and begged the soldiers to spare the life of the old man. The officer, or under-officer, of the party then said, "Yes, we won't trouble about the old people," and touching the cheek of the young girl with his fingers, he added, with a significant laugh, "Pretty youth is better." The sequel need not be written here, although the mother of the girl has told it. (58)

J. H. Morgan's *German Atrocities: An Official Investigation,* includes the following:

> J. G——, Lance-Corporal, King's Own, 1st Batt.:—At the end of November, the second day after we arrived at Nieppe, two of us entered an estaminet and found the landlady crying; she told us that about thirteen Germans violated her daughter and shot her husband against a wall in front of her eyes. She said there were a lot of other cases in Nieppe. (70)

> Private R. McK——, 2nd Royal Irish:—On the advance from the Marne to the Aisne in September, we passed through a village and saw a baby propped up at the window like a doll. About six of us went into the house, with a sergeant, and found the child dead—bayoneted. We found a tottering kind of old man, a middle-aged woman, and a youth, all bayoneted. In another village our interpreter pointed out to us two girls who were crying; he told us they had been ravished. (81)

Such harrowing accounts of "assault," "violation," "ravishing," and that which "need not be written here" provoked understandable outrage, a prime motivator in public support for the war. The reliability of such accounts is difficult to determine from this distance, but clearly if such documents were indeed "plain and unvarnished," the outrage was well justified.

The atrocity document that has received the most critical attention is the government-generated Bryce Report, which was named for Lord James Bryce, the well-respected political figure who chaired a committee charged with investigating reports of German atrocities in Belgium. Essentially, the Bryce Report confirmed what less reputable authors had claimed; Samuel Hynes has described the Report as "remov[ing] the idea of atrocity from the realm of propaganda—the newspaper cartoon and the recruiting poster—and plac[ing] it in sober reality. Thereafter it would be taken for granted by most English people as a truth about the Germans." Rendered in official language ("The style of the depositions," Hynes notes, "is quite uniform . . . plain, circumstantial, and unjudgemental" [55]) and published by the establishment, the factuality of atrocities seemed secure.

The question of exactly what happened in Belgium in 1914 has never really been settled. Some of what passed for fact at the time seems to have been warped by racism; other material was later dismissed because it was uncorroborated or not detailed enough. Susan Brownmiller has argued that reports of rapes have frequently been dismissed because of the ways in which historians have been too often susceptible to sexism and too easily dismissive of rape. "When the war was over, a wholly predictable reaction set in," Brownmiller observes.

> Scholars of the newly refined art of propaganda set about to unravel its mysteries by trying to separate fact from fiction. It was inevitable that a deep bias against women (particularly against women who say they have been raped) would show in their endeavor. There had been some gross lies in the manufacturing of Allied propaganda and these were readily brought to light. . . . But what about the rape of all those women? The crime that is by reputation "the easiest to charge and the hardest to prove" has traditionally been the *easiest to disprove* as well. The rational experts found it laughably easy to debunk accounts of rape. (47)

Brownmiller goes on to demonstrate that, for instance, scholars would dismiss a woman's claim that she had also been robbed, because she was not named, or because her statement had not been attested (47–48). She argues that men may demand proof from raped women that the women may not be in a position to supply or may not want to supply, pointing out that not being able to prove something or being unwilling to have one's name made public does not necessarily have any bearing on the charge being leveled. Brownmiller, in other words, suggests that men are sometimes guilty of dismissing rape as fictional because of a tendency to devise standards of factuality that make it impossible for women to prove what has happened to them. Our understanding of German soldiers' behavior in the summer and fall of 1914 is thus complicated by both racism ("Huns" were assumed guilty at least partly because of their ethnic background) and sexism (women were discredited at least partly because of their inability to produce proof of assault).

Trevor Wilson has analyzed the predicament of Lord Bryce and his committee somewhat differently, arguing that the sexual assaults Belgian women may have suffered pale in comparison to the larger issue—the brutality of the invasion itself. After invading a neutral country, Germany had instituted the policy of *Kriegsverrat,* killing civilians and destroying public buildings and personal property. Such "atrociousness towards Belgium was flagrant, and . . . far more subversive of civilized standards than brutal acts perpetrated upon women and children by bands of soldiers" (190). Wilson thus argues that even if Bryce allowed sloppy investigating methods to shore up atrocity stories, it was in the understandable service of this larger outrage inflicted on Belgium collectively rather than on Belgian women specifically.

While the Kaiser worried about "encirclement," his chief strategists organized the German army for a project of "envelopment," thus articulating an offensive strategy that was nearly identical to the Kaiser's articulation of his worst defensive fear. Count Alfred von Schlieffen, chief of the German general staff from 1891 to 1906, developed a plan to obliterate France in six weeks using seven-eighths of the German army; the other eighth was allocated to the task of holding the Russian front. Convinced that Russia's best defense against a German invasion would always be simply to "withdra[w] within her infinite room" (Tuchman 19), Schlieffen convinced the German general staff that to subdue France should be Germany's first priority. His prescription was that the German army should swing around Belgium as far west as Lille, which, though forty miles inland from the Channel, is far enough west to have been memorialized in a vivid dictum: "[L]et the last man on the right brush the Channel with his sleeve" (Tuchman 25). In their adoption of the Schlieffen Plan, then, Germany appropriated the tactic it most feared. Terrified of encirclement, they struck back with envelopment.

There is an eerie continuity between Britain's rhetoric of accusation at the beginning of World War I (rape) and its predominant metaphors of strategy (push) during the war. The first day of the Battle of the Somme—July 1, 1916—was called "The Big Push" and was celebrated in newspapers at home; "push" expressed a British compulsion to move forward. A similar continuity can be seen between Germany's accusatory rhetoric of encirclement and Schlieffen's plan of wheeling around the edge of Belgium, *enveloping* the French resistance. That the vocabulary of accusation for both countries should correspond so closely to its metaphors of strategy indicates how the way in which a country habitually reads the world is the same way in which it is liable to write the world. England, outraged by rape, responded with a push. The Kaiser, obsessed with encirclement, supported a general staff committed to envelopment.

The degree to which both England and Germany seem to have internalized their own versions of enemy behavior—England committing the act it decried in Germany and Germany committing the act of which it accused the rest of Europe—suggests how each country's perception of the world was based on habitual patterns. The issue of factuality receded before the pressure of such imaginative habits. However, as Scarry has taught us, deeply ingrained perceptual reflexes are felt to have factual authority precisely because the more deeply ingrained they are, the more difficulty we have distinguishing between what we really see and what our expectations are conditioning us to see. When fictive metaphors are mistaken for factual descriptions, it reinforces the tendency to dispute another nation's version of the "facts." What such nations are really arguing about is whose fictions will be allowed to be the official fictions—whose fictions will, by mutual agreement, be endowed with the status of factuality.

One way of endowing cultural fictions with factuality is to move from "making-up" to "making-real"—in other words, to construct artifacts displaying what has been imagined in order to be able to "share" the imaginative object with others (Scarry 21). The differing ways in which England and Germany designed trench architecture may thus be understood as reflecting their differing attitudes toward what kinds of imaginative constructs needed to be affirmed.

German trench architecture was elaborate. As a B.E.F. (British Expeditionary Force) officer describes in a 1916 issue of the *Architectural Review,* one structure near Mametz "was designed to house a whole company of 300 men, with the needful kitchens, provision and munition storerooms . . . an engine-room, and a motor room: many of the captured dug-outs were thus lighted by electricity, . . . [while in] the officers' quarters there have been found full-length mirrors, comfortable bedsteads, cushioned armchairs, and some pictures, and one room is lined with glazed 'sanitary' wallpaper" ("German Trench Architecture" 88–89). The B.E.F. and French army, on the other hand, had a much more makeshift attitude toward their trenches and for the most part merely dug their way far enough underground to afford protection from the strafing of enemy machine guns: "The Allied trench looks, in every way, like the work of men who hoped and meant to move on before long; the German trench looks like the work of men who hoped, or feared, that they would be in it for years. Our [British] trench housing has been much more of a makeshift, a sort of camping out, with some ingenious provisions for shelter and comfort, but not more than the least that would serve" ("German Trench Architecture" 88–89).

Paul Fussell has argued that official B.E.F. attachment to acts of offensive heroism explains the carelessness with which it constructed its trenches: "Since defense offered little opportunity for the display of pluck or swank, it was by implication derogated in the officers' *Field Service Pocket Book.*" It follows then, Fussell explains, that "[o]ne reason the British trench system was so haphazard and ramshackle was that it had originally taken form in accord with the official injunction: 'The choice of a [defensive] position and its preparation must be made with a view to economizing the power expended on defense in order that the power of offense may be increased'" (43). In war, an offensive posture requires movement forward and destruction; to build safe and comfortable fortifications is to make a material investment in defense, which is stationary and constructive. Thus, a blasé attitude about fortification represents the B.E.F.'s testament to the fact that the Allied forces are concentrating on other things. There is no need to make a comfortable life for themselves in the dirt when they are about to move forward and gain control of dirt that is several thousand yards hence.

I would elaborate on Fussell's point by adding that, since England saw itself as driving the Germans out of Belgium and France, it did not invest in physical borders on the western front. The "real" physical borders, which Germany had, to the British mind, illegally crossed, were located elsewhere. That many German trenches were indeed "architectural" structures while English ones were merely dug ones ("dug-outs") shows that Germany, however, viewed the battlefield itself as the site upon which a new national border was being affirmed: Germany understood physical borders as being created by battle right there on the battlefield. The Germans' erection of military architecture that carefully mimicked civilian *domestic* architecture (with full-length mirrors and upholstered chairs) displayed their belief that the borders could be reinvented. Germans were not merely *stopping* in the trenches but *living* in them; they affirmed the "fact" of their belonging there by building *homes*.

British commitment to the war, though staunch, was a commitment to an already imagined, already built culture existing elsewhere. To construct a new world was deemed unnecessary. German commitment, however, was to the ratification of a new vision of itself as a nation, a ratification that required the construction of new material structures that could embody and ensure the durability of the new vision after the war.[2]

The issue of sexual assault stands at the center of both the events of August 1914 and the events in E. M. Forster's *A Passage to India*, published ten years later, in 1924. Adela Quested never accuses Dr. Aziz of rape; the crime is never even named, except to call it an "insult"—"Miss Quested has been insulted in one of the Marabar Caves" (163)—but the way in which the English community rallies around what they perceive as a violated woman parallels the way in which England rallied around Belgium in a number of ways.

First of all, just as the question of German atrocities has undergone numerous transformations and revisions in the light of new facts and old prejudices, the incident in the cave never gets cleared up entirely. Adela begins by feeling certain that Aziz assaulted her, then doubts herself ("Aziz . . . have I made a mistake?" [202]), then drifts back toward certainty. Finally, in the courtroom scene, she withdraws everything. In *Passage*, Forster intentionally leaves the question of sexual assault unresolved: "I tried to show that India is an unexplainable muddle by introducing an unexplained muddle—Miss Quested's experience in the cave. When asked what happened there, I don't know" ("To William Plomer"). Cyril Fielding is as well aware as Susan Brownmiller that sexual crimes are notoriously difficult to verify, as is displayed by his advice to Aziz's friend Hamidullah: "Don't complicate, let the cards play themselves. . . . We're bound to win, there's nothing else we can do. She will never be able to substantiate the charge" (174).

Another link between August 1914 and the incident in the Marabar Caves is the ease with which allegations of assault slide into allegations against a nation. Accusing an individual man of assault quickly escalates into accusing a whole nation of men of demonstrating a propensity to assault women. "In the hands of skilled Allied manipulators," Brownmiller has observed of the early stages of World War I, "rape was successfully launched in world opinion, almost overnight, as a *characteristic German crime,* evidence of the 'depraved Boche' penchant for warfare by atrocity" (43–44). "Modern Germany," William Le Queux stated at the time, "frothing with military Nietzschism, seems to have returned to a primitive barbarism. . . . Germany . . . has for ever lost her place among civilized nations" (preface 5). Similarly, Miss Quested's accusation is immediately articulated as a racial and national issue. After the ill-fated picnic to the Marabar Caves, Cyril Fielding is met at the train by Turton, the Collector, who "could not speak at first. His face was white, fanatical, and rather beautiful—the expression that all English faces were to wear at Chandrapore for many days. Always brave and unselfish, he was now fused by some white and generous heat; he would have killed himself, obviously, if he had thought it right to do so" (163).

Forster is explicit in his analysis of such a "white and generous heat": it blends racism and nationalism (Turton's white face wears the expression "that all English faces were to wear . . . for many days"), and it poses a direct threat to factuality. Turton frowns at Fielding "because he was keeping his head. He had not gone mad at the phrase 'an English girl fresh from England,' he had not rallied to the banner of race. He was still after facts, though the herd had decided on emotion" (165). Just as individual rapes in Belgium became an excuse for indulging a larger racist grudge against Germany, Miss Quested's accusation of Aziz becomes an excuse for indulging a larger racist grudge against Indians. In fact, "The issues Miss Quested had raised were so much more important than she was herself that people inevitably forgot her" (216).

Forster goes on to blend this configuration of events—an alleged assault on a woman that prompts extreme nationalism, disinterest in the facts, and male eagerness to fight and even die—with more explicit reference to what happens in war. McBryde, the District Superintendent of Police, admonishes Fielding that

> "at a time like this there's not room for—well—personal views. The man who doesn't toe the line is lost."
> "I see what you mean."
> "No, you don't see entirely. He not only loses himself, he weakens his friends. If you leave the line, you leave a gap in the line." (171)

That only one official view of the facts is allowed immediately modulates into the language of war: toeing the line of group conformity starts sounding suspiciously like staying in step with a line of advancing soldiers. Modris Eksteins has described British strategy as dominated by the "dream of the 'gap,' the sudden parting of the enemy front" (143), which suggests that the danger of leaving a gap in one's own line would have been a serious preoccupation.

Forster makes it clear that the English community in *Passage* responds to the alleged assault on Miss Quested as a provocation to war: the men gathered at the country club "had started speaking of 'women and children'—that phrase that exempts the male from sanity when it has been repeated a few times" (183). Reference to the formulation of male sacrifice as "women and children first" reminds us of how this marshaling of country club forces draws on patterns of chivalry typical of any war of that era. In another echo of wartime relations, when Mrs. Callendar pipes up that "Mr. McBryde's down there disguised as a Holy Man," she is immediately reprimanded by Turton:

> "That's exactly the sort of thing that must not be said. . . . Mrs. Callendar, be more careful than that, please, in these times."
>
> "I . . . well, I . . ." She was not offended, his severity made her feel safe. (182)

McBryde's ominous suggestion that "these times" require unusual precautions, his patronizing tone, and Mrs. Callendar's willing retreat to the safety of male protection were all familiar patterns of relations between the sexes during the Great War.

Though England went to war in response to the "rape" of Belgium, it did not transform the faces of rape victims into motivating poster images. Instead, beautiful damsels replaced and subsumed the particular victims of rape. Similarly, in Forster's novel, the "crime" against Adela Quested functions as a prompt for a nationalism that subsumes her particular body. At the country club,

> One young mother—a brainless but most beautiful girl—sat on a low ottoman in the smoking-room with her baby in her arms; her husband was away in the district, and she dared not return to her bungalow in case the "niggers attacked." The wife of a small railway official, she was generally snubbed; but this evening, with her abundant figure and masses of corn-gold hair, she symbolized all that is worth fighting and dying for; more permanent a symbol, perhaps, than poor Adela. (180–81)

The dim-witted but beautiful young woman even comments that the situation would be more bearable "if only there were a few Tommies" (184). This Great War nickname for English soldiers further underlines the parallel between the novel and its historical context.

Forster's handling of the community response to Miss Quested's fiancé, Heaslop, points out the incongruous way in which female victims may be used to stir up support and then abandoned in the male activity that follows: "At the name of Heaslop a fine and beautiful expression was renewed on every face. Miss Quested was only a victim, but young Heaslop was a martyr; he was the recipient of all the evil intended against them by the country they had tried to serve" (185). Sexual assault, Forster implies, is a violation that men are adept at turning into something about themselves rather than about its female victims, just as Belgian rape victims were consigned to the background once men stepped into fight.

Forster goes on to suggest that, while insult to a woman can do an excellent job of provoking men into chivalric battles, such chivalry actually obscures varying degrees of hostility against women—hostility that ranges from mild resentment to outright misogyny. On the way to Aziz's trial, for instance, Turton thinks to himself that he doesn't really hate Indians: "After all, it's our women who make everything more difficult out here." This, the narrator tells us, "was his inmost thought, as he caught sight of some obscenities upon a long blank wall, and beneath his chivalry to Miss Quested resentment lurked, waiting its day—perhaps there is a grain of resentment in all chivalry" (214). While the narrator explicitly mentions the way in which chivalry may be attended by resentment, the even stronger juxtaposition of obscene graffiti to that "inmost thought" suggests, even more ominously, that "resentment" might well be too mild a term for the attitude of Turton toward "our women."[3]

Brownmiller has argued that "[w]ar provides men with the perfect psychologic backdrop to give vent to their contempt for women. . . . In the name of victory and the power of the gun, war provides men with a tacit license to rape. In the act and in the excuse, rape in war reveals the male psyche in its boldest form, without the veneer of 'chivalry' or civilization" (32–33). In *Passage,* Forster blends racism and misogyny by describing the English reaction to news about two Indian strikes:

> The Sweepers had just struck, and half the commodes of Chandrapore remained desolate in consequence—only half, and Sweepers from the District, who felt less strongly about the innocence of Dr. Aziz, would arrive in the afternoon, and break the strike, but why should the grotesque incident occur? And a number of Mohammedan ladies had sworn to take no food until the prisoner was acquitted; their death would make little difference, indeed, being invisible, they seemed dead already, nevertheless it was disquieting. (214)

Just as Turton's thought about the troublesomeness of women is juxtaposed against scribbled obscenity, the striking women, whose "death would make little difference," are juxtaposed against feces. Forster clearly suggests that hostility toward women constitutes a strange and disturbing undercurrent to the rhetoric of male chivalry that occurs in response to sexual assault.

Forster began writing *A Passage to India* as early as 1913 but put it aside during the war, when he worked for the Red Cross in Egypt. He did not pick up the novel again until 1922, and even then might not have completed it without the steady encouragement of Leonard Woolf. Critics generally note that this gap between the beginning of work and final publication (1913–24) covers the years of World War I and, if their readings of the novel are pessimistic, generally hold the war responsible for the change in tone from the earlier utopian impulse of *Howards End* (1910). That earlier novel, declares one critic, demonstrates a decidedly utopian impulse, "[b]ut the dregs of Edwardian optimism vanished in the abyss of the Great War" (Rosecrance 185). *Passage,* another affirms, is "certainly Forster's bitterest book": "It is not hard to guess why the optimism which he had shown in 1910 had changed to despair in bitterness by 1924. Between the writing of the two novels had come the First World War and its aftermath: the postwar world was certainly, to a sensitive mind, a much more disquieting place than the prewar world had ever been" (Shusterman 159). Another pair of critics, attending more specifically to the crisis in politics prompted by the war and to Forster's famous comment that "I belong to the fag-end of Victorian liberalism" ("The Challenge of Our Time" 54), state simply that "the Great War 'happened', and liberal humanism died a strange death" (Ebbatson and Neale 18).

Thus, though *Passage* is understood as a novel registering the experience of World War I, the relationship is routinely referred to as an atmospheric, rather than explicit, one. *Passage* was written after the war by an intelligent man who participated (but did not fight) in the war. Like everyone else in Europe, he lost friends to the war. He had not written a novel since before it began, so the cumulative effects of the experience presumably can be felt in the later effort. And they are felt, but not articulated, because when Forster did sit down to complete his novel, he made no mention of war. Instead, he wrote a book about imperialism, racism, friendship, sexuality, religion, work, leisure, and gender. He meditated on the Indian earth, the western predilection for form, the eastern carelessness of it, and existential angst. He structured his novel around three kinds of space (mosque, caves, temple) but no trenches, peopled it with characters of different races and ages and sexes (old English Mrs. Moore, young Indian Dr. Aziz) but not with veterans or war brides.

Yet Forster's description of the Marabar Caves strongly echoes his description of the war, suggesting that, on some level, he used the lessons he learned from the war to structure his novel. Just as Turton becomes annoyed at Fielding because "[h]e was still after facts," Forster, in a letter of 1917, notes that facts tend to be incompatible with war:

> Notes. Human Nature under War Conditions:—
> When a man makes a statement now, it seldom has any relation to the ~~truth~~ facts or even to what he supposes to be the facts. He is merely functioning, generally under the stimulus of fear or sorrow. ("To Goldsworthy Lowes Dickinson")

The Marabar Caves in *Passage* are notable in that "[n]othing, nothing attaches to them. . . . There is little to see, and no eye to see it. . . .

Nothing is inside them . . . if mankind grew curious and excavated, nothing, nothing would be added to the sum of good or evil" (124–25). Moral excavation of the war produced, for Forster, a similar dearth of results, as he explained in his response to news that yet another friend had died in France: "[F]or my own part I've learnt nothing and feel that most people have likewise learnt nothing, despite the assurances of the newspapers to the contrary. I can't even feel that the dead have died in our defence. I didn't want W. R. [Willie Rutherford, who died in France in 1916 or 1917] to leave No 21 [an address or army assignment]. It seemed to me no good and it still seems no good, and the knowledge that his end didn't seem meaningless to him doesn't fill it with meaning for me" ("To Forrest Reid").

Just as the caves collapse meaningful distinctions by reducing all sounds and all voices, language profound and language profane, to a mere "ou-boum," the war represents an ethical black hole to Forster, sucking up possible meanings that then disappear forever. Just as the factuality of the rape of Belgium is never completely resolved, the factuality of the assault on Adela Quested is never completely resolved. Just as England went to war over alleged rape in a way that encouraged racist condescension, the Turtons and Burtons of *Passage* find in Miss Quested's allegations an excuse to indulge their most virulent imperialist condescension against the Indians. And Forster's suggestion that a fixation on sexual assault can be rooted in deeply suppressed misogyny raises disturbing questions about Britain's rally to the defense of Belgian women.

Civilian and combatant modernists both devoted a great deal of energy to delineating the categories of fact and fiction. I would suggest, however, that combatants resisted the modernist willingness to dismiss the category of factuality precisely because combatants—unlike modernists—were involved in defending a specific set of "facts" with their lives, as well as watching friends and comrades defend those "facts" to the death. To dismiss the category of factuality after the war, then—even when it clearly could accommodate neither the experience of combat nor the vagaries of remembering—would have constituted for survivors both an act of disloyalty to those who did die and a diminution of their own efforts. While veterans were honest about the ways in which combat at once overwhelmed and eluded the inherited forms for articulating experience, they could not bring themselves to repudiate those forms, since repudiation would have implicated them in a project of rethinking and reshaping.

On the surface, civilian modernists tolerate factual violation much more blithely than do combatants, privileging what Walter Pater calls "sense of fact" over "mere fact": "[J]ust in proportion as the writer's aim, consciously or unconsciously, comes to be the transcribing, not of the world, not of mere fact, but of his sense of it, he becomes an artist, his work *fine* art" (89). Aesthetic value, Pater asserts, lies in the territory of the perceiving subject. As Michael Levenson has asserted, "'Facts' become a specific literary target" for early modernists like Conrad, and "in the opposition between fact and psychology, deeper interest lies on the psychological side. . . . [I]n Paterian terms, [narrators like Marlow] confir[m] the triumph of 'sense of fact' over 'fact' . . . and embod[y] the psychologistic premise, namely that the meaning of a phenomenon is its presence to a mind" (20).

In Forster's *A Passage to India*, Dr. Aziz takes a very modernist attitude toward facts. Adela insults him with a question about polygamy, so Aziz steps into a cave to escape her and allow his irritation to cool. When he emerges, Adela has disappeared. He sees a car though, so when he rejoins his breakfast party, he tells Fielding and Mrs. Moore that when Adela saw the car she decided to go down and speak to her friend. "Incurably inaccurate," the narrator remarks:

> [H]e already thought that this was what had occurred. He was inaccurate because he was sensitive. He did not like to remember Miss Quested's remark about polygamy, because it was unworthy of a guest, so he put it from his mind, and with it the knowledge that he had bolted into a cave to get away from her. He was inaccurate because he desired to honour her, and—facts being entangled—he had to arrange them in her vicinity, as one tidies the ground after extracting a weed. (158)

To someone invested in factuality at all costs, Aziz's little exercise in fact-tidying amounts to a lie. Forster takes a more indulgent attitude, linking the incident to a larger observation about the nature of Indian sensibilities as opposed to western ones. That Cyril Fielding—one of the most rational English characters in the novel—arrives at a similarly fuzzy conclusion about factuality is therefore surprising, especially since the fact about which Fielding chooses to articulate his newly flexible model of interpretation is the fact of Mrs. Moore's death. Despite death's apparently unyielding insusceptibility to interpretation, Fielding feels "that we exist not in ourselves, but in terms of each others' minds" (250) and reasons out a rebuttal when he receives news of Mrs. Moore's death. "Facts are facts," he certainly admits, "and everyone would learn of Mrs. Moore's death in the morning. But it struck him that people are not really dead until they are felt to be dead. As long as there is some misunderstanding about them, they possess a sort of immortality" (255). Fielding's logic lifts factuality out of the moral realm and resituates it in a perceptual realm, replacing the virtue of external accuracy with the virtue of internal accuracy—that is, with the precise rendering of consciousness.

Forster is also at pains to point out how factuality depends on audience. Soon after the disastrous Marabar picnic, Fielding wishes to ask Adela if there is any possibility that she is mistaken about the assault. McBryde says that his wife could ask Adela that question, but Fielding feels that facts are not immune from the contexts in which they emerge and that different stories might get told to different people:

> "But *I* wanted to ask her. I want someone who believes in him to ask her."
> "What difference does that make?"
> "She is among people who disbelieve in Indians."
> "Well, she tells her own story, doesn't she?"
> "I know, but she tells it to you."
> McBryde raised his eyebrows, murmuring: "A bit too finespun."
> (170)

McBryde assumes that the facts of one's "own story" are independent of the audience before which they are displayed, while Fielding argues that facts depend on audience.

Combatants bickered over issues of factuality, unwilling to abandon their sense of it as a legitimating category, yet unable to fit their experiences of war into its narrow confines and conflicted about the nature of their audience. There are moments during which Robert Graves, for example, exhibits a decidedly modernist preference for the abandonment of a standard of factuality that he claims has been rendered irrelevant by the experience of war: "[T]he memoirs of a man who went through some of the worst experiences of trench warfare are not truthful if they do not contain a high proportion of falsities. High-explosive barrages will make a temporary liar or visionary of anyone; the old trench-mind is at work in all over-estimation of casualties, 'unnecessary' dwelling on horrors, mixing of dates and confusion between trench rumours and scenes actually witnessed" ("Postscript to 'Good-bye to All That'" 33). Yet despite this professed disregard for a strict definition of factuality, Graves vigorously defended the veracity of his war memoirs. After the publication of *Good-bye to All That,* for instance, he carried on a heated correspondence with fellow combatant Siegfried Sassoon over a number of alleged facts in the book.

Sassoon initiated the debate in February 1930 by sending Graves (of whom he had once been fond) a long list of disputed details, complete with page numbers. The accusations provoked exchanges like the following, in which the two men argue about everything from how far a man can ride in a day to whether British officers typically visited prostitutes:

> [7 February 1930, from Sassoon]
> No officer rode into Amiens from Montagne. (It is just possible that the CO did so.) It was 16 miles. So they must have visited your "Blue Lamp" by train and got home early. I challenge you to produce three names of officers who, to your certain knowledge, visited the Blue Lamp from Montagne. Joe Cottrill may have done. Who else? (Graves, *In Broken Images* 201)

[20 February 1930, Graves responds]

Blue Lamp. Richardson and Davies, not to mention Stevens. 1,2,3 and the day before Christmas. Sensational disclosures followed. Want any more?

16 miles. I once rode fifty in a day the following winter.

It doesn't take long to fuck; but perhaps you don't know about that. (Graves, *In Broken Images* 202)

[2 March 1930, from Sassoon]

"*Riding into Amiens.*" When you rode fifty miles, did you have a look at your horse next day? (In your book you say that the dentist was "*twenty miles away.*") My point is that 2 $1/2$ hours each way would fill up a Saturday afternoon (or was it a Sunday?), that I lived in a billet with the transport officer, and heard the fuss about borrowing horses to go for little rides, and knew the capacities of the 1st RWF crocks; and think that your remarks on p. 231 are misleading and give a disproportionate impression of that aspect of Army life (at that time and place).

"*It doesn't take long to *.*" Not a pretty remark, Robert. Yes, I know a little about the chronology, etc., of the act. Isn't it sometimes dependent on the taste, capacity, etc., of the participants? I am also aware that two minutes per man was about the time-limit for "other ranks" (though I should hesitate before I put it into a "powerful war-book"). Anyhow I accept your trio of "Blue Lampers." (C Company remained puritanical.) (Graves, *In Broken Images* 205)

The facts in question here are more that ten years old, yet the fierceness with which each man consults his memory and defends his version of events speaks for the investment of both in an ethic of factuality (after this flurry of insults and counter-insults, they did not correspond for three years). "Such inaccuracies," Sassoon states severely, "are not noticeable to 'the general public', but they are significant to those who shared your experiences. I am testing your book as a private matter between you and me, which is perhaps more important than the momentary curiosity of 50,000 strangers." "I could state you a long list of [inaccuracies]," he threatens—and then proceeds, compulsively, to do just that (Graves, *In Broken Images* 200).

Sassoon's comments imply that the only significant audience to which a veteran could conceivably address himself is one composed of his fellow veterans—despite the fact that it would be the fifty thousand (civilian) strangers who had been, and would continue to be, most vulnerable to misconceptions about the war. That the readers of *Good-bye to All That* who had fought in the war themselves would consult their own memories and experiences (just as he himself was doing) was apparently beside the point for Sassoon. For him, Great War memoirs represented not, as might be expected, an opportunity to set the record straight in the mind of uninformed civilians; rather, they represented the opportunity for yet another shared experience between veterans in which civilians were unable to participate meaningfully—their "momentary curiosity" is immaterial. This view of war memoirs alters the import of his bitter debate about factuality with Graves. If, as Sassoon contends, veterans are writing for their fellow veterans and not for civilians, factual significance is not crucial, since readers could always consult their own experience, accepting or rejecting someone else's version of an event.

At the same time, Sassoon, despite his dogged insistence on documentation and veracity, acknowledges the way in which facts may be cast in various ways in order to give various impressions of an experience to readers. As he tells Graves, "[Y]our remarks on p. 231 [about prostitution] are misleading and give a disproportionate impression of that aspect of Army life (at that time and place)" (Graves, *In Broken Images* 205). What Sassoon acknowledges here is that one can indeed put a spin even on verifiable facts and that a reporter of such facts has an obligation to select his evidence in a manner that gives an accurate view of the larger picture, rather than one which, though it might be strictly true as far as the experience of an individual goes, would, if extrapolated, provide a misleading picture of the whole.

In a suggested solution to one of *Good-bye*'s many enumerated inadequacies, Sassoon proposes a strikingly modernist tactic—the employment of multiple points of limited view. "You cannot correct your story," he tells Graves, "except by making it less one-sided (and less imbued with the omniscience of 12 years afterwards)" (Graves, *In Broken Images* 206). Sassoon's interest in both multiple points of view and the eschewal of wise retrospect corresponds to Levenson's description of how narrative conventions were altered by modernists around the turn of the century. A Victorian author such as George Eliot used a narrator who, as Levenson explains, "is not another character, but a disembodied presence, moving freely over the dramatic scene, and granted prerogatives not allowed to mere mortals." Sassoon prescribes a narrator more along the lines of the ones used by modernists like Conrad, who "makes what amounts to a division of narrative labour": "The third-person narrator provides the precision of physical detail but hesitates to penetrate the individual psyche which George Eliot had so remorselessly invaded" (8).

That Sassoon should berate Graves for his perversion of factuality is somewhat surprising given a work like his own *Memoirs of an Infantry Officer*, in which he makes a point of addressing the problems of producing an accurate account of the war. Despite the rather painstaking chronological frame of the novel, its protagonist George Sherston is at pains to point out the discrepancy between that frame and the unaccountable patterns of remembering that he is forced to rely upon in constructing it. Having chosen to market his Sherston trilogy as fiction, Sassoon could, on the one hand, have created a confident third-person narrator to glide over perceptual difficulties or, on the other, have ignored the erratic habits of a single man's memory. Instead, he chooses both to keep the chronology of the *Memoirs* in place and to point out places where such a structure belies the idiosyncrasies of recollection as well as of experience.

His frank insistence on the unaccountability of his own memory begins early in the novel, when Sherston tells how "[t]here were several of us on board [the bus going to the Army School] . . . and we must have stopped at the next village to pick up a few more. But memory tries to misinform me that Flook and I were alone on that omnibus, with a fresh breeze in our faces and our minds 'making a separate peace' with the late April landscape" (10). Instead of describing the men on the bus (as a Victorian writer might have done) or privileging the texture of his own impression by rendering it in colorful detail, then perhaps shifting to the perspective of the bus driver annoyed at having to make so many stops (as a modernist civilian might have done), Sherston makes a flat admission: this is the way I remember it, but this is probably not the way it really happened—my memory does not agree with the facts. That such an admission appears at all in a *novel* displays the excruciating ambivalence with which soldiers seem to have confronted the failure of factuality as a category.

Incidents crucial to the plot of war recede while irrelevant ones lodge themselves in Sherston's memory: "What we did up in the Front Line I don't remember; but while we were remounting our horses at 71. North two privates were engaged in a good-humored scuffle; one had the other's head under his arm. Why should I remember that and forget so much else?" (62). Sometimes, details that have vanished reappear in the process of rendering their contexts: "Anyhow, my feverish performances were concluded by a peremptory message from Battalion H.Q. and I went down to Bottom Wood by a half-dug communication trench whose existence I have only this moment remembered (which shows how difficult it is to recover the details of war experience)" (92–93). Other times, details that he knows to have been a part of the war resist his efforts at recovery: "Time seems to have obliterated the laughter of the war. I cannot hear it in my head" (82).

That the vagaries of memory pitch a monkey-wrench into the mechanisms of factuality is something upon which combatants and modernists agree wholeheartedly. In a tone far removed from the snippy exchanges with Graves, Sassoon's narrator admits that he has no choice but to tell about his bath rather than attempt to detail anything like a universal experience of the war: "I also remember how I went one afternoon to have a hot bath in the Jute Mill. The water was poured into a dyeing vat. Remembering that I had a bath may not be of much interest to anyone, but it was a good bath, and it is my own story that I am trying to tell, and as such it must be received; those who expect a universalization of the Great War must look for it elsewhere" (17). In Virginia Woolf's *Mrs. Dalloway,* Clarissa articulates the unaccountable nooks and crannies of her memory less defensively but just as honestly when she notes with amazement how, "when millions of things had utterly vanished—how strange it was!—a few sayings like this about cabbages" (4) are what remain lodged in her brain.

Factuality is premised partly on the idea of a witness (as the familiar phrase "observable fact" makes clear) and partly on assumptions about what it is possible to know (which assumptions we refer to when we preface a statement with the words "I know for a fact"). In addition, as the heated exchange between Graves and Sassoon reminds us, we demand that factual accounts employ a judicious selection of detail and a careful placement of emphasis. Accounts of war, judged by a standard test of factuality, ought neither to minimize nor to overemphasize the horror of war casualties; they must have dates right and be assiduously restricted to incidents that were witnessed; rumors, floating in and out of casual conversation, in and out of nightmare, ought to be ignored. As Mary Borden explains in the preface to *The Forbidden Zone*, though, these obligations toward factuality were difficult to fulfill: "To those who find these impressions confused, I would say that they are fragments of a great confusion. Any attempt to reduce them to order would require artifice on my part and would falsify them. To those on the other hand who find them unbearably plain, I would say that I have blurred the bare horror of facts and softened the reality in spite of myself, not because I wished to do so, but because I was incapable of a nearer approach to the truth."

The magnitude, the violence, and the intensity of World War I made impossible the adoption of a position from which anything like "factuality" might have been delineated. Because the movement of armies went beyond the range of any general's peripheral vision, the war was too big to see from a distance; because the chaos of the individual infantryman's experience rendered his view of events incomprehensible, the war was too confusing to see from up close. The degree to which excruciating pain and ghoulish wounds ought properly to have been emphasized overwhelmed the guidelines implicit in a category like factuality. And the stress that eyewitnesses underwent *as* eyewitnesses made the accurate reporting of temporal sequence and duration a near impossibility. In other words, the concept of factuality presupposes a set of basic circumstances which the experience of the Great War exceeded and disrupted in every particular. Though thousands of men witnessed millions of war's images, none of those images was gleaned from a position that allowed the kind of objective certainty we demand of ordinary fact-finding every single day. Modernists were committed to and exhilarated by that project of invention, the results of which we now identify as a privileging of private and psychological facts over public and concrete ones. But when the experiences in question are rapes or wars, the difficulty of determining factuality is transformed from an interesting aesthetic problem into a heartbreakingly physical one, and the elusiveness of factuality becomes deeply disturbing, both emotionally and politically. Soldiers set out merely to fight a war, and when it was over, all they wanted to do was to come home.

FOUR

MAPS

In the early part of the twentieth century, the perception of battlefields became increasingly problematic: they were difficult not only to see in their entirety but even to grasp conceptually. John Keegan has explained that by World War I, the expanded size of battlefields and increased range and volume of weapons had made it impossible for generals either "to be present . . . at each successive point of crisis . . ." or "to survey . . . the line of battle from the front rank." Instead, "[T]he cloud of unknowing which descended on a First World War battlefield at zero hour was accepted as one of its hazards by contemporary generals." A spatial and intellectual shift away from a deadly rain of observable fire and toward a safe, housed "cloud of unknowing," Keegan explains, meant that "[t]he main work of the general . . . had now to be done in his office, before the battle began" (265). Major General J. F. C. Fuller described the situation in similar terms, writing about "the amazing unconscious change which rose out of the Franco-Prussian War, and which in a few years obliterated true generalship, dehumanizing and despiritualizing the general until he was turned into an office soldier" (51).

If the work of a general occurs in the space of an office, then the space of a battlefield—physically expansive, perceptually elusive—must necessarily be shrunk and flattened to the plane of a map. Indeed, generals understood the front by relying on imaginative principles premised on the idea of a map—the geometry of the line, the rhetorical transaction of the synecdoche, and the visual perspective of a singular point of view. I trace in this chapter some of the ways in which modernist civilians and soldiers understood and undercut the limitations of each of these principles by reminding us of the depth that collapses when a mud trench is reduced to an inked line, by imploding the logic upon which synecdoches depend, and by insistently introducing multiple points of view into works that treat both the materials of war and the materials of peace.

Lines provided one of the most powerful methods of organizing the war, dictating the topography of its landscape and the imaginative habits of the men who engineered it. Both systems of defense and conceptions of offense adhered unwaveringly to an ideal of the line; men and materials were installed on the landscape according to its inevitable simplicity, and, for most of the war, muscles and guns invested the ideal with bulk and firepower. Holding the front line, which was dug into trenches and re-peated in the lines of men ordered to move forward and seize enemy trenches, constituted a profound imaginative imperative for generals, who were, Fuller argues, not flexible enough to alter their tactics: "New weapons were introduced yearly; but in its essentials the old tactics re-mained the same, numbers being considered the primary factor. . . . [M]ore detrimental still, numbers added vastly to administrative diffi-culties, that is the handling of the *rear* services; so much so, that general-ship was absorbed into quartermaster generalship, until in the [First] World War all commanders superior to a divisional commander were nothing more than commissary generals" (60–61). Imaginative rigidity, according to Fuller, led to a cycle that entrenched generals even more firmly in their offices behind the lines. As the numbers of troops and dimensions of battlefields increased, generals became increasingly in-volved in the logistics of providing quarters, ammunition, transportation, and so forth.

By World War I, the problem with organizing attacking men into lines was simple and brutal: the machine gun. Used by armies on both sides of no man's land during the war, the machine gun ensured that, no matter how effective a preparatory barrage was, a line of attackers mov-ing forward in rows across no man's land would be vulnerable to any surviving machine-gunners. An expert gunner, firing six hundred shots a minute, could "keep in the air a stream of bullets so dense that no one could walk upright across the front of [his] position without being hit— given, of course, that the gunner had set his machine to fire low and that the ground was devoid of cover" (Keegan 234, 233). It thus took only a very few defensive gunners to decimate a very large number of men organized into an offensive line. As Modris Eksteins states simply: "At-tackers moved forward usually without seeking cover and were mowed down in rows, with the mechanical efficiency of a scythe, like so many blades of grass" (145).

The doggedness of British faith in the geometry of the line was per-haps laid bare with the most brutal clarity in the space of about ten minutes—7:30 to 7:40 A.M. on the first of July, 1916—the first ten min-utes of zero hour on the first day of the Battle of the Somme. This major

offensive, to be executed in large part by Kitchener volunteers, was organized with the inexperience of these "New Army" recruits in mind. Sir
Henry Rawlinson, tapped by General Douglas Haig to head its operations,

> was apparently convinced that untested and undertrained troops, who
> until recently had been committed civilians, could not be trusted to act
> on received infantry tactics. French infantrymen on the right of the
> attack, advancing under fire, would form into small groups and proceed
> by rushes from one piece of dead ground to another, each rush being
> covered by the fire of other groups. Kitchener's novices, it seems to have
> been assumed, could not be trusted to act like this. . . . So both the
> men of the New Armies, who made up some 60 per cent of the attacking
> force, and the more experienced regulars and Territorials, were directed
> to advance in a succession of waves 100 yards apart. Each wave was to
> consist of a line of men, at intervals of two or three paces, moving across
> No-Man's-Land at a steady walk. (Wilson 318)

That these simple, linear orders were carried out with disastrous consci-
entiousness emerges clearly in countless descriptions of the advance,
many of which comment on what appeared to be a weird confusion
between an army at war and an army at parade practice: "On July 1
Britain's volunteers, the flower of Kitchener's New Armies, rose from the
trenches, and successive straight lines in close ranks moved forward at a
slow, steady pace as if on parade" (Schmitt 132). "I could see," one
survivor said, "away to my left and right, long lines of men" (qtd. in
Keegan 249), while another, Lance Corporal E. J. Fisher of the 10th
Essex, testified to the parade-ground mentality, noting that "I looked left
to see if my men were keeping a straight line" (Middlebrook 107). As this
comment suggests, straight lines did not only define the order in which
men climbed the parapet and started out across no man's land but also
dictated a structure that the B.E.F. was expected to maintain even as
German gunners opened fire on them. According to Captain R. Wood of
the 18th Northumberland Fusiliers: "As they moved forward, the sun
gradually shone through the mist and the bayonets glinted. They then
commenced to have losses but, as each man fell, the men behind increased
speed and the pattern was maintained. No man was allowed to stop to
assist casualties and the march continued to the beat of a single big drum,
centrally placed" (Middlebrook 122).

The tactic of advance by *waves* seemed to lend itself with unfortunate
ease to the project of creating a *wake*, leaving behind a visible record of its
motivating geometry—a series of corpse-constructed lines. "There were
very few occasions . . . where the attack was deliberately stopped. Most
had to form up in their waves and walk into the fire-swept zone. . . .
They had to step over the bodies of the dead, torn-off limbs and torsos
mangled by shell fire, or rows of bodies hardly marked but victims of
machine-gun bullets, the eyes already glazing in death" (Middlebrook

117–18). The 10th West Yorks were "practically annihilated and lay shot down in their waves" (Keegan 248). "An artillery officer who walked across later came on 'line after line of dead men lying where they had fallen'" (qtd. in Keegan 249). On the first day of the Battle of the Somme, all told, "the British had lost about 60,000, of whom 21,000 had been killed, most in the first hour of the attack, perhaps the first minutes" (Keegan 260).

The disaster of the first of July may be understood as originating with the relegation of the general to his office, working with a map, for the strategy of that day was, in essence, to simplify the job of the infantry soldiers to the point where the territory over which they were ordered to advance would resemble the abstract clarity of a map. According to John Keegan, the optimism with which both the staff and trench soldiers approached zero hour on that midsummer day relied on the assumption

> that the real work of destruction both of the enemy's defences and men, would have been done by the artillery before zero hour; that the enemy's wire would have been scythed flat, his batteries battered into silence and his trench-garrisons entombed in their dug-outs; that the main task of the infantry would be merely to walk forward to the objectives which the officers had marked on their maps, moderating their pace to that of the barrage moving ahead of them: finally, that once arrived there, they had only to install themselves in the German reserve trenches to be in perfect safety. (218)

The giant mistake of this plan lies precisely in its theoretical beauty—the assumption that all the barbed wire would be flattened, all the batteries silenced, all the troops entombed. These reductive predictions are reminiscent of the mindset that viewed all Germans as barbarians, all Englishmen as honorable, all war as glorious; and they rely on the same faith in reductive representation, the same distance from physical experience. General Haig's response on the second of July to a report that the estimated casualties from the previous day numbered over forty thousand—"This cannot be considered severe in view of the numbers engaged, and the length of front attacked" (Haig 154)—is clearly the response of a man at considerable distance from those forty thousand bodies. Indeed, Haig spent the first of July ten miles north of the battle (Keegan 267).

If the work of a general happens before a battle begins, then his role in battle, Keegan points out, must necessarily shift from a participatory to a prescriptive one. In describing some of the extensive plans composed for individual units on the first day of the Battle of the Somme (thirty-one pages for the XIII Corps, twenty numbered paragraphs for Queen Victoria's Rifles), he comments that "the spirit which informs the plans . . . is a spirit not of providing for eventualities, but rather of attempting to preordain the future" (266). The apparent hubris of this attitude becomes understandable only when contextualized by the knowledge that the generals, far from the front, were consulting not the actual battlefield but maps of it.

In fact, the distance that allowed generals to maintain their belief in the metaphor of the line was legislated by General Haig himself, ensuring a fatal fracture between men who actually looked at the front and men who, by consulting maps, made decisions about how the front should be made to look. In 1915, Haig drew a line on a map at a fairly conservative distance behind the dangerous forward trenches: no staff officer was to venture forward beyond it. The rationale, according to Tim Travers, was that any information that might be gained by such sallies was outweighed by the risk: firsthand information was worth less than the life of a staff officer. According to Travers, "[I]t seems that Haig found his liaison reports sufficient, and in accordance with his Staff College perception that the Commander-in-Chief should set objectives and then leave subordinates to carry out the task, without interference" (109).

Haig's line on a map and the devaluation of eyewitness information that it represented put him at a significant remove from the landscape of war. His order ensured not only that firsthand accounts would devolve into second- and thirdhand ones but also distributed the number of speakers through which information traveled across the military hierarchy of rank. Haig already depended on staff officers for his information; now staff officers were to remain at a remove from the front line and so to become dependent on their subordinates for descriptions of the war. Eyewitnesses, in other words, were put at a further remove from the power to make military decisions, while those with military power were put at a further remove from the physical consequences of their decisions.

"It is clear," according to Travers, "that Corps, Army and some Divisional commanders did not normally visit the front" (109), yet maps seem to have provided these commanders with the illusion of proximity to the landscapes over which they presided. Though it may be apocryphal, the story that Lieutenant General Sir Launcelot Kiggell visited the front at Passchendaele in 1917, "burst into tears and muttered, 'Good God, did we really send men to fight in that?'" (qtd. in Fussell 84) illustrates the dangerous degree to which general headquarters seems to have believed in the reliability of its maps and to have forgotten that representations always need to be checked against the physical realities toward which they point.

Just as generals tried to see the war in advance by using maps and to tell the story of war in advance by giving orders, reporters tried to see the war in retrospect by using maps and to tell the story of war in retrospect by filing reports. In doing so, the journalists, like the generals, relied on the idea of the line. Newspaper accounts of battles used the geometry of the line to structure their accounts of what was happening at the front even while they admitted that it was almost impossible to discern what *was* happening and that what was actually being described was the visual obstructions themselves. Whereas for generals, the slaughter of the line was obscured by attention to maps and satisfaction in their linear logic, for reporters, the slaughter of the line was obscured by attention to visual obstructions and satisfaction in their linear logic.

In reporting the events of July 1, 1916, a London *Times* correspondent first remarks on the virtual invisibility of the event he is supposed to be witnessing, then proceeds unabashedly to make narrative sense out of what he has just admitted he cannot see. The story begins with a description of how, at 7:30 A.M., the "lines of the trenches themselves were only doubtfully visible . . . [as] a dark bank of smoke, mingling with the morning mist, blotted out all the horizon. To the right . . . we saw the line of a white smoke *barrage,* denser than the mist but paler than the fumes of shells, which we made to cover our advance. . . . Behind all the welter and tumult it was impossible to guess what was passing; only one knew that they must be terrible things." Later in the morning, the mists clear and the sun comes out: "But the visibility came too late to enable one to see our men actually moving from their trenches. They had already gone from the ground where one might have seen them, on beyond the German front line, to where a thick veil of smoke still hid everything."

This entire report is structured by the lines the correspondent knows are supposed to order the landscape of the front and the maneuvers of an offensive push. He assumes that the "lines of the trenches" are there, even though they are "only doubtfully visible." From this point on, the report studiously avoids the apparent invisibility of soldiers and instead focuses on the geometry of the various elements that are hiding those soldiers. Smoke and mist are described as a line, a curtain, a veil. Behind or beneath these obstructions, it is "impossible to guess what was passing," for they "hid everything." The story, however, is unflappably optimistic. Readers are assured that "over there, where at night the horizon was all a flicker of lightning, there is nothing but a sullen bank of thick pearl grey. Behind that bank the British Army is winning new glory" ("The Great Battle" 10). Like the generals who attempted to dictate the future, this newspaper story relies more on assumptions than on any information the journalist has gleaned as a "spectator" of the advance of July 1.

It took most of the war to sink in, but strategists eventually began to realize that keeping a defensive front line back a certain distance could spare it from taking the full force of an offensive barrage. The attacking troops might advance further forward than they otherwise would, but once they were within range it was possible to respond with a counterattack. As Cyril Falls explains, the First World War brought "into special prominence one particular aspect of defence in depth, that is, the desirability of muffling and absorbing the shock [of an attack] rather than attempting to break it" (44). Gradually, generals came to understand that the "first essential" of defense was that it "should be conducted not upon a line, or even upon a series of lines, but in a series of zones" (45). Ernst Jünger, in *The Storm of Steel*, claims that the Germans were subject to exactly the same initial misconception about lines, commenting that "[t]he terrible losses, out of all proportion to the breadth of front attacked, were principally due to the old Prussian obstinacy with which the tactics of the line were pursued to their logical conclusion. . . . It was finally given up and the principle of a mobile defence adopted. The last development of this was the elastic distribution of the defence in zones" (110). The shift from the lines to which generals and journalists were so loyal to the zones described by Falls and Jünger must certainly have complicated the narrative of war, but at least it improved its tactics.

A map of a war zone is an abstract representation of a landscape, one that necessarily involves a certain amount of simplification. As John Terraine has pointed out: "On maps the Western Front is usually shown by a continuous line which in 1915 was 475 miles long . . . [despite the fact that it] was never quite as continuous as the maps suggest: flooded areas, rivers, swampy river valleys . . . and abrupt declivities interrupted the lines" (144). In any case, the lines were dug zigzag rather than straight, so as to prevent an enemy from firing down the length of one. Large-scale bombardments created a further discrepancy between the neatness of ink lines and the messiness of mud ditches. As Terraine notes: "[T]he red or blue lines on maps have to be interpreted as small groups of men or individuals crouched in shell-holes or mine-craters, unable to move, unable to communicate, trying just to stay alive" (144). By his recognition that certain lines on certain maps indicated not trenches but people, Terraine puts his finger on a raw nerve: battle maps represented not only simplified landscapes but also physical sites where grisly acts of violence took place on a regular basis. Their clean abstraction thus stirred understandable resentment among those who were not only familiar with what was happening in the war zone but most likely had been victims of its violence. Maps thus provide apt images of the dangerous gap between representation and experience, and they were frequently exploited by combatants as a means for critiquing inadequate or irresponsible representations of war.

Many soldiers recognized that the generals' views of war, so often limited to a study of maps, encouraged a dangerous illusion of having access to the material world of battle when actually what they had access to was only a series of representations. Robert Graves explains how the infantry perceived staff judgment: "Opposite our trenches was a German salient and the brigadier wanted to 'bite it off' as a proof of the offensive spirit of his command. Trench soldiers could never understand the Staff's desire to bite off an enemy salient. . . . We concluded that it was the passion for straight lines for which headquarters were well known, and that it had no strategic or tactical significance" (*Good-bye* 288). In *Un-*

dertones of War, Edmund Blunden makes an almost identical remark about an attack in which his company was ordered to participate: "The German line ran out in a small sharp cape here, called The Boar's Head. This was to be 'bitten off,' no doubt to render the maps in the châteaux of the mighty more symmetrical" (57). Straight lines bear the mark of human construction, Blunden reminds us, and testify to the human capacity to create visible, durable constructs in the material world. By perpetually attempting to "bite off enemy salients"—to straighten out the complexity of pressures that continually defeated their attempts to move forward—generals were attempting to impose upon the battlefield their own visions of the world. Such efforts allowed them to ignore the fact that the ambitious lines they drew on their maps usually resulted not in new lines of trenches on the battlefield but rather in new lines of type in the casualty lists.

Veterans also critiqued the two-dimensionality of maps, noting its lulling, reassuring effects. Blunden, for instance, meditates on whether it strikes "nearer the soul of war to draw lines in coloured inks on vast maps at Montreuil or Whitehall . . . than to rub knees with some poor jaw-dropped resting sentry, under the dripping rubber sheet, balanced on the greasy firestep . . . ?" He answers his own rhetorical question, deciding "That passing by men achingly asleep in narrow chilly firetrenches, their mechanical shifting of their sodden legs to let you go on your way, pierces deep enough" (155–56). "[T]o draw lines" or "to rub knees": Blunden reminds us, as combatants so often do, that the "soul of war" is always lodged in a body and that one is therefore obligated to keep close to the body. The two-dimensionality of colored inks on maps are inadequate precisely because such two-dimensionality suggests no thickness, no depth: how can such inked lines "pierc[e] deep enough"?

The ambulance driver in Helen Zenna Smith's *Not So Quiet . . .* uses the flatness of two-dimensionality to describe her anxiety about falling bombs: "Surely there is no sound anywhere as sickening as the sound of a bomb dropped from the air. A flattening sound, as though the sky were jealous of the earth and was determined to wipe it out of existence. Each time a bomb drops I see myself under it, flat, like the skin of a dead tiger that has been made into a rug with a little nicked half-inch of cloth all round the edges . . . flat, all the flesh and blood and bones knocked flat" (156). Her account emphasizes the tension between two and three dimensions by vividly evoking both the vertical drop of a bomb and the horizontal plane of the earth toward which it plummets; the bomb has a "flattening" sound, as though its mission were explicitly framed in terms of a collapse from three to two dimensions. The image of the tiger rug repeats this collapse; a tiger's three-dimensional body is reduced to a rug—a trophy of two-dimensionality.

Mary Borden, in a sketch called "Bombardment" in *The Forbidden Zone,* shows how aerial perspective flattens three dimensions into two and demonstrates of the way in which such two-dimensionality enables the maintenance of psychological distance. Here, the physical space separating the ground from the sky, which the pilot sees as a map of sorts, ensures the psychological space that separates pilot from civilians and civilians from pilot. The essay fluctuates between the perspective of the pilot dropping bombs on a town and the perspective of the town's inhabitants: from each point of view, the other is a speck, an insect, an "it." Both the people on the ground and the plane in the sky are described as bugs or as like bugs: "The aeroplane continued to descend until it looked from the church tower like a mosquito" (9); "The white beach was crawling now with vermin; the human hive swarmed out on to the sands" (10). In addition, the narrator maintains a controlled distance from both the subjects on the ground and the subject in the air. People don't cry, scream, swear, or exclaim; instead, alterations to the "unconscious map" (7) of the landscape are recorded as "a scream burst[ing] from the throat of the church tower" (8) and the pilot's satisfaction at a direct hit is recorded as a "cavort[ing]" of the "aeroplane . . . whirling after its tail in an ecstasy of self-gratification" (11). This self-conscious display of psychological distance constitutes a pointed reminder of all that is eliminated along with physical proximity.

Another way in which maps were inaccurate can be seen in the phenomenon of medical truces. On a map, proximity to the enemy represents danger, while distance from the enemy represents safety. But because of the way stretcher bearers were spread across the space between no man's land and hospitals behind the front line, and because of the way in which the front line often thrust wounded soldiers into strange proximity with their enemies, the supposed danger of proximate hostility sometimes evolved into compassion instead.

John Keegan has described how, moving backward from the forward trench, the medical stations through which wounded men passed en route to a base hospital in France or Britain were, first, the Regimental Aid Post, then an Advance Dressing Station, next, the Collecting Post, and finally, a Casualty Clearing Station. Plenty of stretcher bearers moved back and forth between the Dressing Station (within medium-gun range of the enemy) and the Casualty Clearing Station (even further behind the lines). But only thirty-two were assigned to the space forward of the Regimental Aid Post. Making the journey of at least an hour between the front line and the Casualty Clearing Station in pairs, then, they could transport, at most, sixteen wounded men to the hospital facility each hour. In other words, the further a soldier proceeded toward enemy trenches, the less he was attended by a system of aid for the wounds he was increasingly likely to receive. At the same time, the further forward of the front line a soldier was wounded, the more his chances of life depended entirely on the compassion of the very men whose lives he had so recently been trying to end. A wounded man lying in no man's land could easily die of his injuries, either because the few stretcher bearers available were tending to other men or unable to reach him or because an enemy soldier, to whom his proximity and immobility made him unusually vulnerable, would finish him off.

But as many firsthand accounts of the war testify, combatants on both sides of the conflict improvised impromptu truces to allow for the removal of wounded men from no man's land. On the first of July, 1916, for example, "In many places, and at a surprisingly early stage of the battle, the Germans offered the British an unofficial and unilateral truce" to allow for the removal of wounded. "[A]t about 2 P.M. on the front of the 56th London Division . . . 'a German medical officer . . . came out with a white flag and said that there was no objection to the removal of wounded on the British side of the wire, so long as no firing took place', and on the VIII Corps' front . . . the Germans allowed stretcher bearers to move freely about no-man's-land between noon and 4 P.M." (Keegan 273–74). Many accounts of the war describe such unofficial truces: Graves tells about spending a whole night retrieving the wounded and dead from no man's land, remarking that "[t]he Germans behaved generously. I do not remember hearing a shot fired that night, and we kept on until it was nearly dawn and we could be plainly seen; then they fired a few shots in warning and we gave it up" (*Good-bye* 195).

The number of wounded saved as a result of such enemy mercy may only have represented a fraction of those saved by the cunning and courage of their comrades in the midst of enemy gunfire. But to diagram the pattern of risk undertaken by that fraction of men who would have died but for such impromptu medical truces would reveal that, while their risk of being killed by German guns would have increased steadily as they moved from London across the Channel into France and then up through the trenches into no man's land, that risk would have suddenly, just shy of death, plunged to zero. Vulnerability could suddenly coincide with invulnerability, and lying at the mercy of one's enemies could suddenly become a guarantee of safety rather than of danger. Medical truces thus demonstrate yet another way in which battle maps, which assumed that danger increased as proximity increased, were untrustworthy representations of the spaces of war.

Another mapping principle that, like the line, was central to the organization of war was the logic of synecdoche, which dictated the relationship between battlefields and nations. Synecdoche, the imaginative maneuver that allows a part to stand for a whole, meant that to control the boundary of the front line carried with it the privilege of drawing boundaries elsewhere on the map of a larger territory. Maps constituted the medium upon which this magnification of power was represented, as is clear by General Douglas Haig's assumption in his diary entry of May 28, 1916: "Beat the Germans here, and we can then make what terms we like!" (146).

Synecdoche relies on the assumption that one knows what smaller space is a part of what larger one. This premise can appear fairly self-evident when looking at a map of Europe: a battlefield occupies so much area on the map of France or Belgium; to gain control of that subset of the landscape would eventually allow the conquering country to play a critical role in redrawing the whole map. The English insistence on limiting battles to battlefields, rather than allowing war to spill over into "civilian" territories, is also embedded in a reliance on synecdoche. If war had spilled over onto English soil, synecdochic calculations would have become much more complicated, as the space of the battlefield began to coincide with the larger spaces assumed to be under negotiation.

James Joyce's *Finnegans Wake* flummoxes the logic that makes synecdochic moves possible. John Bishop, in his study of the *Wake,* includes renderings of two maps that describe one of the book's primary structures: the interconnectedness of "Dublin by Daylight" and "Novo Nilbud ['Dublin' spelled backward] by swamplight" (Bishop 32, 34). "They are two mappings of exactly the same place," he explains, "as really experienced by the same man, though in the antithetical states of wakefulness and sleep" (151). Daylit Map A is naturally idiosyncratic, representing as it does the personal and perceptual priorities, the exaggerations and blind spots, according to which any individual inhabitant will experience any city. Swamplit Map B, however, refers to a different kind of space altogether. It represents, "in the condensed and displaced referential systems typical of dreams, . . . the sleeper's 'knock[ed] out' body" (Bishop 36). Quoting Geza Roheim, Bishop notes how objects vanish as a man falls asleep, and, as they vanish, "the sleeper turns into himself and falls back . . . into his own body. . . . The process of falling asleep is a withdrawal . . . from the object world, . . . [and] the process of dreaming is rebuilding . . . a new environment formed out of the dreamer's body" (Roheim qtd. in Bishop 37).

The two maps, daylit and swamplit, "interpenetrate, each lying simultaneously inside and outside its other. The sleeping body . . . really lies in bed at the place marked 'Chapelizod' in the map of Dublin; but coordinately, the entire ground charted out in the map of Dublin really lies buried in the mound labeled 'headth of hosth' in Relief Map B, where it exists as representation" (Bishop 153). In other words, the sleeping body occupies a fraction of a point on Daylit Map A: a body in a bed at a location on the map. At the same time, Swamplit Map B, drawn to the same scale as its daylit counterpart, occupies a momentary spot in a dream in a brain in a fraction of a point on Daylit Map A. Without changing the conceptual definitions of either externality or internality, the opposition implied by the two maps is thereby both affirmed and reversed: all of Dublin lies in the sleeper's head; all of the sleeper's head lies in Dublin. Such a convoluted state of representational events thwarts the orderly habits of mind groomed by the synecdochic logic of maps. Joyce thus cuts across the ruts of our ingrained assumptions about the relationship between representation and experience by structuring *Finnegans Wake* to accord with the paradoxical dynamic between consciousness and the material world rather than with the narrow logic of a synecdoche.

Joyce's inversion of common mapping logic in *Finnegans Wake* is just one instance of the modernist tendency to seize on unexamined premises and demonstrate their rigidity and limitations. There are occasions, as *Wake* shows, when synecdoche is an inadequate method of representing experience. It is inadequate, for example, for articulating the relation between what goes on inside a person's head (where thoughts or dreams may cover large areas, as maps do) and the position of a person's body (which body, on a map, would be very small). It is also inadequate, as we have seen, for articulating the relation between the length of a line on a map (which may be small and broken into fragments) and the power accessible from such a position (which may be great, if one conceives of power in terms of defensive zones rather than in terms of the length of a line). Modernism encourages the examination of such habits of perception, which, though they may be useful ways of describing some experiences, may be fatally misleading if blindly applied to all experiences. As Virginia Woolf reminds us in "Modern Fiction": "Let us not take it for granted that life exists more fully in what is commonly thought big than in what is commonly thought small" (107). Generals of the Great War would have done well to heed such advice.

The military trains its officers to interpret maps one way—that is, "in exactly the same way as every other officer will interpret" them (Keegan 19). Modernist works, of course, train their readers to interpret in just the opposite way, cultivating an awareness of and an appreciation for multiple points of view. Puns and patterns in a book like *Finnegans Wake,* for example, will not only emerge differently for different readers, but will articulate and modify one another in the course of one and then repeated readings, as memory preserves, erodes, and distorts the accumulated networks of interconnection.

Because the landmarks and geography of Dublin constitute one of the frames of spatial reference to which the *Wake* refers, maps naturally constitute part of the critical apparatus that helps us navigate our way through the text. If generals ensconced themselves on the safe side of the brink between representation and experience, Joyce complicates that position by his assumption that neither representation nor experience are singular. The perpetual alterations wrought by the individual imagination on experience (consciously while awake, unconsciously while asleep) will simultaneously alter the attendant representations, thus producing a plethora not only of maps but of worlds.

While generals devoted troops and artillery to the project of imposing a single theoretical map on a muddy and resistant landscape, modernists like Wallace Stevens cultivate in readers an agility of interpretation that allows them to move around an object, seeing it from all its contradictory perspectives. In "Thirteen Ways of Looking at a Blackbird" (published in *Harmonium* 1923), Stevens flaunts such ability: the speaker indulges in a display of imaginative prowess that demonstrates both the susceptibility of an image to multiple meanings and the potential collision of those meanings. The blackbird may be a metaphor for independent aspects of the self:

> I was of three minds,
> Like a tree
> In which there are three blackbirds.

It may be a metaphor for the distinction between experience and retrospective interpretation:

> I do not know which to prefer,
> The beauty of inflections
> Or the beauty of innuendoes,
> The blackbird whistling
> Or just after.

Or it may be a metaphor for imaginative resistance to the materials at hand:

> Why do you imagine golden birds?
> Do you not see how the blackbird
> Walks around the feet
> Of the women about you?
>
> (*Collected Poems* 92–93)

The trick, the poem implies, is to be able to navigate easily between all the various possibilities without alighting on one and misinterpreting it as the definitive blackbird.

The visual reflex of modernism is to approach its subject from multiple directions. The visual reflex of Great War generals was to approach their subjects from a single direction. They looked down at the maps on their desks, adopting a clear, singular, bird's-eye perspective, with apparently very little consciousness of its limitations and very little attempt to supplement it with other perspectives or other kinds of representation. Major General J. F. C. Fuller's diagnosis of this problem stands in uncanny agreement with Stevens's poem. He advises that generals ought neither to remain only near the front nor only near the rear but rather to move back and forth between the two positions: "The more bird's-eye views—the better; for each is a *real* picture and a *real* situation; that is to say each is moral and physical as well as intellectual" (63). Unfortunately, this gathering of perspectives was not the norm during the war. Instead, generals were content to peer *through* that single theoretical bird's eye, while Stevens busies his speaker with the project of looking *at the bird,* with both eyes open, from multiple perspectives.

William Faulkner uses the strategy of multiple perspectives as a structural principle in *As I Lay Dying* (1930): characters speak the chapters in isolation and the reader only gradually sketches in the various relationships between them. Similarly, the unexpected shifts of narrative glance off each other in Virginia Woolf's *Mrs. Dalloway:* we begin by listening to Clarissa mull over her memories of an old friend, then step back to see her standing on the curb, and finally veer into the mind of a neighbor who also sees her standing on the curb—"A charming woman, Scrope Purvis thought her" (4).

In *Some Do Not . . . ,* Ford Madox Ford uses a difference of opinion between a female pacifist and a male soldier as an example of the way in which perception is isolated and depends not on the object viewed but on the perceiver. Valentine Wannop and Christopher Tietjens look at a casualty list posted on the wall of a shed. She turns on him accusingly, demanding that he "[l]ook at this horror! And you in that foul uniform can support it!" The casualty lists that Valentine points to are "sheets of paper beneath the green roof . . . laterally striped with little serrated lines. Each line meant the death of a man, for the day." Stevens or Faulkner or Woolf would understand Christopher's response: "I support it because I have to. Just as you decry it because you have to. They're two different patterns that we see" (221). Shifts across a series of multiple perspectives—a truism of modernism—thus verbalize the fractured and disillusioning experience of war.

Generals may be understood as having attempted to organize the war into a series of visual lines that would not alter in meaning, regardless of the position from which one viewed them. Lines seemed to work on their own maps and they seemed to satisfy civilians at home. If the soldiers occupying the three-dimensional versions of those two-dimensional geometries rejected such logic (or affirmed its disintegration), the generals didn't have to hear it. Modernists, on the other hand, invented images to display the way in that perspective can completely alter the physical world that constitutes the raw materials of perception. E. M. Forster asserted that "France is not a map, but France, and the German armies do not advance over white paper and retreat leaving it white, but into civilization that they leave a desert" ("Reconstruction" 263). In *Some Do Not . . . ,* Ford invented an image that describes the way in which standing in different places in relation to a text can produce different meanings: "Do you know those soap advertisement signs that read differently from several angles?" Christopher Tietjens asks Valentine Wannop.

"As you come up to them you read 'Monkey's Soap'; if you look back when you've passed it's 'Needs No Rinsing.' . . . You and I are standing at different angles and though we both look at the same thing we read different messages. Perhaps if we stood side by side we should see yet a third" (234). From just such different angles, a view of the trenches produced either the affirmation of linearity or its disintegration; but even at the places where chaos took over and language was drowned out altogether, official voices narrated the "story" of the war, newspaper accounts "documented" it, and generals, relying on the maps at their headquarters, propped up the idea of the front "line."

Soldiers could easily have explained the inefficacy of the metaphor of the line, the misrepresentation of maps, but there were various ways in which language from the front never reached backward into the noncombatant realm. First of all, nobody wanted to hear it. Superiors listening to reports of their subordinates wanted good news and affirmation that their strategies were sound ones. Civilians listening to the stories of combatants wanted optimism and affirmation that what they were sending men off to face wasn't so bad after all. Newspaper editors wanted anecdotes demonstrating pluck and affirmation that their stories would be seen as "doing their part" for the war, and so on. As the narrator in Helen Zenna Smith's *Not So Quiet . . .* explains, letters asserting the splendidness of participating in war are the "only kind of letter home they expect, the only kind they want, the only kind they will have" (30).

There were technological as well as psychological pressures militating against frank accounts of the trenches, for, despite the fact that by July 1, 1916, the Allied telephone and telegraph system was "comprehensive," it stopped at the forward edge of those trenches. In preparation for the "Big Push" of July 1, 1916, lines on poles were installed that would put general headquarters in contact with their forward divisional headquarters; from there on, it was buried six feet underground. "The installation of this 'six-foot bury,'" John Keegan reports, "had been one of the most time-consuming preparations for the offensive, but was justified by the security of communication it provided even under the heaviest enemy shellfire. It had, however, one disabling shortcoming: it stopped at the edge of no-man's-land. Once the troops left their trenches, as at 7.30 a.m. on 1 July, they passed beyond the carry of their signals system into the unknown" (264).

This line beyond which information could not travel backward to staff officers made possible the following entries in General Haig's diary for July 1, 1916:

> The Bombardment was carried out as usual, and there was no increase of Artillery fire, but at 7:30 A.M. (the hour fixed for the Infantry to advance) the Artillery increased their range and the Infantry followed the barrage.

Reports up to 8 A.M. seemed most satisfactory. Our troops had everywhere crossed the enemy's front trenches.

By 9 A.M. I heard that our troops had in many places reached the "1.20 line" (i.e., the line fixed to be reached 1 hr. and 20 minutes after the start).

After lunch, I motored to Querrieu and saw Sir H. Rawlinson. (153)

Even if the telephone lines had reached into no man's land, even if it had been possible to hear the human voice over the noise of the bombs, the splintering of old habits of perception would have made it difficult for soldiers to express what was happening to them. But if war broke apart the fantasy of the linear, it also offered those shards up to the more literary gestures of modernism. The reductive gridding of maps, the rigid geometry of press reports, and the halt of telegraph lines may have muffled the immediate apprehension of how the old forms were failing, but, in the end, the site of that failure constitutes one of the places from which literary modernism can be understood. Conventions that had always made experience seem linked and logical were shattered: Stevens's blackbird emerges from the rubble.

FIVE

WAR CALENDAR

If a reliance on maps displayed Great War loyalty to linear organizations of space, the notion of progress epitomized nineteenth-century loyalty to linear conceptions of time—time that moves steadily forward and morally upward. "In the world view of the nineteenth-century middle class, progress . . . constituted the essence of history" (Eksteins 176); the idea of progress was "one of the most potent that the nineteenth century was to produce" (Keegan 59). "The keys words of the times were 'thought,' 'work,' and 'progress' . . . and both clear thinking and hard work were deemed essential to continued national progress" (Briggs 1). The idea of progress plotted experience onto a calendar where time was an arrow and narratives were reliably chronological.

John Keegan has described how nineteenth-century historians conceptualized war in a way that allowed it to be consistent with this ideal of progress. In his chapter "The History of Military History," Keegan describes how, for generations, war represented a threat to the notion of historical progress because it was thought to deviate from Christian formulations of justice. "Western historians . . . had always . . . tended to depict war as a calamity, a scourge, or a foolishness, unless it could be represented as a crusade . . . or be used to exemplify the life and exploits of great men" (59). Edward Creasy, however, solved the problem. With his Victorian best seller, *Fifteen Decisive Battles of the World* (1851), Creasy invented the "decisive battle" genre of military history, arguing that battles are worthy of our attention because in the end they are responsible for having made the world the way it is. Given the Victorian culture's self-confidence in its own moral credibility, military historians were generally relieved by this argument, for if battles were to be understood as instrumental in making the Victorians what they were, then battles could be scrutinized with clear historical consciences. "Creasy," Keegan explains, "supplied the formula. War had a purpose; it had made the nineteenth century" (Keegan 60).

Creasy's interpretation of war as participating in the orderly procedure of history was an idea firmly ensconced by 1914. By then, according to Modris Eksteins: "In both Britain and France duty was initially associated with patriotism, and the loud patriotism had a strong historic flavor. . . . The war, for most Britons and Frenchmen, was a stage in the march of civilization, in the continuation of progress, both of which were based on what were seen as concrete historical foundations" (178–79). Thus, the metaphor of history's time line, a vector along which time inched steadily forward, was preserved in the popular imagination as well as in the rationalizations of historians.

In a war now infamous for its immobility, though, movement forward across the maps (by generals) and battlefields (by soldiers) of the western front soon proved a nearly impossible task. Machine-gun defenses foiled the possibility of offensive movement, even when infantry advances were preceded by preparatory barrage fire; Keegan reminds us that the word *"barrage,"* borrowed from the French during the war, means "preventing movement" (217). Undoubtedly the glummest testament to the failure of progress during the Great War, however, were the trenches, which displayed the muddy fact that lines that were supposed to move forward rarely did. As a speaker in Ellen La Motte's *The Backwash of War* comments: "There is an attack going on. That does not mean that the Germans are advancing. It just means that the ambulances are busy" (93).

The compulsion to advance is a strong one for minds trained by the military. It is built into rules, like the "Rule on Left and Right," which, according to Barbara Tuchman, dictates that "armies, even when turned around and retreating, are considered to face the direction in which they started; that is, their left and right remain the same as when they were advancing" (viii). In other words, military convention defines left and right—concepts virtually impossible to explain without reference to the body—*not* in reference to the body but in reference to the principle of progress.

If the age-old language of battle choreography takes as a given that an army will be moving forward, military thinking of the early twentieth century tended to satisfy that expectation. The French army took explicit pride in its mobility, for example, as a general staff artillery officer demonstrated in 1909 when responding to a question about 105 mm. heavy field artillery. "Thank God we don't have any!" he exclaimed, adding that "[w]hat gives the French Army its force is the lightness of its cannon" (Tuchman 207). Tuchman describes how the French maintained their loyalty to light artillery in 1911, when the War Council proposed adding 105s to the French Army: "[T]he artillery men themselves, faithful to the famous French 75s, remained unalterably opposed. They despised the heavy field cannon as drags upon the mobility of the French offensive and regarded them, like machine guns, as defensive weapons" (207). Defensive weapons suggested standing still; offensive ones suggested movement, and it was the latter in which the artillery officer took pride.

Loss of mobile warfare seemed to B. H. Liddell Hart a "disease," as his description of the tank specifies: "[The tank] was a specific antidote for a specific disease which first broke out virulently in the World War. This disease was the complete paralysis of the offensive brought about by the defensive power of serried machine-guns, and aggravated by wire entanglements. This disease doomed the manhood of the nation to a slow and lingering end, prolonged only by the capacity to produce fresh victims for the futile sacrifice" (335). It is striking that Liddell Hart's retrospective diagnosis of the Great War strategic disease, quite unselfconsciously, decries not the victimization of an entire generation of young men but rather the terms of their victimization: they were killed while standing still rather than while moving forward. The enervation of "a slow and lingering end" apparently constitutes the difference between disease and war: both kill you, but at least in war, death is kinetic rather than paralyzed.

"I don't know what is to be done. This isn't war," Lord Horatio Herbert Kitchener pronounced (Vansittart 54). Since no one else seemed to know what ought to be done, generals stuck to the tactics in which they had been trained. At Verdun, General Joseph Jacques Césaire Joffre telegraphed an order to his front line that "[e]very commander who . . . gives an order for retreat will be tried by court martial" (qtd. in Liddell Hart 293); "the same axiom ruled on both sides: *Every position lost must be retaken.* Thus, the town of Fleury changed hands sixteen times between June 23 and July 17" (Meyer 61). Likewise, during the Battle of the Somme, "General von Below of the First Army . . . issued an order that any officer who gave up an inch of trench would be court-martialled, and that every yard of lost trench must be retaken by counterattack" (Liddell Hart 331). For the first year and a half of the war, the military leadership of both sides dug themselves into ditches, resigning themselves to a war where progress was measured in meters rather than miles. "Brigadier General Rees . . . described as a 'marvellous advance' the destruction of his Brigade on 1 July 1916, when 'hardly a man of ours got to the German Front Line'" (Travers 85). Instead of altering their expectation of linear progress, military strategists altered their expectation about the scale upon which that progress would be carried out. Instead of abandoning a bankrupt imaginative construct, they blindly reinvested in it—as the daily casualty lists testified.

There are a number of reasons why tacticians did what they did, none of which were perhaps as malicious as their effects must have felt to the troops living in ditches. Perhaps the most important obstacle to abandoning the vector as an organizing strategic metaphor was the absence of an alternative metaphor. Because we habitually incorporate metaphors into our interpretations of the world but just as habitually fail to remember that metaphors are in fact only imposed constructs, it is difficult for any of us to realize the possibility of exchanging one metaphor for another. C. S. Forester described just this quandary in his novel *The General* (1936), in which he depicts the staff's tendency to solve the problem of stalemated trench warfare by administering more of the same: more guns, more troops, more effort, all thrown at no man's land, all swallowed up, over and over. After a description of a debate among senior staff officers about what was wrong with the strategy of 1915, the speaker comments:

> In some ways it was like the debate of a group of savages as to how to extract a screw from a piece of wood. Accustomed only to nails, they had made one effort to pull out the screw by main force, and now that it had failed they were devising methods of applying more force still, of obtaining more efficient pincers, of using levers and fulcrums so that more men could bring their strength to bear. They could hardly be blamed for not guessing that by rotating the screw it would come out after the exertion of far less effort; it would be a notion so different from anything they had ever encountered that they would laugh at the man who suggested it.
> The Generals round the table were not men who were easily discouraged—men of that sort did not last long in command in France. Now that the first shock of disappointment had been faced they were prepared to make a fresh effort, and to go on making those efforts as long as their strength lasted. (195–96)

Forester here raises a double issue: first, that the imaginative nature of constructs tends to sink into invisibility (making us prone, as Elaine Scarry reminds us, to the misapprehension that our assumptions are naturally existing rather than created), and second, that there is a tendency to assume that the amount of material and energy thrown into an effort has a direct relationship to the chances for success. General Douglas Haig's postwar explanation for why he approached the Battle of the Somme the way he did confirms Forester's analysis. At the time, he says, his feeling was: "The greater the force put into it, the more vigorous and sustained the effort, the more loyally the Allies cooperated with each other, the greater the hope" (366).

Haig and general headquarters were under political as well as military pressures: they needed to maintain public support at home as well as Allied support at the front. Haig's explanation of the Somme strategy thus sounds as attentive to rhetorical as to military battle: "To encourage France, to encourage doubters at home, to persuade amateur strategists of the right course to adopt, and to confirm in practice the confidence of the British troops, the urgency of obtaining at least sufficient success to show that the enemy was not invincible on the Western Front and that greater success could be gained with greater forces, was very great" (Haig 368).[1] "To encourage . . . to persuade . . . to confirm . . . to show": these verbs of public presentation were the imperatives driving Haig. The chilling cost of launching that exercise in persuasion, then, may speak less to callousness and more to the extraordinary urgency with which such imperatives were felt and to the incredible difficulty with which any of us would be able to recognize the degree to which we are trapped within our own assumptions.

"The year 1916 saw the advent and acceptance by both sides of a new war, the intentional war of attrition," according to Modris Eksteins (143). Attrition, the formulation of immobility into policy, makes a virtue of defense and endurance, in contrast to the military compulsion to move forward. Eksteins has discussed attrition in terms of German willingness both to alter the rules of war and to engage the German civilian population in the war effort. Because it is for the long haul, a war of attrition necessarily involves all facets of society, not just the military. The distance between the commitment demanded of soldiers and the commitment demanded of civilians is effaced in such a "total war" (156–57). In effect, attrition amounts to a contest between the warring countries' resources, both material and human. Victory is no longer the prize for brilliant strategy or courageous execution of plan but rather the reward for staying power: it belongs to whichever side can, for the longest time, keep its entire economy geared to war, keep the ranks of its military filled, and maintain political support at home. Attrition expands the field upon which war is fought and broadens the criteria according to which winners are determined. War is no longer the exclusive province of the military.

Attrition takes the story out of war by reconstituting its action. War's plot is no longer geared toward battle but rather spreads itself thin over the maintenance of routine. As Ernst Jünger explains, "[A] battle was no longer an episode that spent itself in blood and fire; it was a condition of things that dug itself in remorselessly week after week and even month after month" (109). Jünger here reminds us that war may be understood as frustrating specifically narrative conventions: an "episode," by definition, presents itself sequentially—as beginning, middle, end—while a "condition," because static, forces narrative to circle around either a single moment or a series of moments that overlap and repeat themselves. B. H. Liddell Hart has remarked how the increasing length of battles made description more difficult for the historian: "[U]nless he desires to fill massive tomes with profuse detail, it is difficult to pick out salient features where there are either none, or else so many that they tend to merge into a formless mass" (285). Attrition, which makes war a premise rather than a climax, frustrates narrative convention as emphatically as it frustrates physical movement.

Attrition also takes the heroes out of war by asking of each combatant exactly the same thing: merely to stay alive. This leveling of demand across the ranks of soldiers further contributed to the Great War's frustration of plot. "The hero of this war," Eric Leed has claimed, "was not an 'offensive' but a 'defensive' personality. This required a radical transvaluation of many expectations, values, and images of war. The system of defense fashioned by the superiority of defensive fire over human mobility fundamentally reshaped the idea of military virtue" (105). Leed elaborates on this idea, pointing out that military training is premised on the idea of an offensive personality, which allows (theoretically, at least) a moral and psychological acceptance of the aggressive behavior necessary for war. Trench warfare erodes the usefulness of such a personality, thereby eroding the cast of characters one would expect to populate the narratives of war. When the job of a soldier is not to perform a heroic deed, not to sneak behind enemy lines, not to move at all, but rather to huddle in a ditch and try not to die, traditional notions of plot flounder along with traditional notions of heroism. Readers impatient with modernist novels complain that nothing happens, but nothing happening is precisely what war devolved into when attrition became its organizing policy and staying alive its motivating goal.

When plot flounders and climax is frustrated, resolution falls by the narrative wayside as well, as a brief survey of responses to the armistice displays. For Robert Graves, on duty in Wales in November 1918, news of peace was conflated with news of more casualties, and the Allied victory merely prompted a fresh review of four years' worth of casualties:

> In November came the Armistice. I heard at the same time news of the death of Frank Jones-Bateman, who had gone back again just before the end, and of Wilfred Owen, who often used to write to me from France, sending me his poems. Armistice-night hysteria did not touch the camp much, though some of the Canadians stationed there went down to Rhyl to celebrate in true overseas style. The news sent me walking alone along the dyke above the marshes of Rhuddlan (an ancient battle-field, the Flodder of Wales) cursing and sobbing and thinking of the dead. (*Goodbye* 330)

A walk on a dyke does not wind up the plot of war into the satisfying narrative closure that victory is supposed to represent.

While Graves curses and sobs and thinks of the dead, Vera Brittain describes a war so internalized that its physical cessation is barely noticed: "The immediate result of peace—the cessation of direct threats to one's personal safety—was at first almost imperceptible, just as a prolonged physical pain which has turned from acuteness into an habitual dull ache can cease altogether without the victim noticing that it has gone" (470). Like Graves, she thinks of the war in terms of its casualties, although she renders their psychological effects more precisely than he does: "Only gradually did I realise that the war had condemned me to live to the end of my days in a world without confidence or security, a world in which every dear personal relationship would be fearfully cherished under the shadow of apprehension, in which love would seem threatened perpetually by death, and happiness appear a house without duration, built upon the shifting sands of chance" (470–71). Here, the corpses of war mutate into an architecture of emotion not unlike that discussed in chapter 1: death looms over the house of happiness, which threatens to collapse arbitrarily and without warning.

The armistice did not represent the end of war deaths any more than it represented the end of war's psychological repercussions. In Richard Aldington's *Death of a Hero,* the narrator notes that "[t]he casualty lists went on appearing for a long time after the Armistice—last spasms of Europe's severed arteries" (3). Depictions of London's response to peace frequently underline this sense of war as continuing beyond its deadline, heedless of the conclusion that peace was supposed to represent. In the armistice scene of *The Years,* Virginia Woolf follows an old servant doing errands. Here, news of peace is a deadpan report, eliciting no response and barely interrupting the rhythm of everyday life, much less the booming of the guns:

> A man on a ladder who was painting the windows of one of the houses paused with his brush in his hand and looked round. A woman who was walking along carrying a loaf of bread that stuck half out of its paper wrapper stopped too. They both waited as if for something to happen. A topple of smoke drifted over and flopped down from the chimneys. The guns boomed again. The man on the ladder said something to the woman on the pavement. She nodded her head. Then he dipped his brush in the pot and went on painting. The woman walked on. Crosby pulled herself together and tottered across the road into the High Street. The guns went on booming and the sirens wailed. The war was over—so somebody told her at the counter of the grocer's shop. The guns went on booming and the sirens wailed. (304–305)

When the man on the ladder and the woman on the sidewalk pause, "wait[ing] as if for something to happen," all that does happen is that "[a] topple of smoke drifted over and flopped down from the chimneys"—the most immaterial and arbitrary event imaginable. Instead of the grand vocabulary of victory or even the narrative vocabulary of closure, all we are given is the vocabulary of random drift and of continuation: "The guns boomed again. . . . The guns went on booming and the sirens wailed." The idea of closure is irrelevant to an experience already internalized; for veterans, the war will not end, ever, while for civilians, the peaks of a plot line have been reduced to the monotone of a flat line.

If attrition took the story out of war, modernists took the story out of fiction. With perverse relish, they deliberately disrupted the narrative convention of proceeding forward, arguing that linear chronologies were false representations of the way in which life was actually experienced.[2] Virginia Woolf, for example, criticizes "this appalling narrative business of the realist: getting on from lunch to dinner: it is false, unreal, merely conventional" (*A Writer's Diary* 136). Ford Madox Ford matter-of-factly reports that "it became very early evident to us that what was the matter with the Novel, and the British novel in particular, was that it went straight forward" (*Joseph Conrad* 136). According to David Lodge, the modern novel "discard[s] the traditional narrative structures of chrono-logical succession and logical cause-and-effect, as being false to the essen-tially chaotic and problematic nature of subjective experience" (6). Georg Lukács's assessment of modernism is that it "despairs of human history, abandons the idea of a linear historical development" (qtd. in Howe 17). Alan Friedman has described the change in the structure of the modern novel from its predecessors as a change "from the structure of a ladder to the structure of a cobweb" (414). James McFarlane and Malcolm Brad-bury tell how modernists were interested to free the novel from "onerous plot," rejecting conventions of "linear narrative, logical and progressive order" (393).[3] Modernist impatience with a linear time that moves straight forward from lunch to dinner and with ladder-like narrative structures signals an abrupt shift in ideas about what the novel was and issues to which it should attend.

The linear narrative structures of realist works are based largely on our desire to be told that concepts like logic and chronology are not constructed by language but rather operate independently in the "real world" prior to perception and articulation. By supplying an effect for every cause, winding up every beginning with an ending, and inviting us to look *through* language for a plot rather than *at* it for an idea of how we impose plots on otherwise disorganized experience, realist works confirm our wishful belief that we ourselves are proceeding along a linear path.

The sequentiality of language in realist texts encourages us to trust that experience will present itself as a naturally occurring set of stories. As Catherine Belsey has explained, "reading a realist text is ultimately reas-suring, however harrowing the events of the story, because the world evoked in the fiction, its patterns of cause and effect, of social relation-ships and moral values, largely confirm the patterns of the world we seem to know." The term "realism," she continues, is "useful in distinguishing between those forms which tend to efface their own textuality . . . and those which explicitly draw attention to it. Realism offers itself as trans-parent" (51). The language of nonlinear modernist works, however, is decidedly opaque; David Lodge describes modernism's typical "prose style, however sordid and banal the experience it is supposed to be mediating," as "so highly and lovingly polished that it ceases to be transparent but calls attention to itself by the brilliant reflections glancing from its surfaces" (6). Glittery with riddles, these difficult surfaces force us to confront the ways in which words construct meaning.

Modernist works may be understood as attempting to develop definitions of what constitutes the opposite of progress, as well as ideas about what happens when progress forward along a line reaches some kind of limit. Ford, for example, invented several images that pit linearity against some version of its opposite. One instance, in *No More Parades,* suggests that when the one-dimensional progress of linearity goes too far it becomes dangerous and needs to be immersed into more dimensions—surface and depth. The crisis, which Christopher Tietjens and his wife, Sylvia, both think back on at different moments in the novel, is a sick child: their son had a dangerously high fever and was put into an ice bath. Together, husband and wife watched in controlled panic as the mercury in the thermometer dropped, their attention shifting from the line of mercury to the surface of the ice. The image of linearity here is mercury in a thermometer; the image of its dangerous limit is the potential fatality of a fever; and the image of its spread into more dimensions is a bathtub full of ice cubes.

The sequence of thoughts that leads Christopher to his recollection of this incident are strung together in a way that connects Sylvia to the war. He is at the front, mulling over rumors of the way she is behaving in London; it occurs to him that "she was on the warpath . . . brilliant mixture as she was, of the perfectly straight, perfectly fearless . . . kind. . . . Yet, it came to him, the image of her that he had just seen had been the image of Sylvia, standing at attention . . . whilst she read out the figures beside the bright filament of mercury in a thermometer" (300). In this juxtaposition of two crises, Ford superimposes the strains of a marriage and of a sick child upon the strains of war. Both situations—domestic and military—are taut and linear: Sylvia is "perfectly straight" and stands "at attention"; she is "on the warpath" but also concentrating on the thermometer's "filament of mercury."

Later in the novel, Sylvia recalls the same moment and in similar terms: it occurs to her that when Christopher was putting their son in the bath, his face looked the same then as it does now, as he suffers the stress of front-line service. "She saw him bending, expressionless in the strong lamp-light, with the child in his clumsy arms over the glittering, rubbled surface of the bath. He was just as expressionless then as now. . . . He reminded her now of how he had been then: some strain in the lines of the face perhaps that she could not analyse" (436–37). Ford thus uses linearity—the lines of Christopher's face, the lines of Sylvia's body, and the filament of mercury in the thermometer—as visual homonyms for the linear landscape of war.

In *A Passage to India,* E. M. Forster's Marabar Caves stand as an image of modernist resistance to linearity: the caves refuse to lend themselves to the pressure for plot that is manifested in the novel as the tourist appetite for an itinerary. A visitor to the caves, the narrator remarks, is denied the sense of having come away with anything as palpable as an "experience": "Having seen one such cave, having seen two, having seen three, four, fourteen, twenty-four, the visitor returns to Chandrapore uncertain whether he has had an interesting experience or a dull one or any experience at all" (124). The ladies from England are subject to precisely this disappointment on their picnic: "They did not feel that it was an attractive place or quite worth visiting, and wished it could have turned into some Mohammedan object, such as a mosque, which their host would have appreciated and explained" (141).

Such failure of explanation is repeated over and over during the course of the Englishwomen's outing. They ask about some mounds. What were they—"graves, breasts of the goddess Parvati? The villagers beneath gave both replies" (140). Adela sees what she thinks is a snake, which, when she looks through her field glasses, turns out to be a tree stump. But the "villagers contradicted her. She had put the word into their minds, and they refused to abandon it. Aziz admitted that it looked like a tree through the glasses but insisted that it was a black cobra really, and improvised some rubbish about protective mimicry. Nothing was explained, and yet there was no romance" (140–41). Whereas romance relies on the shimmering nebulous, the problem here is outright contradiction. How can one be confident that one has had an experience if it becomes impossible to tell one's friends about it or to record it in one's journal? To witness a mysterious, inexplicable shape is romantic; to witness either a tree stump or a snake—who knows which?—is just frustrating.

Lack of explanation leads to narrative frustration for Mrs. Moore, when she withdraws from the group touring the caves and sits down to write a letter. "Dear Stella, Dear Ralph," she begins, then stops, realizing that "[n]o, she did not wish to repeat that experience." For what the caves have done is to reduce all language to a single word, making narrative progress impossible: "If one had spoken vileness in that place, or quoted lofty poetry, the comment would have been the same—'ou-boum'" (149).

On the train journey to the Marabar Caves, Aziz's English guests are disappointed by the failure of the sunrise to present itself as an event. The narrator describes this disappointment in a sexual vocabulary, drawing attention to the way in which the novel undermines plot by undermining our assumptions about the predictability of sexual narrative. Using metaphors of sexuality, the narrator describes how the expectation of climax fell flat: "They awaited the miracle. But at the supreme moment, when night should have died and day lived, nothing occurred. . . . Why, when the chamber was prepared, did the bridegroom not enter with trumpets and shawms, as humanity expects? The sun rose without splendour" (137). Just as the sunrise belies the expectations aroused by the language of sexual encounter, the alleged sexual assault that supposedly constitutes the main event of the novel builds to a courtroom climax and then swiftly deflates:

> Victory on this side, defeat on that—complete for one moment was the antithesis. Then life returned to its complexities, person after person struggled out of the room to their various purposes, and before long no one remained on the scene of the fantasy but the beautiful naked god. Unaware that anything unusual had occurred, he continued to pull the cord of his punkah, to gaze at the empty dais and the overturned special chairs, and rhythmically to agitate the clouds of descending dust. (231)

Victory here is momentary—a crisis like the crisis of fever in *No More Parades* and similarly poised against a context of messy complexity that is the opposite of crisis. Meanwhile, the character with the lowest social standing, the "beautiful naked god" operating the fan, is "[u]naware that anything unusual had occurred." Clearly, even the experience of a momentary climax like victory is an experience only available from particular perspectives: it disappears here from the perspective of a person who is situated both above and below the courtroom plot—a man who "sat on a raised platform near the back . . . and seemed to control the proceedings," yet one who "had no bearing officially upon the trial" and indeed "did not understand why the Court was fuller than usual" (217).

What Forster offers as an alternative to plot is his idea of passage, worked out in the last section of the book during the Hindu celebration of a divine birthday. The celebration is accompanied by the presentation of a number of images of the god, no one of which is privileged, no one of which is ever settled upon. The "God to be born was largely a silver image the size of a teaspoon" (283), yet celebrants play a game with a child and a red ball that represents "the fondling of Shri Krishna under the similitude of a child" (289). Finally, "No definite image survived" at all; "at the Birth it was questionable whether a silver doll or a mud village, or a silk napkin, or an intangible spirit, or a pious resolution, had been born. Perhaps all these things! Perhaps none!" (290).

At the end of the book—"the climax, as far as India admits of one" (315)—Hindus prepare "to throw God away, God Himself, (not that God can be thrown) into the storm. Thus was He thrown year after year, and were others thrown—little images of Ganpati, baskets of ten-day corn, tiny tazias after Mohurram—scapegoats, husks, emblems of passage; a passage not easy, not now, not here, not to be apprehended except when it is unattainable: the God to be thrown was an emblem of that" (314–15). Just as the book's title promises a passage to India yet seems to document various journeys away from it (Mrs. Moore dies on her passage back to England); just as the nonexperiences do and do not add up to a plot (the difficulty of describing the Marabar picnic); just as the images of absence are simultaneously empty of meaning and laden with meaning ("empty as an Easter egg" [125]); so, the notion of passage suggests that meaning is only accessible the moment one discards it. The most one can aim for is "husks, emblems of passage," because as soon as one has experienced a passage, or read about one, it ceases to satisfy; because passage is "not to be apprehended except when it is unattainable."

Combatants' accounts of the war respect the conventions of linearity in that they proceed by the calendar—frequently appearing to be either reconstructions or fictional versions of veterans' trench diaries. Chapter titles of Siegfried Sassoon's novel *Memoirs of an Infantry Officer* are typical in their adherence to straight chronology: "At the Army School," "The Raid," "Before the Push," "Battle." Most chapters begin with sentences that further orient both soldier and reader within the baffling context of war by anchoring experience to such details as location, timing, or weather: "I have said that spring arrived late in 1916, and that up in the trenches opposite Mametz it seemed as though winter would last forever" (first sentence, chapter 1, page 9); "I came back from the Army School at the end of a hot Saturday afternoon" (first sentence, chapter 2, page 21); "One evening about a fortnight later I was down in that too familiar front-line dug-out with Barton, who had just returned from leave and was unable to disguise his depression" (first sentence, chapter 3, page 41); "On the morning of a Battalion move I made it my business to keep out of the way until the last moment" (first sentence, chapter 4, page 58). Within the chapter describing the attack of July 1, 1916, the protagonist, Sherston, transcribes his journal entries, each of which is carefully marked with the time from his watch: there are a dozen such passages recorded between the hours of 7:45 in the morning and 8:15 that night.

Despite this apparent respect for the conventions of chronology, though, combatant novels can be extremely confusing to read. For one thing, the cast of characters is liable to be huge, making it difficult to mark time according to habitual temporal landmarks such as the deaths of familiar characters. Individual soldiers—subject to the vagaries of a vast bureaucracy, dependent on their immediate superiors for the granting of leaves or transfers, moving up the line with their companies and carried back on stretchers at random, perpetually losing their friends to death or hospitals or other assignments—come into contact with hundreds of strangers in moments of emergency that make strangers memorable, even if they disappear forever within fifteen or twenty minutes. Because virtually all war narratives reproduce this aspect of the experience, keeping track of individuals with whom a protagonist comes into contact is not only impossible but also futile. Even if one were capable of keeping character sketches straight, such a filing away of information would serve no purpose, for only a fraction of the men warranting one-paragraph descriptions ever reappear in the story.

Such vast lists of characters mean that occasionally a narrator will mourn the death of someone he has never even mentioned, only to find himself defending his sorrow to the reader. "Another shell, bursting on a small party of non-commissioned officers as they were about to leave the trenches after relief, robbed us instantly of Sergeant Clifford," Edmund Blunden reports, and then immediately acknowledges that though Clifford has not figured in his story at all up to this point, he was nonetheless a man whose "sweetness of character" had "for months past [made him] invaluable in all necessities" (181).

Enid Bagnold, who wrote about her experiences as a V.A.D. at the Royal Herbert Hospital in Woolwich, called her account *A Diary without Dates* and makes a point of describing the difficulty of marking time in a hospital. When a new V.A.D. shows up for duty, Bagnold speculates about the aching feet and empty stomach that the new woman will record in *her* diary that night. As Bagnold runs through the litany of how she's sure the new woman feels, she notes that "I get a glimpse of the passage of time and of the effect of custom." It seems that the only way she can visualize time is by realizing how far away she herself is from these early responses: "With me the sickness and the hunger and the ache are barely remembered. It makes me wonder what else is left behind. . . . The old battle is again in my mind—the struggle to feel pain, to repel the invading familiarity" (116). Here, the routine of hospital work erases not only the passage of time but the ability to feel; familiarity seems to confound the forward movement of the calendar.

Bagnold reports that her patients mark time by observing the anniversaries of wounds that sent them to the hospital. Wounds, in these cases, constitute strange new birthdays—the beginnings of different lives with different bodies. "Sometimes a man will whisper, 'Nurse . . .' as I go by the bed; and when I stop I hear, 'In ten minutes it will be a twelvemonth!' and he fixes his eyes on me" (121). Bagnold admits that she doesn't "yet understand this importance they attach to such an anniversary." But she does "know that for some of them, for [example, for] Waker, that moment at two o'clock in the morning changed his whole career. From that moment he was paralysed, the nerves severed; from that moment football was off, and with it his particular ambition. And football, governing a kingdom, or painting a picture—a man's ambition is his ambition, and when it is wiped out his life is changed" (122). These men realize that their wounds have altered the trajectory of their lives and construct new calendars accordingly.

Ellen La Motte's account of war, like Bagnold's *Diary without Dates*, is titled in a way that pits war against chronology: she documents not linear movement, a flowing current of events, but rather *The Backwash of War*. During 1915 and 1916, when she wrote the sketches that constitute

The Backwash of War, "the lines moved little, either forward or backward, but were deadlocked in one position." As she explains:

> Undoubtedly, up and down the long reaching kilometers of "Front" there was action, and "moments of intense fright" which produced fine deeds of valor, courage and nobility. But where there is little or no action there is a stagnant place, and in that stagnant place is much ugliness. Much ugliness is churned up in the wake of mighty forces, and this is the backwash of war. Many little lives foam up in this backwash, loosened by the sweeping current, and detached from their environment, one catches a glimpse of them—often weak, hideous, or repellent.
>
> There can be no war without this backwash. (vii–viii)

La Motte does not deny the possibility of progress in other places (though there was precious little of it in 1915 and 1916), but she emphasizes that for every current, there is a wake and a backwash. Movement forward generates movement backward. Similarly, where there is no movement at all, there is a stagnant place, and this, too, is implicated in the ugliness that La Motte describes as war's backwash.[4]

Over and over, in modernist accounts of war at the front line and of war behind the lines, in the combatant spaces of France and in the civilian ones of London, time is squished into an experience akin to sucking quicksand. "By night it was cold, by day roasting hot. . . . There was little to do," Blunden reports from the front. "The men drowsed and yawned. Time went by, but no one felt the passage of it, for the shadow of death lay over the dial" (186). Similarly, in Virginia Woolf's *Mrs. Dalloway,* Peter Walsh, after the war, in the middle of London, is arrested by the fact that, years ago, Clarissa refused to marry him. "As a cloud crosses the sun," the narrator reports, "silence falls on London; and falls on the mind. Effort ceases. Time flaps on the mast. There we stop; there we stand. Rigid, the skeleton of habit alone upholds the human frame. Where there is nothing, Peter Walsh said to himself; feeling hollowed out, utterly empty within" (73–74). And like both Blunden and Walsh, Helen Zenna Smith records the apparent elimination of time along with its attendant emptiness: "The months pass, each day a replica of the last" (214). Despite the fact that she seems to be "living by the clock," it is a mechanical process, for "inwardly I am nothing. . . . I am content to drift along in the present. The past is gone; I have no future" (216–17). The clocks of modernism seem, at such moments, to cease ticking altogether.

The sheer noise of trench warfare flummoxes the orderly progress of plot by flummoxing language itself: characters speak but we can't hear them. For all soldiers know, crucial explanations disappear into noise that is simultaneously meaningless (in terms of verbal import) and fatally meaningful (in the noise that signals shells, machine guns, grenades). At the beginning of *No More Parades,* Ford registers this drowning out of words by giving bombs the verbs of language while human speakers grunt inaudibly and inarticulately, never saying anything that makes it into quotation marks. "The two men squatting on their heels over the brazier" at the beginning of the novel "began to talk in a low sing-song of dialect, hardly audible. It went on and on, monotonously, without animation. It was as if one told the other long, long stories to which his companion manifested his comprehension or sympathy with animal grunts." Meanwhile, a bomb begins to speak: "An immense tea-tray, august, its voice filling the black circle of the horizon, thundered to the ground. Numerous pieces of sheet-iron said, 'Pack. Pack. Pack'" (291). Blunden also describes weapons as possessed of voice, when telling how precisely the timing of an attack was carried out. While the men were required merely to move at the appropriate moment, the guns were required to speak at that moment: "Orders had been admirably obeyed; the waves extended, the artillery gave tongue at the exact moment" (108).

Blunden describes the ability to speak as rising and ebbing at least partly in response to the volume of noise. At the moment of a retreat, he and a friend "looked silently at one another, and went. We immediately passed the bodies of two men just killed, the sweat on their faces, and with shouts of uncontrol we ran for life through the shelling and the swamps." Having reached safety, they "emerged short of breath. Beyond, one of my signallers whom I had not seen lately approached us, and showed the inimitable superiority of man to fate by speaking, even then and there, in appreciation of the German artillery's brilliance . . . [until a] machine-gun, at long range, interrupted this conversation, and moved us on" (188). In this sequence of events, the speaker moves from silence to "shouts of uncontrol," finally "emerg[ing] short of breath" from his run, not yet having spoken a word. His appreciation of the signaller's remarks thus seems as much prompted by admiration of the ability to speak at all as by the fact that the man is complimenting the Germans on their admirable job of shelling ("exactly as if he had been talking of a fast bowler, or art for art's sake" [188]). Finally, the machine gun "interrupt[s] the conversation"—as if *it* were speaking. Noise thus constitutes another way in which war frustrates the articulation of forward progress.

Perhaps the most important way in which war belies conventions of narrative linearity is the way in which incidents absolutely crucial to the history of the war (as constructed afterward) are the very incidents least susceptible to narrative. For civilians, battles constitute the landmarks of war and give it shape. Yet combat at close range is about as disordered, incomprehensible, and illogical an experience as it is possible to imagine. Battle does not lend itself to conventions like plot or closure. In fact, soldiers participating in a battle often have no idea what is going on. Martin Middlebrook's research on the fate of Kitchener's armies on July 1, 1916, focuses on the accounts of "junior ranks [actually participating in the attack] whose view was a very local one and . . . collectively depict almost indecipherable chaos" (Keegan 262). "The singular part of the battle," Blunden remarks of another offensive, "was that no one . . . could say what had happened, or what was happening. One vaguely understood that the waves had found their manœvre in No Man's land too complicated. . . . But the general effect was the disappearance of the attack into mystery" (90). The fact that we are so familiar with battles suggests that historical accounts of war take this "disappearance . . . into mystery" as a starting point for narrative, rather than as an obstacle to it. Personal accounts, on the other hand—both fictional and nonfictional—tend faithfully to reproduce the failure of calendrical time as a way of describing the experience of war.[5]

Modernist intolerance with linear narrative structures emerged from a concern to render the contents of consciousness rather than the flow of external events. Virginia Woolf's famous suggestion that we "record the atoms" of experience, "however disconnected and incoherent in appearance" ("Modern Fiction" 107), clearly keeps faith with an internal conception of time, rather than one that could be represented by a series of uniform boxes on calendars. Civilian modernists thus privileged the *internal* by inventing narrative structures that could mimick the particles of which they imagined consciousness to be composed. Combatant modernists, in contrast, responded to explicitly *external* events when they disrupted narrative linearity, for it was their experience of combat that belied time lines of years and calendars of boxed days.

This difference in motivation between civilian and combatant texts emerges clearly in two book reviews published in the October 1928 issue of the *Nation and Athenæum*. Both the review of Siegfried Sassoon's *Memoirs of a Fox-Hunting Man* and the review of Virginia Woolf's *Orlando* remark on the way the texts disrupt narrative linearity. Both reviews describe the tactics with which this disruption is effected, which for Sassoon involves a focus on the external and for Woolf a focus on the internal. Sassoon's reviewer claims that "[t]he book has not the vestige of a plot. . . . His relations with other people never become in the least complicated or explicitly emotional" (Mortimer 150); Woolf's reviewer points out that "[i]nstead of beginning with a man more or less at the beginning and going on with him, as time goes on with him, more or less to the end, she likes to draw a sphere round a moment of his consciousness and examine its contents, which are very surprising. To traverse a succession of such spheres is strenuous work for a reader accustomed to be drawn smoothly along a straight and trusty slab of human life" (Gates 148). Sassoon's *Fox-Hunting Man* has no plot because it is all exterior; Woolf's *Orlando* has no plot because it is all interior.

I have said that modernist language is usually difficult and opaque, refusing to soothe us with the illusion that language can ever be transparent. War memoirs, in general, do not take this attitude toward language.

Robert Graves bluntly addresses the issue of style in one of his less-than-friendly exchanges with Sassoon: "My theories about how people should write. I have none. But I can only read with pleasure books written to be read not written to show how they were written" (*In Broken Images* 202). Graves clearly thinks of himself as a man who travels light—he claims no theories about how people should write, no attitude about language. His assertion that he is not interested in books "written to show how they were written" places him squarely in what David Lodge calls the "antimodernist" camp, which "regards literature as the communication of a reality that exists prior to and independent of the act of communication. Antimodernist writing thus gives priority to content, and is apt to be impatient with formal experiment, which obscures and hinders communication" (6–7).

Yet Graves seems to contradict his own scorn for novels "written to show how they were written" when he congratulates Edmund Blunden for his handling of form in *Undertones of War*. In that book, Blunden's narrator tells how, in his navigations along the front line one morning, "Kenward, the corporal and I saw a sentry crouching and peering one way and another like a birdboy in an October storm. He spoke, grinned and shivered; we passed; and duly the sentry was hit by a shell." Witnessing this death instantly prompts Blunden to remark on the sticky issues of representation that war always poses: "So that, in this vicinity a peculiar difficulty would exist for the artist to select the sights, faces, words, incidents, which characterized the time. The art is rather to collect them, in their original form of incoherence" (156). Graves singles out this passage for specific praise in a complimentary review, stating that "Blunden is about the first man I have read who has realized that the problem of writing about trench-warfare lies in the 'peculiar difficulty of selecting the sights, faces, words, incidents which characterized the times,' and that the solution is 'to collect them in their original form of incoherence'" ("Trench History" 420). Furthermore, a reviewer of Graves's own *Goodbye to All That* remarks that "Mr. Graves . . . does not concentrate on any particular phase of the conflict; he portrays whatever came his way" (Hellman 121), suggesting that Graves himself followed a principle of (apparent) nonselection in his own book. In other words, though Graves resists nonlinearity in theory, he finds that resistance to the linear does a better job of telling war than conventional notions of plots that move forward, underlining once more the way in which modernist inflections accommodated the experience of trench warfare.

I have been arguing that combatant novels are surprisingly modernist and difficult in their handling of time, yet contemporary reviewers tended to praise combat novels for their clarity, objectivity, and adherence to the facts. Blunden's *Undertones of War* was deemed "impressive as a record" (Hill 7) and admirable for the way in which we "see what he sees, feel what he feels, without intervention" (Morley 994). Sassoon's *Memoirs of a Fox-Hunting Man* was considered "clear and simple" (Schriftgiesser 3), "the honest record of an average man" (Canfield 5). Graves's *Good-bye to All That* displayed "candor, level-headedness, good sense" (Matthews 23) and painted an "accurate picture . . . refreshingly untainted by affection" (Whitridge 706).

Given soldiers' admissions of the ways in which war makes linear plots and categories like factuality seem suddenly frail and inadequate, how is it that such books are understood by their contemporaries as "clear and simple"? If combatant works and modernist works both gum up the conventions of narrative, how is it that modernist novels seemed so alien and combatant ones so accessible? The explanation, I would suggest, lies not in form but in content. For civilians, war is a strange and inaccessible experience, so for glitches to appear in renderings of it is not as noticeable as it is for glitches to appear in the representation of everyday life. When smiles flicker across the faces of the dead in a work by James Joyce, when ghosts haunt the houses of Henry James, and when Woolf takes liberties with her narrators, we are ruffled by the way in which these tactics seem not to conform to the ways in which we usually understand experience—*our* experience, for we have mostly all seen bodies in coffins and walked the corridors of empty houses. Consulting ourselves as our own expert witnesses, we reject the modernist tendency to be disoriented by that which we have an investment in trusting. A disoriented soldier is not threatening in the same way, since most of us are liable never to have to test his version of the experience of combat against a version of our own.

Thus, no matter how many times linearity is disrupted in a war memoir—no matter how painfully a narrator falters—their modernist erasures of connective logic sink for us into virtual invisibility, precisely because we expect war to be chaotic. To read modernist *civilian* narratives, on the other hand, is to be forced to read our own homes through a grid that we may want to believe is more fitting to war, to participate in a world where disorientation is a quality of our collective civilian consciousness. That the safety and organization we think of as inherent to a civilian culture are merely imaginative structures, easily replaced by the imaginative structures that also suit war, suggests that we are negotiating a dangerous world indeed. If we were to acknowledge that interchangeability, peace would begin to seem as dangerous and as disturbing as war.

THE SHAPES OF OBJECTS

SIX

FORGETFUL OBJECTS

Virginia Woolf's story "Solid Objects" (1920) marvels at the ability of objects to evoke astonishingly different worlds while standing in close proximity to one another and juxtaposes that ability against the human intolerance for such proximities. At the beginning of the story, the narrator is so far away from two friends that their bodies do not seem to be bodies at all, but are perceived instead as "one small black spot" (79) on a beach. By the end of the story, large psychological distances separate the previously indistinguishable bodies: John and Charles still speak the same language yet seem suddenly to be "talking about different things" (86). Their friendship ends, the possibility of relationship canceled by differences in their perceptions of the potential meaning of the "solid objects" of the story's title.

John's preoccupation with objects begins at the beach when, as he is digging absentmindedly in the sand, he happens upon "a full drop of solid matter." The "smoothing of the sea had completely worn off any edge or shape, so that it was impossible to say whether it had been bottle, tumbler, or window-pane; it was nothing but glass" (80). Whereas, to the narrator, two pages previously, nothing had seemed "so solid" as the bodies of the two men, the lump of glass almost immediately usurps visually the apparent solidity of Charles: John holds it up "so that its irregular mass blotted out the body and extended right arm of his friend." The sky, the beach, and the body of Charles suddenly become backdrops to the object on which he concentrates, no longer significant in themselves but only for the way in which they affect the color of the sea glass, whose "green thinned and thickened slightly as it was held against the sky or against the body." The lump of glass "pleased [John] . . . puzzled him; it was so hard, so concentrated, so definite an object compared with the vague sea and the hazy shore" (81). The appealing solidity of the glass has already replaced—both visually and verbally—the solidity of the young men's bodies.

John begins, questlike, to search for other objects that remind him of the lump of sea glass. He hunts for objects in curiosity shops, on side-walks, "in the neighbourhood of waste land where the household refuse is thrown away" (82). Clearly, the solid objects that intrigue him are those have been used, that are suggestive of a past. That the past the objects represent is inaccessible to him doesn't matter—in fact, the ambiguity of an object's significance opens up imaginative possibilities. Perhaps, for example, the lump of glass "after all . . . was really a gem; something worn by a dark Princess trailing her finger in the water. . . . Or the oak sides of a sunk Elizabethan treasure-chest had split apart, and, rolled over and over, over and over, its emeralds had come at last to shore" (80–81). He is absorbed and delighted by a piece of broken china shaped like a starfish:

> Set at the opposite end of the mantelpiece from the lump of glass that had been dug from the sand, it looked like a creature from another world—freakish and fantastic as a harlequin. It seemed to be pirouetting through space, winking light like a fitful star. The contrast between the china so vivid and alert, and the glass so mute and contemplative, fasci-nated him, and wondering and amazed he asked himself how the two came to exist in the same world, let alone to stand upon the same narrow strip of marble in the same room. (83)

Broken, discarded, of cryptic yet compelling significance, the lumps and shards of history are buried in the sand, strewn about on sidewalks, or tucked onto the shelves of junk shops, as indicative of balked promise as the "smooth oval egg of a prehistoric bird" (82). John, a young man filled with high promise himself, glimpses the resonance of objects, re-turns to it, and gradually becomes so engrossed by it that the project of accumulating and displaying such relics consumes him. His attentiveness to the narrative possibilities that objects represent and his appreciation of the drastically different worlds from which they emerge usurp his ability to attend to human relationships and to appreciate the possibility of inhabiting the same world as the people around him. His friend, involved in politics, is invested in shaping the present; John, involved in solid objects, is invested in excavating the past. The two projects admit of no common ground, either spatial or imaginative, and that lack of common ground proves intolerable. When Charles realizes that the "mere appear-ance" of John "upon a [political] platform was out of the question" (86), he decides that friendship between them is impossible. The two of them are as radically isolated from each other as the lump of glass and the

fragment of china are from each other—that the two men or the t
objects "came to exist in the same world" is amazing. While John fin
this phenomenon of simultaneous proximity and distance almost irresi:
ibly compelling, though, Charles finds it deeply disturbing.

In this chapter, I suggest that many people in the 1920s felt about
objects in ways similar to the way John and Charles do. On the one hand,
objects seem to them to suggest the ambiguous contexts from which they
emerge, with a vividness that obscures the inhabitants of the present
moment: John feels them in this way, as does a veteran in Rebecca West's
Return of the Soldier, which I discuss later. In Ernest Hemingway's *A
Farewell to Arms,* Frederick Henry also relies on the ability of objects to
evoke a different world, although he uses it to discard the past rather than
to be overwhelmed by it. On the other hand, objects may evoke nothing
at all: this is how Charles experiences them, and it is the condition to
which the international style of architecture aspired. According to this
view, the very idea of historically resonant objects is threatening; like
Charles, international-style architects recoiled from such evocative artifacts.

Modernist writers endow material objects with the luminous ability
to evoke memories, while modernist international-style architects endow
material objects with the ability to escape memory. Both strategies result
in forgetfulness, for when characters in modernist texts are confronted
with these resonant artifacts, they discard them as a way of leaving the
past behind. I will argue here that both the persistence with which writers
describe objects as pieces of the past and the persistence with which
international-style architects describe objects as having shaken off the
past are rooted in attitudes toward the war. Objects in modernist texts
and buildings in modernist sketchbooks are forgetful objects, one way or
another—designed to display either the erasure of history or the possibility of pitching it into the garbage.

In postwar Britain, the immediate past was by no means rejected, but it
was confined to a specific category of artifacts. Britain erected hundreds
of monuments to the war dead, both on the Continent and in its own
cities and villages, but architectural memorialization of the dead and
missing was kept distinct from the design of architecture that would be
used and inhabited by the living. Though monuments like the Cenotaph
were artifacts that civilian traffic patterns were forced to move *around,*
memorial architecture was never something that civilians had reason to
move *through* in the course of their everyday lives. The War Graves
Commission had deliberately organized their memorials in this way: "It
had set its face against buildings of practical utility, knowing that ultimately they must invite association with their function rather than with
the sacrifices the dead had made" (Longworth 97). The advantage of this
separation of the war into a specific architectural category is the very one

anticipated by the commission: architecture associated with the war is *only* associated with the war. The disadvantage of this separation is that the war is isolated from civilian experience—in effect, continuing the isolation that, during the war, roused the ill feeling of many combatants. In this way, Britain remained as invested in the distinction between soldier and civilian as it was in August 1914, when Germany's lack of distinction between the two categories was construed as justification for entering the war.

A survey of London's *Architectural Review* from the years 1916 through 1919 reveals little evidence that British architects saw the war as impinging on either their profession or their professional imaginations. In the few articles that mention the war, two responses emerge: attention to architectural damage and anxiety about the building market. Most of the war-related articles concern themselves with the documentation of buildings that were bombed and battered by the Germans—destruction that tended to be offered up as proof that Germans were now treating European architecture as barbarically as they had treated Belgian civilians in the late summer of 1914. The *Architectural Review* reprinted an article by American architect Whitney Warren in which he argues that German war policy clearly signals the "moral degeneracy" of a "stunted" nation:

> If the war in Europe has accomplished nothing else, it will have performed an important service in correcting previous existing misconceptions as to the national characteristics of Continental peoples. The homely solid German has proved to be the degenerate of Europe—as moral degeneracy alone explains . . . the sordid grimness of acts of pillage, rapine, and destruction to which the countries over which they have passed have been subjected. . . . From a nation so stunted in full development such a martyrdom of mutilated cities, a decapitation of cathedrals, and assassination of architecture should perhaps have come as no surprise. (Warren 19)

In his eagerness to indict Germans for their moral stuntedness, this writer exchanges the vocabulary of architectural damage for the vocabulary of physical wounding: cities are not destroyed but "mutilated," cathedrals not damaged but "decapitat[ed]." Architecture is not described as wrecked, demolished, obliterated, reduced to rubble, or even vandalized, but rather *killed*—the implicit verb running throughout the commentary, since killing is the necessary preamble to "martyrdom" and "assassination"—giving buildings the moral import of bodies.

While it is understandable that architects would be particularly aggrieved by the wartime destruction of buildings, it is notable that this destruction is characterized as peculiarly German, allowing it to be dismissed as irrelevant to British moral and architectural concerns. If Germans can be construed as singularly guilty of crimes against architecture, if the war can be construed as having "performed [the] important service" of exposing Germans as moral trolls—ethically "stunted"—then the English can be construed as singularly innocent of crimes against architecture and the war as having vindicated (or at least not sullied) the English character. Such vindication leads naturally to a postwar sense of relief: having denied complicity in the war, one can wash one's hands of the war once it is over. This view clearly supported the British tendency to keep memorial architecture in a category distinct from all other kinds of architecture: if the war could be understood as having challenged neither personal nor collective consciousness, then no new outlook need be architecturally expressed.

In 1919, the *Architectural Review* ran a two-part article in which two different architects considered the topic of "Peace and the Art of Architecture." This pair of articles demonstrates the degree to which the British architectural community understood the war to be an experience that would find its material registration only in war monuments, while all other forms of architectural design would proceed either without reference to the war or with the goal of reestablishing prewar conditions.

In part I of the piece, Ernest Newton observes reassuringly that "I do not think that our life has been so much modified by the war that any great difference will be required in the planning of country houses," but notes that it is impossible to ignore the shortage of servants. Then, claiming to foreground women's contribution to the war effort in the postwar architectural imagination, he, in fact, effaces those very contributions. Due to the current lack of domestic help, he predicts that "[i]t is likely . . . that for some time to come, instead of the demand for 'cupboards,' so well known to architects, the demand will be for 'labour-saving appliances.'" He proposes a ready solution to this quandary, however, "ventur[ing] to suggest that the best labour-saving device is for everybody to do some housework herself." "The war," he notes, "has produced W.A.A.C.'s, W.R.N.'s, W.R.A.F.'s, and Land Girls, who have found real pleasure in doing hard work of all kinds." Thus, "The happy home possessing daughters need not worry too much about the servant problem" (Newton 160).

In other words, the war has taught women to be servants. Postwar architecture, the author suggests, finds itself in the happy position not only of reensconcing women in the domestic sphere, but of positioning them there in the role of domestics. While the writer claims to be honoring women's war work, he undermines the profound implications of that work: independence, public service, clout in the labor force, and the radical enlargement of options for women. This architect, instead, sees his job as imposing architectural restriction on such options: stuff these newly independent women, he advises, into the cubbyhole not even of wives but of servants.

If part I of "Peace and the Art of Architecture" encourages architects to forget women's participation in the war, part II urges them to forget the war—all of it—by concentrating instead on the abstract concept of victory. Walter H. Godfrey argues that while the other arts are "engendered by suffering," architecture springs from and articulates the public celebration of victory, serving "as a crown to momentous national enterprises that have achieved for their peoples a full and spacious reward. The great conventions of architecture, the 'styles' which compel the homage and the amazed admiration of the world, were conceived by men under the stimulus of victory" (Godfrey 160). His notion of peacetime architecture is that it ought to confirm the dualities of war and to relish victory rather than represent anything about the actual experience of war. If Godfrey is aware of the fact (discussed in chapter 5) that many veterans found the concept of victory irrelevant to their experience of the armistice, he obviously sees such an attitude as too sour to warrant mention.

It is unlikely that all architects in Britain agreed with the judgmental myopia that viewed Germany as singularly ill bred for doing in war what is generally done in war or that all architects saw postwar women as better fit for the scullery than for any public space or that all architects viewed the war in the simplistic terms of a victory that could be chalked up on the national slate. But British architects did tend to see the war as an experience best expressed by the war monument. Apart from erecting monuments, Britain did not attend to the architectural registration of war, focusing instead (and this is understandable) on the crying need for more housing. A generation of young men had left for the war from their parents' homes and schools but returned needing homes of their own. Two weeks after the armistice, Lloyd George gave a famous speech at Wolverhampton, in which he asked rhetorically: "What is our task? To make Britain a fit country for heroes to live in" ("What Happened Last Time" 5). As the *Architectural Review* described the situation, "[P]hysical reconstruction was almost synonymous with housing" ("What Happened Last Time" 3). The concern with monuments and with this market of houses for heroes thus constituted the British architectural response to the Great War.

Architectural response to war was much more explicit on the Continent, at least to those who documented the emergence of what became known as the international style. To these men—architectural historians like Reyner Banham and Nikolaus Pevsner, along with architects like Ludwig Mies van der Rohe and Le Corbusier—German expressionism, in particular, was understood as a specifically postwar phenomenon, unfortunate for its interference with the otherwise rational and understandable development of the international style. Often, in fact, what was understood as the registration of war in the forms of expressionism was singled out as responsible for what were understood as its regressive elements.

Nikolaus Pevsner, for example, seems taken aback when he detects evidence that the war influenced the course of architectural development. With a Victorian belief in progress, Pevsner's *Outline of European Archi-*

tecture (1960) analyzes the architecture of the first quarter of this century by identifying what he sees as the steady emergence of a machine-age aesthetic, which he endorses as a brave break from the past and an appropriate expression of the times. While the idea of linear progress may seem to contradict the act of breaking with the past (since time lines sketch relationships, not breaks), Pevsner documents progress by first articulating the new premise he sees as launching the international style— the incorporation of the materials, processes, and forms of mass production—and then looking for movement forward from that point:

> [B]y 1914 the leading architects of the younger generation had coura-geously broken with the past and accepted the machine-age in all its implications: new materials, new processes, new forms, new prob-lems. . . . The twentieth century . . . is a century of masses and it is a century of science. The new style with its refusal to accept craftsmanship and whims of design is eminently suitable for a large anonymous clien-tele and with its sheer surfaces and minimum of mouldings for the industrial production of parts. (401, 404)

But, as Pevsner reports, the progression from a more craftsmanlike aes-thetic to a sheer and industrial one hit an odd glitch: "[O]ne might have expected . . . that the new style, once established, would carry on with-out crisis. But curiously enough the years between 1920 and 1925 were not years of straight progress on the lines laid down by the pioneers of 1900–14" (404–405). This unfortunate transgression of the "lines" that had previously been "laid down," according to Pevsner, is directly attrib-utable to the Great War: "[T]he troubled mood of 1919, of irretrievably lost confidence in peace and prosperity, of men returning from years spent in violent and primeval conditions, twisted the new architecture and designs into an Expressionism in some ways more akin to Art Nouveau than to the style of 1914" (405). In this formulation of architectural history, the violence of the war is "primeval," constituting an evolution-ary step backward, which, "curiously enough," makes itself felt in the design of buildings produced by veterans of the experience. Unlike the British sense that war's violence could be confined to the architectural category of monuments and filtered out of all other categories, Pevsner sees war as having interfered, on the Continent, with the emergence of the machine-age style that he is trying to document. For him, war is wrenchingly, architecturally, regressive—an experience that "twisted" the "lines" previously "laid down," thus foiling "straight progress."

He goes on to name some of the most famous examples of this expressionist deviation: Fritz Höger's *Chilehaus* (1923; figure 6.1) in Hamburg, Hans Poelzig's *Grosses Schauspielhaus* (1919; figure 6.2) in Berlin, and Erich Mendelsohn's Einstein Tower (1920–21; figure 6.3) in Potsdam.[1] It is not surprising that these are buildings with lines and edges that are not straight or with straight lines that loom threateningly;

Figure 6.1. Fritz Höger: Chilehaus, *1923 (British Architectural Library, RIBA, London).*

just as the conception of historical time as a straight line moving forward helped both to produce and to shore up a military conception of space as bounded by front lines and dug into trenches, the conception of architectural development as a straight line moving forward helped both to produce and to shore up an architectural conception of space as bounded by straight lines and plugged into boxes. Indeed, Pevsner has elsewhere described the eventual predominance of the international style as "the victory of the cube over the sharp angle and the curve" ("Finsterlin" 357).

Although registration of the war is not usually the primary concern of architectural critics in their discussions of expressionist design, the war does appear in a matrix of assumptions about expressionism that may be roughly summed up as follows: as opposed to the "rational" lines, cubes, white surfaces, and flat roofs of the international style, the curves, textures, pitched roofs, and sharp angles of expressionism constituted an idiosyncratic and "emotional" deviation from reasonable forms. Not infrequently, architectural historians decided that the source of this deviation was rooted in the experience of the Great War.

For example, Poelzig's *Grosses Schauspielhaus*, "whose form would have been unthinkable five years earlier or five years later" (Pehnt 16), "was described as 'a child of the war . . .' in a contemporary magazine" (Sharp 54). Notable for "the avoidance of all hard, straight lines in the ground plan" and for "the concavities and convexities that conjure forth wizardries of light and shade," the building, one critic argues, establishes Poelzig as "the master of a new emotion in architecture"; it prepares "the spectator for something extraordinary, something that would seduce him from reality" (Scheffauer 121–22). These appreciative comments relish the theater's unusual icicle-like forms, but another critic's observation that Poelzig's "industrial work of the early twenties soon became much more straightforward" (Hitchcock 344) is more typical, suggesting that the *Grosses Schauspielhaus* was merely a temporary veering off from some reasonable theoretical norm.

Figure 6.2. Hans Poelzig: Grosses Schauspielhaus, *1919 (Bildarchiv Foto Marburg; Art Resource, New York).*

Figure 6.3. Erich Mendelsohn: Einstein Tower, 1920–21 (British Architectural Library, RIBA, London).

Mendelsohn's Einstein Tower is often described as emanating from the trenches of the Great War as well. Reyner Banham's analysis of Mendelsohn begins with "the well-known sketches of the War years" ("Mendelsohn" 85), a time during which Mendelsohn was not only serving in the German army but also thinking about architecture: he wrote *Reflections on New Architecture* at the front between 1914 and 1917 (Sharp 181). Banham judges that the Einstein observatory "gave tangible form to all the tendencies latent in the wartime sketches" ("Mendelsohn" 87), clearly implying that the building's form derived from the experience of war. In his account of Mendelsohn's movement away from designs like the molded shape of the Einstein observatory and toward ones that were more "chunkily rectangular," Banham describes the shift as one in which Mendelsohn seemed "to reject Expressionism as the employment of the insane, and to substitute for it a more sensible and humane view of the world." He explicitly describes the flaunting of straight lines as architecturally wild: "The curvilinear Expressionist manner is screwed up to a pitch of contorted frenzy." But this frenzy, he reports, is followed by something more controlled: "Sketches reveal . . . imagination run mad in the Expressionist pleasure-pavilions . . . of 1920, succeeded at once by a sharp rectangular style" ("Mendelsohn" 89, 85, 89, 88). Thus, descriptions of both the *Grosses Schauspielhaus* and the Einstein Tower locate the source of their expressionist forms in the war and perceive those forms as out of control (a contemporary critic, Manning Robertson, described the Einstein Tower as "'a monument to complication and bewilderment'" [qtd. in Sharp 119]). Both buildings are succeeded, according to these critics, by a settling down into more reasonable, understandable—that is, linear and boxy—forms.

Höger's *Chilehaus* is not linked explicitly to the war but its form is unacceptable to certain critics for the same reasons that Poelzig's and Mendelsohn's buildings are. Far from boxlike, the *Chilehaus* presents "a silhouette of the shrillest Expressionist order" (Hitchcock, *Architecture* 344). This building is not only constructed in brick, which "In the late twenties . . . was upheld as the antithesis of 'white' or International Style modern architecture" (Pehnt 128), but its surface is enlivened in a number of other ways. "Höger and his staff preferred irregular, second- and third-grade bricks because these gave added animation to the wall texture. . . . Close-set piers separate the window-strips . . . [so that] the façade opens and closes to the passer-by" (Pehnt 127–28)—much in the same way that the "Monkey's Soap . . . Needs No Rinsing" advertisement changes depending on one's perspective in Ford Madox Ford's *No More Parades* (see chapter 4). In addition, "The number of different light values appearing simultaneously on the façade at any time of the day Höger calculated to be at least fifty, including shadows and reflections" (Pehnt 128).

Although Pevsner seems uncomfortable with the link between architecture and the war, moody veterans figure explicitly in his theory that "men returning from violent and primeval conditions twisted the new architecture and designs into an Expressionism." He quickly moves on, however, to a reformulation that, ignoring soldiers, pictures the postwar architectural situation as a purely abstract tension between two styles, one of which plays dirty: "the new style of 1914, temporarily doped by the fumes of Expressionism, re-established itself and developed in some countries into the accepted, leading style for all kinds of jobs" (409). Now, instead of the war constituting a human experience that affected how human beings designed buildings, it is the "fumes of Expressionism" that drugged the prewar "style of 1914" out of its disciplined state. This description attempts to disengage architecture from its sources in human experience and imagination, picturing it instead as operating in a pristine world of architectural representation. Pevsner's own metaphor, however, subverts such a picture. People, not buildings, are susceptible to fumes, as anyone who had lived through World War I would have been aware: the introduction of gas as a weapon had been one of the war's notorious features.

Banham, like Pevsner, described expressionism as a deviation from a vector of development, though it was, he asserts, a phase of reevaluation that needed to be passed through before progress could carry on: "[T]he resolute paring-down to one particular set of formal and structural solutions that took place in the early Twenties seems to have been a necessary phase of self-discipline and brain-cleansing before development could resume" (*Theory and Design* 163). Banham's evaluation is kinder to expressionism in that he sees it as having served a function. Like Pevsner, though, he assumes that the resumption of "development" required the imposition of new "self-discipline" and "brain-cleansing," an assumption reminiscent of the antidote Pevsner implied was necessary for recovery from the doping of architecture by expressionist fumes.

Both Pevsner and Banham, to varying degrees, seem to regard expressionism as an unfortunate incident, one that needs to be gotten beyond, thus implying that the war, itself, is an unfortunate incident that needs to be gotten beyond. In such a view, war is perceived as a temporary binge, producing an aesthetic hangover that just needs to be slept off.[2]

It was not just architectural historians who denigrated reference to the war in the design of buildings. Architects themselves resisted the idea that war had had an effect on architectural form. When asked a strongly leading interview question by Peter Blake about the effect of the war on his work, Ludwig Mies van der Rohe dismisses the possibility:

> BLAKE: In your early work there was a tremendously sudden break. Whereas you had been working in the classical tradition up to the beginning of World War I, in 1919 you seem to have broken completely with everything you had done before.

> MIES: I think the break started long before. The break started when I was in the Netherlands working on the problem of the Kröller museum. There I saw and studied carefully Berlage. I read his books and his theme that architecture should be construction, clear construction. His architecture was brick, and it may have looked medieval, but it was always clear. (Blake, *Four Great Makers* 94–95)

In his question, Blake refers to the sharp difference between early Mies designs like the Kröller house (1912; figure 6.4)—a low classical building with colonnades—and his 1921–22 glass skyscraper projects (figures 6.5 and 6.6), which provided some of the early definitive images of modern architecture. Mies, however, claims a continuity between the two designs,

Figure 6.4. Ludwig Mies van der Rohe. Project: Kröller House. The Hague, The Netherlands. 1912. Drawing. Present whereabouts unknown. Photograph © 1996 The Museum of Modern Art, New York.

Figure 6.5. Ludwig Mies van der Rohe: Friedrichstrasse Skyscraper, 1921. Presentation Perspective (north and east sides). Charcoal, pencil on brown paper, 173.5 × 122 cm. The Mies van der Rohe Archive. The Museum of Modern Art, New York. Photograph © 1996 The Museum of Modern Art, New York.

Figure 6.6. Ludwig Mies van der Rohe: Glass Skyscraper, 1922. Model. No Longer Extant. Photograph courtesy The Mies van der Rohe Archive, The Museum of Modern Art, New York.

privileging the architectural, rather than the cultural, context in which he was working. At least one critic—Philip Johnson, a disciple of Mies— agrees with him about the relation between the Kröller house and its architectural context. According to Johnson, both Peter Behrens and Hendrik Petrus Berlage provided a meaningful context in which to understand the design of the Kröller house, for "the former contributed the reduction of Neo-Classic shapes to simple rectangular blocks, the latter, the practice of structural honesty . . . namely, that those parts of a building resembling supports should actually support and, conversely, that all the supporting elements should be evident" (16).

Still, the distance between the Kröller house and the glass skyscrapers seems very great. While the Kröller house clearly draws on a number of familiar classical conventions, each of the skyscraper designs, according to Johnson, was "shocking when it appeared" (22). It is this distance, this shock, to which Blake's question refers. The Kröller house is "a rather low-slung, extended complex of one-story wings and colonnades grouped around a central, two-story-high block facing on various interior patios." It is "neoclassical" in its details (Blake, *The Master Builders* 177), whereas the 1921 *Friedrichstrasse* skyscraper project is a "sheer cliff of crystal . . . a staggering piece of imagination" (Blake, *The Master Builders* 180) and the 1922 skyscraper design "was even more extraordinary than the first one: in plan it consisted of a complex of free forms; each floor was enclosed by a continuous curtain or skin of glass . . . yet this curved glass skin was made up of dozens of identical flat window units that changed direction on every mullion line, like the sides of a polygon" (Blake, *The Master Builders* 182).

Blake wonders whether the war could account for such a radical shift. Mies, however, dismisses the link by not even deigning to mention it, forcing architectural historians interested in the relationship between building design and historical context to make oblique comments about the connection without offering any firm evidence of a relationship. Kenneth Frampton's vagueness is typical when he observes that Mies, in 1914, was "a tyro architect of romantic classical persuasion. But he was to emerge from the crucible of World War I with a very different artistic and emotional outlook. . . . It was as though the reality of modernization and the traumatic experience of the first industrialized war had decisively transformed the members of his generation" (35). This kind of cautious speculation is similar to the hazy links that critics sometimes sketch between literary modernists and the war.

Le Corbusier, another leading architect of the international style, distances himself from the war by first linking it to expressionism and then describing how abhorrent he finds expressionism. The designs of Hermann Finsterlin (figures 6.7 and 6.8) and Bruno Taut are singled out as examples of the repellent movement:

> In the depths of our being, larva, toads and beasts which haunt the memories of the primordial world re-emerge again today. . . . [W]e see them in this new crisis of the spirit which followed the war: frightening dreams of Hermann Finsterlin . . . with their viscous ejaculations recalling underwater horrors, or those viscera, or impure acts of beasts. He was pretending to extract out of this architectural creations . . . Bruno Taut publishes in his review houses where one finds the same distracted neurasthenia. (qtd. in Jencks 60–61)

Le Corbusier clearly finds the expression of a postwar "crisis of the spirit" disturbing: his aesthetic shudder blends metaphors of wet, dreamy sexual deviance ("ejaculations . . . horrors . . . impure acts of beasts") with a temporal collapse in which recent history sinks into the mud of prehis-

Figure 6.7. Hermann Finsterlin: Formal Study for Casa Nova, *1920. Reproduced from* Visionary Architecture: From Babylon to Virtual Reality (*Munich: Prestel, 1994*) *by permission of the author, Professor Christian W. Thomsen, and Ms. Gabriella Finsterlin Reisser, Stuttgart.*

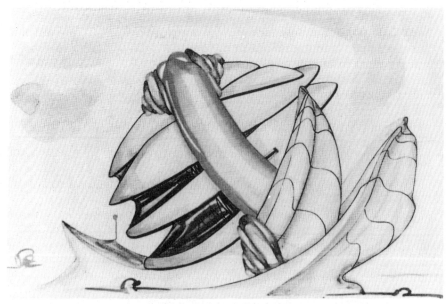

Figure 6.8. Hermann Finsterlin: Glass Dream II, *1920. Reproduced from* Visionary Architecture: From Babylon to Virtual Reality (*Munich: Prestel, 1994*) *by permission of the author, Professor Christian W. Thomsen, and Ms. Gabriella Finsterlin Reisser, Stuttgart.*

tory, the Great War becoming just one more layer on the sediment of a disgusting reptilian "primordial world." Wolfgang Pehnt has asserted that "It was not until the International Style . . . that history was rejected as a source of inspiration and point of reference" (49); Le Corbusier's description of expressionism demonstrates the wholeheartedness with which advocates of the international style put the nasty past behind them.

Although they were not always consistent in their positions, international-style architects generally differed from their expressionist predecessors both in their attitudes toward *cultural* history (their refusal to acknowledge that the war might register itself on design) and toward *architectural* history (their insistence on a new style free of historical architectural conventions). Le Corbusier articulates an unrelenting insistence on the new in *Towards a New Architecture* (1922): "We throw the out-of-date tool on the scrap-heap. . . . This action is a manifestation of health, of moral health, of *morale* also" (13). In contrast, the expressionists, with their lack of emphasis on regulating principles, took a much looser attitude toward history: having just emerged from the war, addressing the problems it raised seemed natural. Further, they felt "no contradiction as yet between their demand for originality and their appeal to particular periods of history or to exotic cultures. What they looked for in history was not models that they could copy but confirmation of what they themselves wanted to do. They had no respect for tradition at all. They just took what they could use, transforming what they had taken into something else" (Pehnt 49). In other words, while the dictates of the international style enforced forgetfulness, expressionism forgot or remembered, as the spirit moved its individual practitioners.

Walter Gropius complicates the simplified distinctions that are often made between expressionism and the international style. Of the four "giants" of modern architecture—Mies, Le Corbusier, Gropius, and Frank Lloyd Wright—only Gropius fought in the war. Mies, who was not qualified to be a German officer since he did not have a university degree, enlisted in the engineers and spent the war building roads and bridges (Blake, *Mies* 23). Swiss-born Le Corbusier spent the first two years of the war in his hometown, La Chaux-de-Fonds, and then moved to Paris, but did not participate in the war. Wright, an American, lived in Wisconsin until 1916 and then moved to Tokyo.

Gropius, who fought for Germany, was straightforward in his acknowledgment that the war had affected him not only personally but architecturally:

> The full consciousness of my responsibility in advancing ideas based on my own reflections only came home to me as a result of the war, in which these theoretical premises first took definite shape. After that violent interruption, which kept me, like many of my fellow architects, from work for four years, every thinking man felt the necessity for an

intellectual change of front. Each in his own particular sphere of activity aspired to help in bridging the disastrous gulf between reality and idealism. . . . I saw that an architect cannot hope to realize his ideas unless he can influence the industry of his country sufficiently for a new school of design to result. (Gropius 48, 51)

Gropius did, in fact, preside over a new school of design. After the war, he succeeded Henri Van de Velde as director of the Weimar School of Arts and Crafts, which he merged with the Weimar Academy of Fine Arts, creating the now famous *Das Staatliche Bauhaus Weimar*—commonly referred to as the Bauhaus (Gropius 51–52).

Gropius's response to the war-generated imperative for "an intellectual change of front" has been charted differently by different historians. If they assume—as Stephen Bayley, Philippe Garner, and Deyan Sudjic do—that a handicraft aesthetic evolves naturally into an industrial aesthetic along a continuum of progress, then they see Gropius's initial organization of the Bauhaus around cooperation between artistic designers and craftsmen as a move backward:

> [T]his medievalism represents a regression on Gropius's own pre-war position, when he had already begun to investigate the possibility of industrializing the building process. Some commentators have tried to associate this backward step with Gropius's experiences during the slaughter of the First World War, in which the machine's potential for destruction was so starkly revealed. But it also reflected the economic realities of life in Weimar, a small city in which handicrafts and crafts-based industries were vital. Gropius was able to stress the value of the school in the regeneration of the local economy. (Bayley et al. 91)

Though the authors draw our attention to the complexity of Gropius's position, they are clearly uncomfortable with that complexity. The passage begins by dismissing historians who "have tried" to make a connection between Gropius's experience in the war and his organization of the Bauhaus. They then seem to accept the very connection they have skimmed over, implying that their only reservation about such an interpretation is the way in which it may oversimplify the architect's motivations, ignoring "economic realities." The authors' discomfort with historians who stress the trauma of the war on Gropius's architectural psyche can be understood as springing from their commitment to a hierarchical paradigm: expressionism, handicrafts, and acknowledgment of the war precede, and are less sophisticated than, modernism, mass production, and a deliberate forgetfulness regarding the war. The extent to which response to the war determined Gropius's organization of his school is partly a matter of speculation, but his incorporation of handicrafts and expressionist teachers into his scheme is undeniable. These historians thus reason that Gropius must have reversed his course along the vector of development: "this medievalism represents a regression" and is a "backward step."

Marcel Franciscono, more at ease with the possibility that apparently contradictory motivations might coexist in a single person and free from the compulsion to hierarchize positions, charts a different course by identifying two ideologies of design prevalent at the beginning of the century. First, there was "modern architecture and applied design based upon directness and sobriety of expression and the use of industrial materials, forms, and techniques," as institutionalized by the Deutsche Werkbund (founded in 1907), and second, there was "what we loosely think of as the subjectivity or exaggerated emotionalism of German painting and sculpture." The Bauhaus, he states in his introduction, inherited both these streams of thought: "As a school and a working community of widely differing artists, the Bauhaus was in a real sense the only viable attempt ever made to synthesize them or at least hold them in equilibrium" (Franciscono 4). Franciscono thus offers an interpretation of Gropius that is able to take into account both the architect's wish to incorporate his experience of the war into his organization of the Bauhaus and also his sensitivity to other pressures and motivations. In this view, Gropius appears unusually willing to abide complexities not tolerated by other leading practitioners of the international style.

International-style intolerance for that which does not necessarily fit is demonstrated by Le Corbusier's historical pattern-finding in *Towards a New Architecture* (1923), where, as Banham remarks,

> [t]his interfusion of the Mechanical and the Classical achieves a kind of apotheosis in the chapter on Automobiles. Here on a pair of facing pages the reader finds, at the top, the Basilica at Paestum on the left, the Parthenon on the right, and, below, a Humber of 1907 and a Delage of the early Twenties. On reflection the reader realises that this is supposed to be read from page to page, implying an equivalent progress between Humber and Delage and between Paestum and Acropolis, but the immediate response seems always to be to read down the page, thus producing an image of contrast. (Banham, *Theory and Design* 223)

Le Corbusier thus schools us in the art of reading history on a scale that is broad but reductionist. By limiting his interest to a narrow array of objects that seem to him to constitute evidence of progress along a straight line, he gains a sense of historical continuity but sacrifices eccentricity and diversity—precisely what international-style architecture sacrificed by its insistence on straight lines of development.

Le Corbusier's demand that a new architectural historical precedent must be invented is thus a qualified demand. He was not unwilling to situate himself in relation to tradition, but he wished to choose his influences from the distant rather than the recent past, thus positing his own laws of design within the context of a pristine thread of development from venerable ancestors. Both he and Mies were brutal in their denunciations of contemporaries and stubborn in their denials of any influence those contemporaries might have had on their own work: Charles Jencks makes clear that for "every positive point" Le Corbusier makes, "there is someone or something which is destroyed" (59). When asked in an interview to name philosophers and historians who had influenced him, Mies neglects to name even one: "I was interested in architecture all my life. And I have tried to find out what was said about architecture. I have tried to find out what can influence architecture. I feel that architecture belongs to certain epochs; it expresses the real essence of its times. It was to us a question of truth. How can we find out, know, and feel what is the truth?" (Blake, *Four Great Makers* 103). This declaration of abstract loyalty to architecture eliminates all its lumps and personalities, smoothing out history into various expressions of "essence" and claiming thus to approach "truth."

While the architectural modernism of the international style attempted to construct forgetful objects—buildings that had been "purged of the paraphernalia of historical reminiscence" (Curtis 8)—literary modernists, probably because they were contemplating objects constructed by others rather than building them themselves, tended to view objects as saturated with a past, which could be gotten rid of only by discarding those resonant objects. Stephen Kern, in his analysis of modernist attitudes toward the past, demonstrates that the discrediting of history was not limited to architecture, but spread across literary and philosophical studies as well. Kern cites, among others modernist precursors, Friedrich Nietzsche's *The Use and Abuse of History* (1874), a tirade against the burden of historical consciousness, in which Nietzsche declares, with typical vinegar, that "One who wished to feel everything historically would be like a beast who had to live by chewing a continual cud" (qtd. in Kern 52). Kern also points out that in Henrik Ibsen's *Ghosts* (1881), the past haunts the present: "I almost think we are all ghosts," Mrs. Alving laments. "It is all kinds of dead ideas and all sorts of old and obsolete beliefs. . . . There must be ghosts all over the country. They lie as thick as grains of sand" (63). Nietzsche's unappetizing metaphor of historical regurgitation recalls Le Corbusier's disgust with expressionist drawings, which seemed to him more like the exercise of "viscera" than of vision; Ibsen's ghosts recall Le Corbusier's "larva, toads and beasts which haunt the memories of the primordial world" and "re-emerge today." Similarly, Rebecca West's comment that "It is sometimes very hard to tell the difference between history and the smell of skunk" (qtd. in Vansittart ix) recalls Nikolaus Pevsner's derogatory "fumes of Expressionism."

Hayden White has discussed the discrediting of history in the decades prior to the First World War, arguing that the war finished off whatever legitimacy history still retained by 1914. Before the war, he states, "there was a growing suspicion that Europe's feverish rummaging among the ruins of its past expressed less a sense of firm control over the present than an unconscious fear of a future too horrible to contemplate" ("Burden of History" 119). Then, as he notes:

> [The war itself] did much to destroy what remained of history's prestige among both artists and social scientists; for [it] seemed to confirm what Nietzsche had maintained two generations earlier. History, which was supposed to provide some sort of training for life . . . had done little to prepare men for the coming of war . . . and when the war was over historians seemed incapable of rising above narrow partisan loyalties and making sense of war in any significant way. ("Burden of History" 120)

White and Kern both provide long lists of authors (including Virginia Woolf, Paul Valéry, William Butler Yeats, Franz Kafka, and D. H. Lawrence) who make historians the scapegoats of their works. White argues that the modernist tactic of superimposing past and present "implicitly condemned the historical consciousness by suggesting the essential contemporaneity of all significant human experience" ("Burden of History" 115). All these writers "reflect the currency of the conviction voiced by Joyce's Stephen Dedalus, that history is the 'nightmare' from which Western man must awaken if humanity is to be served and saved" ("Burden of History" 115), in much the same way that Le Corbusier viewed the "frightening dreams" of expressionist architects as something to be rejected and replaced by an architecture liberated from historical paraphernalia.

Kern carries this observation one step further, suggesting that, as the historical past fell out of favor, interest in the personal past began to replace it. "New theories about memory and forgetting and new studies in child developmental psychology appeared and were synthesized in psychoanalysis, which popularized as never before the notion that the individual past remains active and continues to shape adult behavior" (61). This shift in focus, according to Kern, represented a desire to exercise some control over the past, a more plausible goal if limited to the individual rather than encompassing the large forces that shape whole cultures.

I would argue that literary modernism's handling of the material world constitutes a specific manifestation of Kern's premise that post-Freudian preoccupations centered around personal rather than national histories. More specifically, the material world in modernist works tends to soak up personal history, making apparent the way in which the past is always witness to the present. In "The Jolly Corner" (1909), for example, Henry James creates a character haunted by an alternative present, the imagination of which is made possible by a past compellingly embodied in objects and architecture. Spencer Brydon is hypersensitive to the deposits of history within "the jolly corner," his childhood home. Brydon speaks

> of the value of all he read into it, into the mere sight of the walls, mere shapes of the rooms, mere sound of the floors, mere feel, in his hand, of the old silver-plated knobs of the several mahogany doors, which suggested the pressure of the palms of the dead; the seventy years of the past in fine that these things represented, the annals of nearly three generations, counting his grandfather's, the one that had ended there, and the impalpable ashes of his long-extinct youth, afloat in the very air like microscopic motes. (552)

This past is accessible because it *is* palpable, as we understand from the narrator's description of Brydon's past as a number of transparent layers of history. The "presences of the other age" are "all overlaid" with these other experiences yet are "still unobscured": Brydon and his friend Alice Staverton "had communities of knowledge, 'their' knowledge . . . of presences of the other age, presences all overlaid, in his case, by the experience of a man and the freedom of a wanderer, overlaid by pleasure, by infidelity, by passages of life that were strange and dim to her, just by 'Europe' in short, but still unobscured, still exposed and cherished" (548).

As Brydon mulls over the question of what he might have become had he not moved from New York to Europe thirty-three years ago, the strength of his conviction that one's material world inevitably shapes one's whole personality becomes clear: "'What would it have made of me, what would it have made of me?'" (554) he asks himself. One's personal history, we are given to understand, is a series of possibilities only one of which is ever bodied forth, and Brydon's articulation of the issue—that a different world would have "made" him differently—suggests a strong faith in the exterior forces and material world that shape a temperament, a profession, a series of habits.

It is architecture that frames the possibility for an encounter with this parallel personal history. Brydon prowls the empty house at night, confident that this is the site where he might be able to confront his ghostly alter-self (or anti-self), "rejoicing above all, as much as he might, in open vistas, reaches of communication between rooms and by passages; the long straight chance or show, as he would have called it, for the revelation he pretended to invite" (558). Unobstructed views and long hallways provide both literal and metaphorical "communication"—architecturally, between rooms, and personally, between the past as it has been played out into the present and the past as it might have been played out differently into a different present.

E. M. Forster's *Howards End* (1910) also describes the past as coagulating into objects. In *Howards End,* family history is embodied in the family furniture: "Round every knob and cushion in the house sentiment gathered, a sentiment that was at times personal, but more often a faint piety to the dead, a prolongation of rites that might have ended at the grave." Margaret Schlegel acknowledges but resents this inherited history, now that she is responsible for moving it from one house to another. "Chairs, tables, pictures, books, that had rumbled down to them through the generations, must rumble forward again like a slide of rubbish to which she longed to give the final push and send toppling into the sea" (149). This relation between objects and history is still visible in texts written after the war, as in Elizabeth Bowen's *The Death of the Heart* (1938), where furniture represents a compelling past, frightening to those who have merely to witness it without having established any relation with it. Matchett, who takes care of the family's furniture, makes this solemnly plain when she declares that "furniture like we've got is too much for some that would rather not have the past. If I just had to look at it and have it looking at me, I'd go jumpy, I daresay. But when it's your work it can't do anything to you" (101).

A bereaved mother in May Sinclair's *The Tree of Heaven* (1918) articulates one of the reasons why furniture, in particular, becomes an especially poignant trace of the past. Its echoes of the human form, the human skeleton, become the physical marker of the absent body: "Her mind turned and fastened on one object—the stiff, naked wooden chair standing in its place before the oak table by the window. She remembered how she had come to Michael there and found him writing at his table, and how she had talked to him as though he had been a shirker and a coward" (401–402). The notion that her sons retain a spiritual presence is no comfort at all to this mother, who encouraged them to enlist and must now live with their deaths at the front: "I don't *want* them all changed into something spiritual that I shouldn't know if it was there. I want their bodies with me just as they used to be. I want to hear them and touch them, and see them come in in their old clothes" (403). Thus, for this woman longing for physical presence, the straight-backed chair becomes a physical reproach—a painful memory of the dead son she urged toward his death.

When the past that has pooled into objects is a past that includes the war, characters sometimes take advantage of that reification as a way of discarding an experience they would just as soon forget. If memories are conceived of as residing in certain objects, it becomes possible to place, manipulate, or discard those memories. In Ernest Hemingway's *A Farewell to Arms* (1929), for example, the imperative of war disappears with the objects of war. Frederick Henry is able to walk away from his job as an ambulance driver as easily as he does precisely because the objects and people attaching him to the military—his ambulances and his men— disappear. Henry uses an analogy to explain the logic of his desertion: "You had lost your cars and your men as a floorwalker loses the stock of his department in a fire. There was, however, no insurance. You were out of it now. You had no more obligation. If they shot floorwalkers after a fire in the department store because they spoke with an accent they had always had, then certainly floorwalkers would not be expected to return when the store opened again for business" (232).

To shoot a floorwalker after a fire because of his accent is to shoot him not for having lost his merchandise, but for the way he inflects (and has always inflected) his experience. While his cars and men are there, Henry feels, his obligation is there. When they disappear, however, only imaginative imperative would bind him to the military—an imaginative imperative he never felt. Like the hypothetical floorwalker shot for his accent, the army would thus be shooting Henry for a lack of involvement always there but only now made visible by his desertion.

The veteran in Rebecca West's *The Return of the Soldier* (1918) begins the novel having achieved accidentally the same forgetfulness that Frederick Henry manages for himself on purpose: Chris Baldry returns home from the war having forgotten everything that happened to him between his first flush of adolescent love (for a woman now impoverished and married to someone else) and his startling jolt into consciousness, years later, on a stretcher at the front. One moment he holds Margaret in his arms, telling her that his love for her is changeless, and the next, "as he spoke her warm body melted to nothingness in his arms. . . . He was lying in a hateful world where barbed-wire entanglements showed impish knots against a livid sky . . . and the stretcher bearers were hurting his back intolerably" (86). Chris's impression that he has moved directly from a sensuous appreciation of Margaret's body to a stark consciousness of his own speaks to a notion of experience that centers almost exclusively on the fate of the body and relegates to amnesia any relics of less urgent consideration. The plot of Chris's life that happened in the interim between embrace and injury (marriage to Kitty, death of a young son, maintenance of an estate, progress into middle age) has been erased.

The intervening, forgotten years are accessible to Chris only through the objects that witnessed those years and filled his world as he moved through them. Upon his return to Baldry Court, one of the first manifestations of Chris's amnesia is his responsiveness to the oldest articles in the house—things that had been there before his relationship with Margaret and that thus participate in a continuity he still recalls. "Dipping his head he would glance sideways at the old oak panelling; and nearer things he fingered as though sight were not intimate enough a contact, his hand caressed the arm of his chair, because he remembered the black gleam of it, stole out and touched the recollected salt-cellar. It was his furtiveness that was heartrending; it was as though he were an outcast and we who loved him stout policemen" (59).

Objects play a large part in the efforts of Jenny—Chris's cousin and the narrator of the story—to negotiate a peace between Kitty (the forgotten wife) and Margaret (the old love, emphatically remembered). "I tried," Jenny admits, "to make my permanent wear . . . a mood of intense perception in which my strained mind settled on every vivid object that came under my eyes and tried to identify myself with its brightness and its lack of human passion. . . . I was afraid that when I moved my body and my attention I might begin to think" (125–26). But while Jenny focuses on neutral objects (like the branches of a tree) as a way of hypnotizing herself out of thought and away from sorrow, Chris and Margaret relish the memory of the objects they had shared together. Jenny's perception of this intimacy is painful to her: "It was not their love for one another that caused me such agony at that moment; it was the thought of the things their eyes had rested upon together" (129). Chris cherishes the distant past as encountered through household objects. But the war past is a burden.

Chris is finally jerked back into the present by two objects that had belonged to his now-dead son—a jersey the little boy had worn and a ball with which he had played. Margaret argues against showing these objects to Chris—she would rather have him forgetful than in pain—but Kitty is adamant. She wants Chris back in the present, since it is replete not only with painful memories of war and of a child lost but with her own place in his life. The ball and the jersey work instantly: Chris returns simultaneously to his women—Kitty, Jenny—and to his knowledge of the war. Now he walks

> not loose limbed like a boy, as he had done that very afternoon, but with the soldier's hard tread upon the heel. It recalled to me that, bad as we were, we were not yet the worst circumstance of his return. When he had lifted the yoke of our embraces from his shoulders he would go back to that flooded trench in Flanders under that sky more full of flying death than clouds, to that No Man's Land where bullets fall like rain on the rotting faces of the dead. (187)

As Jenny understands, the past that Chris wishes to escape is not the past of his marriage (cold though it seems compared to his romance with Margaret) or even the past of his son (painful though that death also is); the most painful past is the past of the war.

Elaine Scarry, in her analysis of war's structure, has pointed out that "[w]hat is remembered in the body is well remembered; [in war,] the bodies of massive numbers of participants are deeply altered; those new alterations are carried forward into peace. So, for example, the history of the United States participation in numerous twentieth-century wars may be quietly displayed across the surviving generations of any American family—a grandfather whose distorted feet permanently memorialize the location and landing site of a piece of shrapnel in France, the feet to which there will always cling the narration of a difficult walk over fields of corn stubble. . . . [T]he record of war survives in the bodies, both alive and buried, of the people who were hurt there" (112–13). Chris Baldry's body, which has returned from the trenches physically whole—more or less free of the wounds Scarry describes as embodied memories—nevertheless records the returning consciousness of war in his body. Memory has physical weight, as we see in Chris's gait: he appears to walk as if carrying a literal, physical burden, even though the real burden is a mental one. Having been pulled out of his amnesia by a set of objects, Chris involuntarily returns to the job of embodying the memories of war.

West's story demonstrates the tension between the felt responsibility of remembering the war and the longing to forget it. Veterans who returned from the war missing pieces of their bodies suggested a memory of war that would remain indelible: even today, as Scarry points out, the "history of World War I, in which two out of every three young Frenchmen either died or lost a limb, is still visible in all the windows of the subway cars—'LES PLACES NUMÉROTÉES SONT RÉSERVÉES PAR PRIORITÉ 1° AU MUTILÉS DE GUERRE . . .'—an inscription that each day runs beneath the standing city as though in counterpoint to and partial explanation for that later story recorded above" (113). Helen Zenna Smith's narrator in *Not So Quiet . . .* makes the same link between memories and wounds. As the narrator realizes, her friend Edwards will never be able to forget these days and nights of war and horror. All her life she will have the reminder with her in the Australian husband with one leg. Limp, limp, limp . . ." (57).

Veterans' ambivalence about the project of remembering the war emerges over and over in books written after the war. As is always noted in discussions of war books, the novels and memoirs that now form the core of the war canon did not, for the most part, begin to appear until the late twenties, and even when they did, they were often presented as attempts not to remember but to forget. Samuel Hynes quotes a paragraph from an early edition of Robert Graves's *Good-bye to All That*: "The objects of this autobiography, written at the age of thirty-three, are simple enough: an opportunity for a formal good-bye to you and to you and to you and to me and to all that; forgetfulness because once all this has been settled in my mind and written down and published it need never be thought about again" (Hynes 429). Graves here articulates his paradoxical desire both to remember and to forget: he wants to have written down his memories of the war into a book so that he can forget the war by throwing the book away—pitching it out of his consciousness like psychic garbage. Once it is all written down, "it need never be thought of again." But that gloss on the book's title—a confession of its forgetful motive—was later itself erased by being deleted from subsequent editions of *Good-bye to All That*. Contemporary readers are thus presented with a title that seems to refer to a dismissal of the war and a text that seems to reanimate it, lacking Graves's explanation that by shoving his experience of war into the space of public imagination he is attempting to clear it out of the space of his own memory.

I have previously discussed both combatant homesickness and the common combatant feeling that home was no longer a house in a civilian neighborhood but rather a place at the front surrounded by other soldiers. The armistice-day scene in Ford Madox Ford's *A Man Could Stand Up*— (1926) is a poignant enactment of this imaginative alteration of home, replete with the disposal of objects as an attempt to forget. Finally "at home" and with the war over, the first thing Christopher Tietjens does is to sell the furniture from his London apartment. His lover, Valentine Wannop, "had seen him going to sell his furniture. Madly! Running to do it. You do not run when you are selling furniture if you are sane" (650). Valentine creeps up the stairs to the apartment, only to find it empty—"All white, again with stains on the walls from which things had been removed." And yet:

> This room was inhabited. As if set down in a field, the room being so large, there camped. . . . A camp-bed for the use of officers, G.S. one, as the saying is. And implements of green canvas, supported on crossed white wooden staves: a chair, a bucket with a rope handle, a washing-basin, a table. The bed was covered with a flea-bag of brown wool. She was terribly frightened. . . . These things looked terribly sordid and forlorn. Why did he place them in the centre of the room? Why not against a wall? It is usual to stand the head of a bed against a wall when there is no support for the pillows. (650)

The reason, of course, that Tietjens does not stand his bed against the wall is that he is not at home in his apartment; he is merely camping there. He arranges his belongings (gear from his home at the front, not furniture from the home front) in the civilian space of his cleared apartment exactly as if he were still inhabiting the combatant space of the war. Tietjens spend the night of November 11, 1918, with his pals from the war in a way that extends the war's reach rather than attempts to leave it behind. While many of the examples in this chapter have described attempts to forget the war (and, presumably, the selves that negotiated and responded to the war), Tietjens here displays his acceptance of the fact that it is his prewar civilian self that has become inappropriate and needs to be discarded. He handles his belongings accordingly.

For those whose wounds were invisible—for soldiers who returned whole (at least outwardly), and especially for civilians whose memories of the war were exclusively imaginative and unembodied, the pouring of memory and of history into disposable objects became at times and for some an appealing solution to the problem of the ugly, wartime past. For others like Tietjens, however, the war reshaped the self so radically that homecoming itself had to be reimagined.

SEVEN

GLASS OBJECTS

Throughout this book, I have argued that the content of war sometimes prevents us from recognizing profound overlaps between civilian and combatant modernism. In this final chapter, I link literary modernism and expressionist architecture not by arguing that civilians' attention to glass corresponds to soldiers' attention to glass but rather by arguing that the material of glass provides an opportunity for civilian modernists to meditate on the single most important way in which their experience differs from combatants. The difference is at once humbling and invigorating for civilians, because it consists, on the one hand, in the obvious but crucial acknowledgment that the physical experience of war must always remain inaccessible to civilians and, on the other hand, in the obvious but crucial imperative that it is imaginative experience that must be altered if war is going to be avoided in the future—for only in imaginative, representational form can modernism teach the lessons of war without perpetuating it.

I argue in this chapter that modernist self-consciousness about the nature of representation frequently prompts civilian modernist writers to prefer opaque to transparent language and to portray internal realities at least as vividly as external ones and that these preferences often emerge in connection with meditations on glass. I suggest that a similar self-consciousness about the nature of representation informs expressionist architecture—a primarily postwar phenomenon frequently understood as springing directly from the war. Expressionist fascination with visual shenanigans rather than the display of architectural structure, with perceptual rather than physical reality, is visible in the way expressionist architects handle glass in their designs and talk about glass in their writing. Expressionist treatment of glass links them to civilian literary modernists and distinguishes them from those architects whose designs were eventually characterized as constituting the international style.

Glass is a particularly appropriate material for ruminations on representation both because it links spaces visually while separating them physically and because it can, like language, glide back and forth between clarity and opacity. The potential for transparency inhabits glass, as it does words, but so does the potential merely to reflect back images of ourselves—of our frustrated expectations that glass will expose without participating, that words will communicate without interfering. In the experience of reading language, words may seem to efface themselves before the demands of information, or they may call attention to the idea that meaning is completely susceptible to and determined by the categories according to which we organize information. In the experience of reading architecture, glass may seem inconspicuous for its transparency or conspicuous in its reflectiveness; it may expose structural bones or shimmer with mirrored light, splintering attempts to fit together an idea of the building's interior or of what makes it work structurally.

In the early decades of the twentieth century, the issue of transparency riveted both architectural and literary modernists. In architecture, the development of steel and reinforced concrete skeleton construction opened up new possibilities for the use of glass as a building material. Because these skeletons—instead of masonry walls—now held up the weight of buildings, glass could be wrapped around the exterior surfaces without regard to structural considerations. This ability to use glass extensively made it possible to conceive of space in new ways.

International-style and expressionist architects differed in their opinions about the proper use of glass in building design. Architects who helped to develop the international style—men like Le Corbusier, Ludwig Mies van der Rohe, and Walter Gropius—emphasized "volume—space enclosed by thin planes or surfaces as opposed to the suggestion of mass and solidity" (Barr 13) and the use of glass to expose architectural structure. As Mies explained, "We can see the new structural principles most clearly when we use glass in place of the outer walls, which is feasible today since in a skeleton building these outer walls do not actually carry weight." Otherwise, he states severely, "the structural system . . . is hidden in a chaos of meaningless and trivial forms" (qtd. in Banham, *Theory and Design* 268). International-style architects tried to make clear in their designs the difference between structure and cladding. They believed that designers should make the two systems visually distinct, giving strict priority to the display of structure and resisting any impulse to lavish attention on cladding or exterior ornament. Unless a building's glass skin permitted the clear and immediate apprehension of structural bones, "there is a conflict between its true character as an enclosed steel cage and the apparent mass of its vertical buttressing and pyramidal composition" (Hitchcock and Johnson 42). The premise here is clear: "true character" is a matter of structure—what physically is holding up the building. Visual effects unrelated to or even misleading about structure ("apparent mass," for example) are deemed false.

The international style was codified by a Museum of Modern Art architectural exhibition in 1932, for which Henry-Russell Hitchcock and Philip Johnson wrote the exhibition catalog. Though the authors claimed not to be issuing architectural prescriptions (over thirty years later, Hitchcock still claimed that "we merely described . . ." [Hitchcock foreword x]), they did acknowledge the imperative mode of the essay, even as they claimed that it was inevitable: "In stating the general principles of the contemporary style, in analysing their derivation from structure and their modification by function, the appearance of a certain dogmatism can hardly be avoided. In opposition to those who claim that a new style of architecture is impossible or undesirable, it is necessary to stress the coherence of the results obtained within the range of possibilities thus far explored" (21). Coherence thus emerges as another premise of the international style: the various components of a building must work together to convey a single, coherent impression.

Throughout the catalog, the moralism of this "stat[ement] of general principles" is striking. For instance, regarding the use of glass and "as a corollary of the principle of surface of volume there is the . . . requirement that the surfaces shall be unbroken in effect, like a skin tightly stretched over the supporting skeleton. . . . Hence the breaking of the wall surface by placing windows at the inner instead of at the outer edge of the wall is a serious fault of design. . . . For the glass of the windows is now an integral part of the enclosing screen rather than a hole in the wall as it was in masonry construction" (45). This catalog does not describe; it preaches. Drawing on a vocabulary of aesthetic moralism, it frames its concerns in terms of rights and wrongs, requirements (of good design) and faults (of bad design).

Expressionist architects, on the other hand, treated glass much more whimsically. In their utopian, idiosyncratic, and mostly unexecutable designs,[1] glass might be used in a single building as prism, crystal, mirror, or blends of all three. Part of a primarily German and explicitly post-World War I movement, expressionist architects flaunted the dictates of international-style "coherence." While fascinated by glass, they did not insist that it be used to teach the public lessons about structure. This was possible, in part, because expressionists did not employ the moral aesthetic vocabulary that international-style architects used to describe the distinction between skeleton and cladding, the way windows should be treated, or the need for coherence. Wolfgang Pehnt has pointed out that expressionists were more interested in the startling artistic effects that their buildings could create than in the strict expression of structure and that international-style architects, not surprisingly, criticized expressionists for such "untruthfulness." "Dishonest it certainly was," Pehnt remarks, "if we take as our criterion of form that it should appropriately illustrate structural conditions. The Expressionists, however, did not accept such premises" (20). "Truth," if expressionists had been inclined to use the term at all (and usually they were not) was, for them, as liable to emerge from the perceptual experience of a building as it was to be gleaned from a demonstration of the physical structure that supported its weight.

These different attitudes about the use of glass as a building material are easily visible in several famous examples. In Mies van der Rohe's famous (never built) skyscraper projects (see figures 6.5, 6.6), the glass skin is self-effacing and notable for its ability to expose the steel skeleton it sheathes. That walls no longer need to bear the building's weight is made plain. "These buildings," Hitchcock and Johnson comment admiringly in their Museum of Modern Art catalog, "would have been pure volume, glazed cages supported from within, on a scale such as not even Paxton in the nineteenth century would have dreamed possible" (33). In Bruno Taut's expressionist Glass Pavilion of 1914 (figure 7.1), however, the elements of structure and surface blend. Colored panes of glass that form the walls of the building are handled in a way that seems perceptually, as Pehnt comments, in "opposition to the law of load and support" (18). As far as an observer can tell, the wall holds up the building, yet the wall is made of glass. Here, the mechanics of structure are conceived of as being no more valid an aspect of the "truth" than the fact that a wall of colored glass is capable of concealing structural principles.

For all the impassioned rhetoric, boundaries between the categories of expressionism and the international style are not, of course, impermeable. Mies's skyscraper design of 1922 seems, for example, to owe its character not only to the international-style commitment to the display of structure but also to the expressionist interest in a play of reflection off the glass panes of its irregular silhouette. Mies himself, in fact, has told how "I discovered by working with actual glass models that the important thing is the play of reflections and not the effect of light and shadow as in ordinary buildings. . . . At first glance the curved outline of the plan seems arbitrary. These curves, however, were determined by three factors: sufficient illumination of the interior, the massing of the building viewed from the street, and lastly the play of reflections" (qtd. in Johnson 182). This interest in the "play of reflections" sounds decidedly expressionist and is reminiscent of Fritz Höger's calculation of the number of light values visible in his *Chilehaus*. Similarly, Bruno Taut designed buildings after his Glass Pavilion that seemed to owe more to the international style than to expressionism. Still, the generalization holds, at least as far as any generalization may. International-style architects followed rules

Figure 7.1. Bruno Taut: Glass Pavilion, 1914 (Akademie der Künste, Berlin).

about the exposure of structure, which often dictated the ways in which they were willing to use glass. Expressionist architects followed no rules at all and used glass with as much quirkiness as they used any other material.

Expressionists were more likely to rhapsodize about the romantic possibilities of glass than to lecture about its architectural rectitude. In *Glass Architecture* (1914), for example, science fiction visionary Paul Scheerbart, as one critic has observed, "deemphasize[d] the material nature" of architecture (Bletter 87). His projected urban renovations included the replacement of all brick and mortar walls with glass ones, extensive use of colored glass (even cars and boats were to be made of it), and cities that floated on water, perpetually rearranging themselves into new patterns—glassy, colored, floodlit. Clearly, such theoretical landscapes were compelling for their fantastical visual effects, not for solidity or "truthfulness." To Scheerbart, glass offered itself as a path between an architecture of stubborn materiality and an architecture capable of modulating into diaphanous immateriality.

Much as expressionist architects handled glass in a way that encourages us not to *see through* glass but to *see* glass, so modernist writers handled language in a way that encourages us not to see through language but to see language. By eschewing conventions of storytelling, they force us to look instead at ways in which we depend on language to organize experience into a story. Of course, language is the only possible material for a writer, while glass is one of many for architects; but language may be handled with vastly different intentions by writers, who may choose to regard it either as a self-effacing window through which content may be unambiguously viewed or as a multifaceted crystal that communicates, but not without simultaneously drawing attention to its own form. In the hands of writers like Virginia Woolf and James Joyce, language tells its own structure as much as it tells a story. How opacity insinuates itself into the process of constructing meaning thus emerges as a central preoccupation for both modernist writers and expressionist architects.

Detractors of literary modernism often use terms of analysis similar to the ones that international-style architects used in their pronouncements on the need for "truth" or "coherence" in architecture. Georg Lukács, for example, was famously indignant with what he saw as the modernist inability to confirm, with confidence, "the objective world"; he fumes about how, for them, it remains "inexplicable" (25). Just as international-style architects like Mies van der Rohe and Le Corbusier assumed that glass could articulate the "truth" about structure, so early critics of modernism assumed that words could articulate the "truth" about reality. Meanwhile, modernist writers and expressionist architects ducked moralisms altogether: they were too absorbed by their experiments with the interplay between verbal form and verbal content, too busy tracing the complex relationships between physical fact and perceptual experience in buildings, to worry about any preconceived idea of truth.

Both architectural expressionists and literary modernists examined ways in which perceptual experience belies physical facts. In Paul Scheerbart's expressionist vision of glass architecture, the colored glass of a floating city offers itself as a material valuable for its ability to modulate visually into nebulousness. In a description of a house he designed for himself, expressionist architect Bruno Taut tells how a lamp of Luxferprisms hanging over his dining room table made the table seem to disappear: "Against the black plane of the table gleam crockery, glass and flatware—but one can no longer call it a table setting, for the table has vanished!" (qtd. in Banham, *Well-Tempered* 132). Taut obviously relishes this act of disappearance; material truth and perceptual truth are of equal interest to him. In a remarkably similar visual image, Katherine Mansfield describes in "Bliss" (1920) a dark table that seems visually to melt and a glass bowl that seems visually to float. A woman arranges fruit in a bowl: "When she had finished with them and had made two pyramids of these bright round shapes, she stood away from the table to get the effect—and it really was most curious. For the dark table seemed to melt into the dusky light and the glass dish and the blue bowl to float in the air" (93). In both cases, the emphasis is on a temporary escape from the laws of material reality. Taut understood that crockery and flatware are not really floating in midair; Mansfield's character knows that her glass dish is not floating either. What both relish, however, is the illusion of float—the way in which the perceptual contradicts the physical.

Similarly, in Virginia Woolf's *The Waves* (1931), objects dissolve into Scheerbartian immateriality: "That is the corner of the cupboard;" Rhoda says to herself, as she falls asleep, "that is the nursery looking-glass. But they stretch, they elongate" (27). Later she observes that "things are losing their hardness; even my body now lets the light through; my spine is soft like wax near the flame of the candle" (45). "I begin," Bernard says at the end of the book, "to doubt the fixity of tables, the reality of here and now, to tap my knuckles smartly upon the edges of apparently solid objects and say, 'Are you hard?'" (288).

Such moments in which perception constitutes reality may be understood as one of the broad preoccupations underlying Woolf's whole novel. One of her most consistent techniques for addressing this issue is her description, through a sequence of chapter prefaces, of how different qualities of light can alter perception of the material world. As the following catalog of imagery indicates, light creates a demand for analogy by continually modifying our apprehension of material surfaces. The narrator is thus set the task of inventing different images for the same objects as day progresses and sunlight changes in the room and on the beach:

> The sun laid broader blades upon the house. . . . Everything became softly amorphous, as if the china of the plate flowed and the steel of the knife were liquid. (29)

> The sun fell in sharp wedges inside the room. Whatever the light touched became dowered with a fanatical existence. A plate was like a white lake. A knife looked like a dagger of ice. (109–10)

> [D]aggers of light fell upon chairs and tables making cracks across their lacquer and polish. (165–66)

> Lined with shadows their weight seemed more ponderous as if colour, tilted, had run to one side. Here lay knife, fork and glass, but lengthened, swollen, and made portentous. (208)

The attentiveness with which the narrator works to capture this sequence of perceptual modulations suggests Woolf's loyalty to the idea that perception constitutes the only reality to which we have access.

Woolf demonstrates the fickle elusiveness of material reality using a method with which expressionists would have been comfortable—the dematerialization of objects. In *The Waves,* strong emotions change the way characters experience objects, as Neville observes while waiting with taut anticipation for the arrival of his friend Percival. "And every moment he seems to pump into this room this prickly light, this intensity of being so that things have lost their normal uses—this knife-blade is only a flash of light, not a thing to cut with. The normal use is abolished" (119). That the knife-blade should dissolve into a flash of light is a logical extension of the perceptions registered in the chapter prefaces just cited, for there the sun itself is described as laying "blades" on the house, as well as gradually changing the material state of the knife from "liquid" to "ice" to something "lengthened, swollen." In other words, the knife that in the prefaces appears not to be able to cut is actually experienced by Neville, in all his tension, as literally not being able to cut. The narrator's language—telling how the sun deals out its store of blades and how the knife first melts, then freezes, and finally expands—describes, momentarily, a reality that Neville actually experiences; it is a reality not unlike the one that Taut described when telling about the disappearance of the table top in his dining room.

Woolf's descriptions of the material world shuffle a set of familiar perceptual puns on water, ice, and glass. China "flow[s]," steel seems "liquid," and the plate melts into a perceptual "lake" because of the way the sun hits them through the windows: we understand intuitively that the logic of these images relies on the principles of light, heat, and melt—on a glide between substances that may either flow or harden. A decade after *The Waves* was published, Wallace Stevens draws on the same set of images in a poem called "The Glass of Water" (published in *Parts of a World* 1942). Assuming his podium voice, Stevens here carefully explains the modernist position on such transformations:

> That the glass would melt in heat,
> That the water would freeze in cold,
> Shows that this object is merely a state,
> One of many, between two poles.

> (*Collected Poems* 197)

In other words, objects—the constituents of objective reality—are not necessarily stable, but rather are susceptible to perceptual ebb and flow. The implications of Stevens's argument make antimodernists cringe, for, in their judgment, faithfulness to individual perceptual realities rather than to the pool of shared objective ones makes modernist writing unnecessarily difficult, apolitical, and solipsistic. For the literary modernist or the expressionist architect, however, the unstable nature of reality itself constitutes a perfectly sufficient justification of their strategies. As architectural historian Rosemarie Bletter has pointed out, Scheerbart and Taut were intrigued by glass precisely for its properties of perceptual transformation: "[G]lass architecture . . . because of its reflective properties looks already *as if* it were undergoing such changes" (97). Glass architecture may, in other words, employ the verbal technique of simile: perceptual changes are *like* physical ones.

Katherine Mansfield's story "Prelude" (1920), by drawing parallels between, on the one hand, children's difficulty in attending to the merely literal and, on the other, the secret anxieties and dreams of a mother, implies that the difference between children and adults is not a difference of perceptual expertise but rather of honesty. Children, unlike adults, can admit that the margins between reality and the imagination are by no means secure. The child Kezia peers through panes of colored glass at the yard below: "One was blue and one was yellow. Kezia bent down to have one more look at a blue lawn with blue arum lilies growing at the gate, and then at a yellow lawn with yellow lilies and a yellow fence." So far, Kezia seems to have kept hold of the fact that the lawn, the lilies, and the fence change because she is looking at them through different panes of glass. But this confidence soon falters: "As she looked a little Chinese Lottie came out on to the lawn and began to dust the tables and chairs with a corner of her pinafore. Was that really Lottie? Kezia was not quite sure until she had looked through the ordinary window" (14). As her certainty wobbles, so do the boundaries separating interior world from exterior one, private from public reality.

That the act of perceiving itself can become a frightening experience is soon made clear, as Kezia stands at yet another window, looking out. At first, "She liked the feeling of the cold shining glass against her hot palms, and she liked to watch the funny white tops that came on her fingers when she pressed them hard against the pane." But as she stands there, twilight settles into night, and anxiousness strays toward panic. Kezia "wanted to call Lottie and to go on calling all the while she ran downstairs and out of the house. But IT was just behind her, waiting at the door, at the head of the stairs, at the bottom of the stairs, hiding in the passage . . ." (15). Her sudden fear, though partly connected with the procedure of dusk into dark, is also closely associated with the physical act of perception. Just as looking at the world through the viewfinder of a camera makes us more conscious of the act of seeing, Kezia's awareness of the materiality of the glass pane (it's cold, she's pressing her fingers against it) provides a physical analogue for the act of perception that then takes on a life of its own in the character of IT. Mansfield's characters inhabit worlds that are perpetually threatening to come alive, in part because the boundary between the literal and the metaphorical is shifty. Perception is always potentially threatening.

By positioning readers, at random moments and without warning, within the perceptual reality of childhood, Mansfield violates our expectation that the material world constitutes public ground and the imagination private deviation from that ground. Matters of the imagination wield as much narrative clout as matters of the shared world when the writer places them side by side in unapologetic, disorienting sequence. During these moments of imposed childhood, we find ourselves suddenly clumsy in making the usual distinctions between literal and metaphorical reality; Mansfield thus exposes the convention of bifurcation itself. The pairings that testify to our investment in orderly perimeters—private/public, interior/exterior, figurative/literal—begin to merge, and the messiness of their merging seems, at least momentarily, more accurately to capture the nature of experience than does any previous categorical neatness. Like Taut, pointing out how his dining room table is both there and not there, Mansfield focuses our attention on moments of perception that would ordinarily make us flinch, precisely because those acts of flinching mark the boundary between physical and perceptual reality.

"Water, because of its intrinsic capacity to reflect, belongs to glass architecture; the two are almost inseparable," Paul Scheerbart declared (58). Like Stevens's glass of water that is "merely a state, / One of many, between two poles," like the shifts and dissolves of domestic objects in *The Waves*, and like the unpredictable loomings of the imagination in "Prelude," expressionist architects purposely situated their work in a region hovering somewhere between materiality and immateriality. In Scheerbart's imagination, glass and water blend together in a ribbon of transparent continuity, just as they do in Stevens's "The Glass of Water":

> Here in the centre stands the glass. Light
> Is the lion that comes down to drink. There
> And in that state, the glass is a pool.

> (*Collected Poems* 197)

Here, the poem's title tilts toward pun, its inflection slightly adjusted: the glass of water is not only a container filled with liquid but also the sheen of light on a pool—a momentary glassiness on the water's surface resulting from a momentary conspiracy of light and wind and fish. Glass is a pool when light is a thirsty lion, yet glass retains the echo of a cup, precisely because the fluctuation between meanings—glass tumbler of water, glassy surface of water—is as rapid and untrappable as the behavior of light.

Mansfield, in a letter to John Middleton Murry about Woolf's *Night and Day* (1919), criticized it for its apparent heedlessness of the war. She disliked the novel, confessing that "[m]y private opinion is that it is a lie in the soul. The war has never been: that is what its message is. I don't want (G. forbid!) mobilisation and the violation of Belgium, but the novel can't just leave the war out. . . . I feel in the profoundest sense that nothing can ever be the same—that, as artists, we are traitors if we feel otherwise: we have to take it into account and find new expressions, new moulds for our new thoughts and feelings. . . . We have to face our war" ("To John Middleton Murry" 380). Henry James worried that "[t]he war has used up words; they have weakened, they have deteriorated like motor car tires . . . we are now confronted with a depreciation of all our terms . . . with a loss of expression through an increase of limpness, that may well make us wonder what ghosts will be left to walk" (qtd. in Buitenhuis

61). And Walter Gropius asserted, as I discussed in chapter 6, that, after the war, "every thinking man felt the necessity for an intellectual change of front" (qtd. in Benevolo 398–99).

Despite this sensitivity to the way in which war was understood as affecting language, modernism has to believe that interior experience is at least as profound if not more profound than exterior experience, because otherwise the physical experience disappears with the physical body, and otherwise the implications generated by the physical experience of war have to be reexperienced physically in order to be understood. Otherwise, the only way to learn the lessons of war would be to keep fighting wars, and the only people who would ever learn the lessons of war would be soldiers—who, though they learn their lessons well, too often take their education with them straight to the grave. Modernism thus tries to internalize the perceptual and imaginative repercussions of war—to transform them into imaginative material and at the same time always to point toward the battlefield, toward the physical experience of war, and toward the body, as Enid Bagnold does when she articulates her own movement toward the physical experience of war as a step across a threshold into a territory on the other side of a set of glass doors. In her book, part I is "Outside the Glass Doors" and part II, "Inside the Glass Doors"; the glass boundary is the one separating the outside from the inside of a hospital—a boundary whose crossing transforms soldiers into patients (63–64). She is one step closer to the physical experience of war, but only one step.

In Tennessee Williams's *The Glass Menagerie* (1944), glass is an image suggesting both the fragility and the power of imaginative reality. Standstill in this play is not the result of flawed strategy and machine guns but of imaginative lethargy: "People go to the *movies* instead of *moving*!" (201), Tom Wingfield declares. Yet the play's absent father, a World War I veteran and "telephone man who fell in love with long distances" (145), presides over the Wingfield family with remarkable authority. The father's appearance on the set of Williams's play is denoted by a blown-up photograph of him in a World War I doughboy's cap, smiling *"as if to say 'I will be smiling forever'"* (144). The photograph is, however, only a thin emblem of the father's imaginative clout, his palpable presence in the Wingfield household.

The glass menagerie of the play's title signals not only Laura's fragility and beauty but also the compelling richness of the imaginative world into which she withdraws. If the responsibility for Laura is part of what Tom tries finally to escape by joining the merchant marines, that responsibility seems at the same time to be the one thing that it is impossible to escape, for the play ends with Tom's confession that Laura has managed to maintain a torturing imaginative proximity to him. Apparently, the more profoundly she withdraws from the exterior world of work and social relations, the more profoundly her presence is ensconced in Tom's psyche; the more she turns inward from physical to imaginative experience, the more deeply Tom internalizes her. The image that Williams provides for this instance of imaginative persistence is glass.

Laura's glass menagerie is consistently paired with the victrola and the phonograph records left behind by her father. Both the glass animals and the records represent opportunities for retreat—when her mother discovers that she has dropped out of business college, for example, Laura immediately moves over to the victrola. Both Tom and Amanda link the glass collection to the record collection: "So what are we going to do the rest of our lives?" Amanda queries dramatically after the business college fiasco. "Stay home and watch the parades go by? Amuse ourselves with the glass menagerie, darling? Eternally play those worn-out phonograph records your father left as a painful reminder of him?" (155–56). Later, Tom gently reminds his mother that Laura "lives in a world of her own— a world of little glass ornaments, mother. . . . She plays old phono- graph records and—that's about all—" (188).

Laura has taken up her father's record collection and combined it with her glass collection in a way that both repeats and alters the psycho- logical dynamic the father represents. While Mr. Wingfield has escaped into the expansiveness of physical space (a space delineated by long- distance telephone lines), Laura retreats into the expansiveness of imaginative space. While his fate suggests a male escape into the "adven- ture" of war or of moving west, hers suggests a female retreat into the claustrophobia of domesticity. Most important, though, the absences into which both Laura and Mr. Wingfield eventually devolve absolutely domi- nate the people left behind. For Tom, the absence delineated by the aban- doner (his father) and the absence delineated by the abandoned (his sister) are equally insistent and oppressively present.

"The last we heard of him," Tom remarks at the beginning of the play, "was a picture postcard from Mazatlan, on the Pacific coast of Mexico, containing a message of two words: 'Hello—Goodbye!' and no address" (145). Like the "whizz bangs" mailed home from the western front during World War I, this postcard represents a thin pretense of actual connection. It confirms that the sender is alive, but beyond that is notable more for its lack than its offer of information; and, like the hostility with which soldiers endowed the Field Service Cards when they named them after bombs, the father's teasing "Hello—Goodbye!" warps the postcard cliché greeting that wishes you were here. The sender exists, but only as an inaccessible idea, the silhouetted shape of a father who should be around but isn't, who could be around but chooses not to be. He has gone as far west as possible, stopping only when he reached the edge of Mexico and perhaps not even there, yet his smiling doughboy presence constitutes the play's "fifth character," as conspicuous during the action of the play as Laura will become after the play's conclusion.

The absent soldier and the glass menagerie thus preside together over the unfortunate cast of Williams's "memory play."

In Virginia Woolf's *Mrs. Dalloway* (1925), glass objects provide a site at which the narrator can attend self-consciously to the issue of representation, confronting the fact that, though civilian modernism may register the effects of war, the language in books and the buildings of home are always inherently at a remove from the physical experience of combat. Glass objects are an appropriate site for self-conscious analysis of this problem since architectural glass is at once able to separate spaces physically and to connect them visually: glass windows enable us to get a look at what is on the other side of a wall and at the same time to be protected from what we see.

Not long before arriving at Clarissa Dalloway's party, Peter Walsh muses about the difference between the England of his youth and the one he sees now,

> more than suspecting from the words of a girl, from a housemaid's laughter—intangible things you couldn't lay your hands on—that shift in the whole pyramidal accumulation which in his youth had seemed immovable. On top of them it had pressed; weighed them down, the women especially, like those flowers Clarissa's Aunt Helena used to press between sheets of grey blotting-paper with Littré's dictionary on top, sitting under the lamp after dinner. She was dead now. He had heard of her, from Clarissa, losing the sight of one eye. It seemed so fitting—one of nature's masterpieces—that old Miss Parry should turn to glass. (246)

A "whole pyramidal accumulation" seems, at least in retrospect, to have been pressing down on Peter and his generation in the same way that Miss Parry used a dictionary to press flowers between sheets of blotting-paper. The pressure she applies with the dictionary repeats the apparently "immovable" pressures that weighed them down; her gesture both figures and overlaps with an entire set of cultural circumstances. While she clearly is not responsible for these pressures, she just as clearly participates in them. Peter believes that Miss Parry is dead, suggesting that at least part of the explanation for the shift in the "whole pyramidal accumulation" is that those invested in it are being replaced by the next generation.

Helena Parry emblematizes and illuminates the past. "She belonged to a different age, but being so entire, so complete, would always stand up on the horizon, stone-white, eminent, like a lighthouse marking some past stage on this adventurous, long, long voyage, this interminable . . . life" (247). The eye that formerly enabled her to see has been replaced by a glass object that now marks her inability to see, a failure of vision that seems to Peter "fitting." The juxtaposition of Peter's sense that Miss Parry participates in oppressive generational pressures and his recollection of her failing vision links the two ideas: not being able to see is associated with—or even constitutes—the "whole pyramidal accumula-tion" that had seemed to be flattening the generation below it. Glass is the material that replaces the eye and marks failed vision rather than being the material through which the eye can see.

As it turns out, Miss Parry is a guest at Clarissa's party:

> She ascended staircases slowly with a stick. She was placed in a chair (Richard had seen to it). People who had known Burma in the 'seventies were always led up to her. . . . For at the mention of India, or even Ceylon, her eyes (only one was glass) slowly deepened, became blue, beheld, not human beings—she had no tender memories, no proud illu-sions about Viceroys, Generals, Mutinies—it was orchids she saw, and the mountain passes and herself carried on the backs of coolies in the 'sixties over solitary peaks; or descending to uproot orchids (startling blossoms, never beheld before) which she painted in water-colour; an indomitable Englishwoman, fretful if disturbed by the War, say, which dropped a bomb at her very door, from her deep meditation over orchids and her own figure journeying in the 'sixties in India. (271)

Peter had imagined Miss Parry—associated in his mind with the weight of generations and with partial, glassy blindness—to be dead. Instead, she carries on, walking with a stick, being placed in chairs, and having people led up to her. At the mention of India, her eyes "beheld, not human beings" but orchids. She becomes fretful if disturbed from these medita-tions by bombs at her doorstep, for all her vision—tenuous as it is—is turned inward toward herself and backward toward the past. The blighted vision marked by the glass eye is redundant, because the imaginative energy Miss Parry directs at orchids rather than at people precedes her partial blindness, because the self-absorption that is inter-rupted by war does not rely on the physical mechanics of vision. Miss Parry, turning to glass, becomes an image of the nineteenth century that not only refuses to die but also refuses to look ("parry" derives from the French *parer*—to ward off—an imaginative and perceptual warding off, in this case). She is a civilian thoroughly engaged by her own past and thoroughly disengaged from the war, an "indomitable Englishwoman."

While Miss Parry's glass eye suggests failed sight, both literally and figuratively, the glass of windowpanes sketches a boundary and a dis-tance that Clarissa Dalloway sees through clearly and bridges easily. She "watched out of the window the old lady opposite climbing upstairs. . . . Somehow one respected that—that old woman looking out of the window, quite unconscious that she was being watched. There was some-thing solemn in it—but love and religion would destroy that, whatever it was, the privacy of the soul" (191–92). Here, visual access—across the way, through the window—suggests an imaginative proximity that is limited but sympathetic. Clarissa respects that which is inaccessible—"the privacy of the soul"—but at the same time (and unlike Miss Parry) attends to the other person, her old neighbor across the way. Clarissa's acknowledgment of the space that separates her from her neighbor enables her, paradoxically, to succeed in crossing that space, at least up to a point. What it comes down to, in her mind, is a simple imaginative and architectural fact: "[H]ere was one room; there another. Did religion solve that, or love?" (193). The rooms are indisputably separate, both guarding and providing an architectural analogue to "the privacy of the soul," yet the visual access that the window provides is attended by a degree of sympathetic imaginative attention.

During the party, Woolf positions Clarissa's thoughts on her neighbor beside her thoughts about Septimus Smith, the Great War veteran who has committed suicide. She muses about Septimus, who has thrown himself from a window; in the same room, a few minutes later, she watches her neighbor through a window. The old woman and the young veteran fluctuate back and forth in Clarissa's mind, two characters isolated in space but adjacent in Clarissa's imagination: "It was fascinating, with people still laughing and shouting in the drawing-room, to watch that old woman, quite quietly, going to bed. She pulled the blind now. The clock began striking. The young man had killed himself; but she did not pity him; with the clock striking the hour, one, two, three, she did not pity him, with all this going on. There! the old lady had put out her light!" (283). The neighbor and the veteran are linked for Clarissa by the strokes of the clock: sound can traverse space as swiftly as a thought. Solitary as the young man and the old lady are, each prompts Clarissa's imaginative and nearly simultaneous attention.

Clarissa tries to imagine the physical experience of Septimus Smith's suicide. "He had killed himself—but how? Always her body went through it first, when she was told, suddenly, of an accident; her dress flamed, her body burnt. He had thrown himself from a window. Up had flashed the ground; through him, blundering, bruising, went the rusty spikes" (280). Clarissa's intuition, of course, is accurate: she answers her own question about how he killed himself in a way that perfectly accords with the narrator's report of him "fl[inging] himself vigorously, violently down on to Mrs. Filmer's area railings" (226).

Just as Clarissa realizes the method of Septimus Smith's suicide, she intuits, with surprising accuracy, one part of the reason why he does it—not the part that has to do with the war, but the part that has to do with Holmes and Bradshaw, men who ignore the role war plays for Septimus and advise their patient to ignore it too. Just as the old woman prompts Clarissa's protective feelings about "the privacy of the soul," Septimus prompts a similar insight about one of the men who had treated him: "Sir William Bradshaw, a great doctor yet to her obscurely evil . . . capable of some indescribable outrage—forcing your soul, that was it—if this young man had gone to him, and Sir William had impressed him, like that, with his power, might he not then have said (indeed she felt it now), Life is made intolerable; they make life intolerable, men like that?" (281).

Septimus does, in fact, feel borne down upon by both Bradshaw and Holmes; Bradshaw has indeed "impressed him, like that" with a power and a weight reminiscent of Miss Parry's dictionary: he has a "heavy look" and declares, with chilling predictive accuracy, that Mr. Warren Smith's is a "case of extreme gravity" (144), as if anticipating the gravity that ensures his death.

Bradshaw's potentially insidious powers of impression are combined, in Septimus's own mind, with flawed vision, just as Helena Parry's "pyramidal accumulation" is combined in the mind of Peter Walsh with her glass eye. Septimus sees his wife Rezia "mount[ing] the appalling staircase, laden with Holmes and Bradshaw, men who never weighed less than eleven stone six . . . who different in their verdicts (for Holmes said one thing, Bradshaw another), yet judges they were; who mixed the vision and the sideboard; saw nothing clear, yet ruled, yet inflicted" (224–25). Once again, weight is associated with faulty vision: first, Miss Parry's dictionary, the pressure of her generation, and her glass eye; then, the men who weigh at least eleven stone six, make statements about gravity with heavy looks, and see nothing clearly. Failures of vision—the glass eye, the irrelevant sideboard, the lack of clarity—begin to emerge as deeply implicated in the veteran's suicide: the "gravity" of his case is at least exacerbated, if not prompted by, the weight of Miss Parry, of Holmes and Bradshaw, and of a whole collective generational failure of vision.

Haunted by a dead friend killed in the war, tormented by experiences that no one around him acknowledges, much less understands, Septimus Smith scribbles a postcard that Clarissa Dalloway seems to read: "Once you stumble, Septimus wrote on the back of a postcard, human nature is on you. Holmes is on you" (139); "Once you fall, Septimus repeated to himself, human nature is on you. Holmes and Bradshaw are on you" (148). As removed as Clarissa is from Septimus, from the war in which he fought honorably but is not able to leave behind, she attends to him, concentrates on him, and gets it, at least as far as she is able, right. The glass eye that in Helena Parry's body suggests failed vision, the mixture of vision and sideboard that in Bradshaw suggests implacable weight, is counterpoised against Clarissa Dalloway's sharp, intuitive attention (she knows instinctively the oppressiveness of Bradshaw, the method of suicide) and the lightness of her body, which throughout the book is described as shot through with "a touch of the bird" (4). Standing on the other side of a window while her neighbor goes to bed or on the other side of London while Septimus sits on a windowsill, Clarissa accepts the limits of vision but also believes in the possibility of vision—perceptual, psychological, imaginative.

I would suggest that this simultaneous self-consciousness about both the limits and the possibilities of vision typify the modernist approach to World War I. Miss Parry ignored a bomb on her doorstep while Clarissa attends, however briefly, even posthumously, to the experience of a troubled veteran. Dr. Holmes advises Septimus to "[t]hrow yourself into outside interests; take up some hobby" (138). "'Try to think as little about yourself as possible,' said Sir William [Bradshaw] kindly" (149). Clarissa, however, realizes that such prescriptions are not a help but a refutation, a blind and even hostile forcing of the soul. Woolf suggests that civilians can at least begin to approach the experience of war by directing imaginative energy toward it, and that they will meet with a modicum of success if they do the job carefully and thoughtfully. The suggestion is modest but honest: to claim access to more would be presumptuous.

Wallace Stevens uses glass as the material from which a voice that speaks war can be imagined, emanating from "The central man, the human globe, responsive / As a mirror with a voice, the man of glass, / Who in a million diamonds sums us up" ("Asides on the Oboe," published 1942 in *Parts of a World*). Glass is the appropriate material from which to fashion an image of this figure, for it simultaneously erases him by its transparency and reflects us by its mirrorlike qualities. "One year," the poem tells us,

> . . . death and war prevented the jasmine scent
> And the jasmine islands were bloody martyrdoms.
> How was it then with the central man? Did we
> Find peace? We found the sum of men. We found,
> If we found the central evil, the central good.
> We buried the fallen without jasmine crowns.
> There was nothing he did not suffer, no; nor we.
>
> It was not as if the jasmine ever returned.
> But we and the diamond globe at last were one.
> We had always been partly one. It was as we came
> To see him, that we were wholly one, as we heard
> Him chanting for those buried in their blood,
> In the jasmine haunted forests, that we knew
> The glass man, without external reference.

(Collected Poems 250–51)

Here, the poetic project is strangely completed by the problem of articulating war—or of speaking at all during wartime. While not seeming to participate in that violence, the words of the glass man suddenly seem to constitute a world of their own. And, like other words of other modernist writers, the words of the glass man in this poem do not even necessarily seem to address the corpses in the bloody forests. But the poet imaginatively occupies that space of corpses, and listeners are approaching that place when they finally "know" the glass man, in all his comprehensiveness, his multiplicity of voices and views, his ability to "sum us up" in a "million diamonds."

The impulse of "Asides on the Oboe" is to bridge the many gaps that war imposes, to find a way of expressing war that doesn't choose sides ("We found, / If we found the central evil, the central good"), that doesn't limit its experience of the war to either battlefront or home front ("we heard / Him chanting for those buried in their blood . . ."). At the same time though, the awkward, concocted distance between the speaker and the war he articulates is obvious. Corpses are only obliquely strewn between the lines of the careful poem, which is not given the conspicuousness of a dramatic soliloquy but rather the intimacy of "Asides," and which, despite its evocation of theater, is figured as musical—"on the Oboe"—rather than dramatic—on a stage. We are told that "death and war prevented the jasmine scent," not that bombs scorched it out of existence. We do not see wounds or blood; the poem skims over corpses when it tells that "the jasmine islands were bloody martyrdoms."

Glass becomes an emblem both of the fragility of the project that attempts to span the gaps that war imposes and an image of how—despite the fact that war, lived through, is a physical experience—it is perception, in the end, that must be revised. War's violence scars and kills those that experience it. Soldiers may send us postcards from its dangerous spaces, but without a broader change in perceptual habits, war will never make its way into the general consciousness, and its lessons will have to be repeated generation after generation. The position of the civilian speaker will always be suspect because it will always be relatively safe, but it is the view from that position that must be altered. For only when we learn to negotiate the space between representation and war will we be able to navigate history along a path that avoids war. And only when we learn to look both through the glass and at the glass will the writers and architects of modernism be able to invent the possibility of that path and to lead us along it.

NOTES

Introduction

1. The degree to which the space between front line and home front protected civilians varied by country and even within countries. British civilians were subject to zeppelin raids, though the casualties from them were relatively low; I discuss air raids on Britain in chapter 1. German civilians suffered food shortages during the Allied naval blockade. The distinction between front line and home front was absolute for most Americans, but it collapsed completely for the Belgians and incompletely for the French.

2. While literary critics almost invariably use the word "modernist" as the adjective springing from the noun "modernism," architectural critics tend to describe the buildings and ideas that constitute modernism as simply "modern." Because my formal training is primarily literary and because I am trying to sketch out common ground between the two disciplines, I use the word "modernist" in reference to both literature and architecture.

Chapter 1

1. Soldiers' incomprehension of the civilian desire to learn the precise particulars of death (seen both here and in Robert Graves's poem "The Leveller") seems to spring from the acceptance of what Bäumer expresses here—that the specifics of death are inconsequential compared to the end result of death. Unlike the War Graves Commission, which was anxious to respect the equality of sacrifice across the classes, soldiers were not so much concerned with social democracy as they were acutely conscious of the ultimate futility of distinguishing between one death and the next.

2. At Loos, Ploegsteert, Passchendaele, and Louveral, the memorials to the missing are combined with the cemeteries; at Thiepval and Ypres (the Menin Gate), they are separate.

3. Only the inscriptions are individualized. Each headstone is marked with a cross, star of David, or other religious icon. Each family was permitted to choose an epitaph, but all the headstones are exactly the same.

4. American battle memorials are separate from memorials to the missing. Due to the much less extensive American involvement in the war, however, the whole issue of corpses was a different matter for Americans. The U.S. government, for example, managed to return corpses to any family wishing to bury a soldier at home.

5. Gavin Stamp explains how the tradition of burying soldiers changed: "After Waterloo, for instance, while the bodies of officers were taken home for burial, the private soldier was left in unmarked mass graves. Nevertheless, in the course of the Nineteenth Century the feeling grew stronger that all the dead in battle should be properly commemorated. By order of Queen Victoria in 1870, the dead of Waterloo were belatedly honoured by what was probably the first national memorial to the dead (as opposed to a monument to victory), which was built in the St Ever Cemetery, Brussels. Significantly, it was in the American Civil War—the first 'modern war' not least by being popular and total—that proper cemeteries were established for all ranks, and a similar concern was manifested by both participants after the Franco-Prussian War. As wars became larger in scale and were fought by conscripted soldiers rather than by small professional armies, so the popular concern for the fate of the individual soldier increased" (6).

Chapter 2

1. See Vicki Mahaffey's *Reauthorizing Joyce* (26-32) for an illuminating discussion of Father Flynn.

2. I am indebted to Elaine Scarry for this formulation of the relation between sleep and death.

Chapter 3

1. My conception of the ways in which boundaries between countries are invented and substantiated is indebted to Elaine Scarry's article "Consent and the Body: Injury, Departure, and Desire" in *New Literary History* 1990, 21: 867-96.

2. This analysis of the imaginative positioning of the war is also indebted to and supported by Modris Eksteins's analysis of the different reasons for which Germany and Britain were fighting. Eksteins points out that England had a sense of its own identity and its aged and indisputable place in world history while Germany had always been plagued not only by a lack of geographical boundary setting itself apart from the rest of Europe but by a history of divisive issues even within Germany itself: "No nationally organized industry like the English cloth trade existed to develop commercial ties, no national religion to encourage religious unity. For many Germans the greatest achievement in Germany history was the Reformation. That a development which divided the German-speaking peoples instead of uniting them should be so regarded spoke volumes on German identity" (64). Thus, Eksteins argues, the project of forging a national identity from a collection of religions—each of which had a stronger sense of itself as a separate unit than as connected to the larger political identity of a German state— was a difficult but extremely compelling imaginative imperative. Britain, on the

other hand, maintained a much more conservative attitude about what was being fought for in the Great War. If for the Germans the purpose of World War I was "to change the world," for the British it was "to preserve a world. The Germans were propelled by a vision, the British by a legacy" (119).

3. Turton's idea that women are actually often responsible for such problems mimics the familiar tendency to blame the victims of sexual assault by suggesting that they "asked for it."

Chapter 5

1. According to an editor's note, this quotation is taken from "the 'Memorandum on Operations on the Western Front, 1916–18,' deposited by Haig in 1920 at the British Museum with instructions that none of it should be published before 1940. The document was actually written by Haig's successive Chiefs of Staff, Lt.-General Kiggell and General Sir Herbert Lawrence, but Haig himself carefully revised it and added some notes of his own" (Editor's Notes on Appendices 365).

2. Stephen Kern has analyzed a number of ways in which time began to be understood differently in the beginning of the twentieth century. My discussion here is indebted to chapter 1 ("The Nature of Time") in his book *The Culture of Time and Space,* especially for its presentation of the quotations from Ford Madox Ford and from James McFarlane and Malcolm Bradbury.

3. While I have limited the discussion here to the polarities of progress and immobility, modernist interest in moving backward and forward through time was matched by a similar interest in the scientific community around the turn of the century. See Stephen Kern's observations about the sensation produced by early cinema's ability to play with the speed and direction of film (29–30). Also, quantum physics and relativity (ideas that Einstein was working on in the first fifteen years of the twentieth century) are, as Timothy Ferris has noted, "time-symmetrical; their equations work equally well when run forward or in reverse" (35).

4. Published in 1918 and 1916, respectively (much earlier than most of the canonical male veterans' accounts of war), both Bagnold's and La Motte's books got them into trouble. According to Jane Marcus, Bagnold was dismissed from her position as a V.A.D. after the publication of *A Diary without Dates* (126). La Motte reports in a 1934 introduction that *The Backwash of War* was suppressed in the summer of 1918. "Until this happened," she notes, "it went through several printings, but the pictures presented—back of the scenes, so to speak—were considered damaging to morale. . . . From its first appearance, this small book was kept out of England and France. But it did very well in the United States, until we entered the War" (v).

5. See John Keegan's *The Face of Battle* (35–45) for an analysis of narrative conventions regularly imposed on battles.

Chapter 6

1. In *An Outline of European Architecture,* Nikolaus Pevsner lists the *Chilehaus* and the *Grosses Schauspielhaus* as the "most famous examples" of expressionism and goes on to list the Einstein Tower as "important for the future"

(405). In an article of 1962, "Finsterlin and Some Others," he lists all three buildings as among the "most familiar examples" (353) of expressionism.

2. Interestingly, while Reyner Banham adopts a linear model of development in order to describe the workings of dominant architectural ideology across time, in an article written in 1959, the year before he published the statement just quoted, he argued persuasively that Bruno Taut and Paul Scheerbart—men closely allied with the expressionist movement—had been persistently and unfairly underemphasized in architectural histories precisely because their inclusion would disrupt just such a sense of orderly evolution. Banham claims that the influence of Taut's Glass Pavilion at the Cologne Exhibition of 1914 is neglected, for example, at the expense of buildings designed by men we associate with the international style—Walter Gropius's 1914 Model Factory and Ludwig Mies van der Rohe's glass skyscraper projects. His reasoning is that, by focusing on men who were later strongly associated with the "rational" architecture of the 1920s, promoters of the international style could invent a retrospective history in which they represent themselves and their style as the culmination of all that went before, a line of development pointing inevitably toward a certain conclusion. Banham objects to this retrospective plotting of progress because of what it leaves out: "The official history of the Modern Movement, as laid out in the late Twenties and codified in the Thirties . . . is only possible because the living matter of architecture, the myths and symbols, the personalities and pressure-groups have been left out." Historians of the international style, he charges, have invented a family tree that emphasizes only certain branches: "Quite suddenly modern architects decided to cut off half their grandparents without a fa[r]thing" ("Glass Paradise" 89). Ulrich Conrads and Hans Sperlich make a similar argument in their book *Fantastic Architecture* (1960), which they describe as "a collection of what had to be discarded in order to arrive at an orderly definition of present architecture in terms of certain theories" (6).

Chapter 7

1. Germany's devastated postwar economy both created and reinforced the problem of actually building expressionist schemes. Because no one had money to build, the expressionists soon adopted the attitude that they might as well indulge their wildest impulses, thus producing a set of designs notable for their material impracticality, but also striking for their imaginative abandon.

WORKS CITED

Aldington, Richard. *Death of a Hero*. 1929. Garden City, N.Y.: Garden City Publishing, 1972.

"At the Cenotaph." *Times* [London] 21 July 1919: 15 +.

Bagnold, Enid. *A Diary without Dates*. 1918. London: Virago, 1978.

Banham, Reyner. *The Architecture of the Well-Tempered Environment*. Chicago: University of Chicago Press, 1969.

———. "The Glass Paradise." *Architectural Review* Feb. 1959: 87–89.

———. "Mendelsohn." *Architectural Review* Aug. 1954: 85–93.

———. *Theory and Design in the First Machine Age*. 2nd ed. New York: Praeger, 1970.

Barbusse, Henri. *Under Fire: The Story of a Squad*. Trans. Fitzwater Wray. New York: Dutton, 1917.

Barr, Alfred H. Preface. *The International Style*. By Henry-Russell Hitchcock and Philip Johnson. 1932. New York: Norton, 1966.

Bayley, Stephen, Philippe Garner, and Deyan Sudjic. *Twentieth-Century Style and Design*. New York: Van Nostrand Reinhold, 1986.

Belsey, Catherine. *Critical Practice*. 1980. London: Methuen, 1986.

Benevolo, Leonardo. *The Modern Movement*. Vol. 2 of *History of Modern Architecture*. Trans. H. J. Landry. 2 vols. 1966. Cambridge, MA: M.I.T. Press, 1971.

Benstock, Shari. *Women of the Left Bank: Paris, 1900–1940*. 1986. Austin: University of Texas Press, 1987.

Bishop, John. *Joyce's Book of the Dark: Finnegans Wake*. Madison: University of Wisconsin Press, 1986.

Blake, Peter. "A Conversation with Mies." Ed. Gerhardt M. Kallmann. *Four Great Makers of Modern Architecture: Gropius, Le Corbusier, Mies van der Rohe, Wright*. Record of a Symposium held at the School of Architecture,

Columbia University, March–May 1961. New York: Da Capo Press, 1970. 93–104.

———. *The Master Builders: Le Corbusier, Mies van der Rohe, Frank Lloyd Wright.* 1960. New York: Norton, 1976.

———. *Mies van der Rohe: Architecture and Structure.* Baltimore: Penguin, 1960.

Bletter, Rosemarie Haag. "Paul Scheerbart's Architectural Fantasies." *Journal of the Society of Architectural Historians* 34 (May 1975): 83–97.

Blunden, Edmund. *Undertones of War.* 1928. New York: Harcourt, Brace, 1965.

Borden, Mary. *The Forbidden Zone.* Garden City, NY: Doubleday-Doran, 1930.

Bowen, Elizabeth. *The Death of the Heart.* 1938. New York: Knopf, 1939.

Bradbury, Malcolm, and James McFarlane. *Modernism 1890–1930.* 1976. London: Penguin, 1991.

Briggs, Asa. *Victorian People: A Reassessment of Persons and Themes 1851–67.* Rev. ed. 1955. Chicago: University of Chicago Press, 1972.

Brittain, Vera. *Testament of Youth: An Autobiographical Study of the Years 1900–1925.* New York: Macmillan, 1933.

Brophy, John, and Eric Partridge, eds. *Songs and Slang of the British Soldier: 1914–1918.* Rev. 2nd ed. London: Eric Partridge Ltd. at the Scholartis Press, 1930.

Brownmiller, Susan. *Against Our Will: Men, Women and Rape.* New York: Simon and Schuster, 1975.

Buitenhuis, Peter. *The Great War of Words: British, American, and Canadian Propaganda and Fiction, 1914–1933.* Vancouver: University of British Columbia Press, 1987.

Campbell, Joseph and Henry Morton Robinson. *A Skeleton Key to* Finnegans Wake. 1944. New York: Viking-Penguin, 1986.

Canfield, Mary Cass. "The Record of an Average Man." Rev. of *Memoirs of a Fox-Hunting Man,* by Siegfried Sassoon. *New York Herald Tribune Books* 3 Feb. 1929: 5.

Cather, Willa. *One of Ours.* 1922. New York: Vintage–Random House, 1971.

———. *The Professor's House.* New York: Grosset & Dunlap, 1925.

Conrads, Ulrich and Hans G. Sperlich. *Fantastic Architecture.* Trans. and ed., Christiane Crasemann Collins and George R. Collins. 1960. London: Architectural Press, 1963.

Curl, James Stevens. *A Celebration of Death: An Introduction to Some of the Buildings, Monuments, and Settings of Funerary Architecture in the Western European Tradition.* New York: Scribner's, 1980.

Curtis, William J. R. *Modern Architecture Since 1900.* Oxford: Phaidon, 1982.

De Sola Pinto, Vivian. "My First War: Memoirs of a Spectacled Subaltern." Panichas 67–84.

Ebbatson, Roger and Catherine Neale. *E. M. Forster: A Passage to India.* 1986. London: Penguin, 1989.

Eksteins, Modris. *The Rites of Spring: The Great War and the Birth of the Modern Age.* Boston: Houghton Mifflin, 1989.

Eliot, T. S. *The Waste Land.* 1922. *The Complete Poems and Plays 1909–1950.* New York: Harcourt, Brace, 1971. 37–50.

Falls, Cyril. *The Nature of Modern Warfare.* New York: Oxford, 1941.

Ferris, Timothy. "How the Brain Works, Maybe." Rev. of *The Emperor's New Mind: Concerning Computers, Minds, and the Laws of Physics,* by Roger Penrose. *New York Times Book Review* 19 Nov. 1989: 3 + .

Ford, Ford Madox. *Joseph Conrad: A Personal Remembrance.* Boston: Little, Brown, 1924.

———. *A Man Could Stand Up—.* 1926. Rpt. in *Parade's End.* New York: Vintage–Random House, 1979.

———. *No More Parades.* 1925. Rpt. in *Parade's End.* New York: Vintage–Random House, 1979.

———. *Some Do Not . . .* 1924. Rpt. in *Parade's End.* New York: Vintage–Random House, 1979.

Forester, C. S. *The General.* 1936. Boston: Little, Brown, 1947.

Forster, E. M. "The Challenge of Our Time." 1946. *Two Cheers for Democracy.* Ed. Oliver Stallybrass. 1951. London: Edward Arnold, 1972. 54–58.

———. *Howards End.* 1910. New York: Vintage–Random House, 1921.

———. "Our Graves in Gallipoli." *Abinger Harvest.* New York: Harcourt, 1936. 32–35.

———. *A Passage to India.* 1924. New York: Harcourt Brace, 1984.

———. "Reconstruction in the Marne and the Meuse." *Albergo Empedocle and Other Writings.* Ed. George H. Thomson. New York: Liveright, 1971. 263–68.

———. *Selected Letters of E. M. Forster.* Ed. Mary Lago and P. N. Furbank. 2 vols. Cambridge: Belknap-Harvard, 1983–85.

———. "To Forrest Reid." 10 Jan. 1919. Letter 193 of *Selected Letters of E. M. Forster.* Vol. 1. 298–99.

———. "To Goldsworthy Lowes Dickinson." 5 May 1917. Letter 165 of *Selected Letters of E. M. Forster.* Vol. 1. 250–51.

———. "To William Plomer." 28 Sept. 1934. Letter 300 of *Selected Letters of E. M. Forster.* Vol. 2. 124–25.

———. "What I Believe." 1938. *Two Cheers for Democracy.* Ed. Oliver Stallybrass. 1951. London: Edward Arnold, 1972. 65–73.

Frampton, Kenneth. "Modernism and Tradition in the Work of Mies van der Rohe, 1920–1968." *Mies Reconsidered: His Career, Legacy, and Disciples.* Organized by John Zukowsky. Chicago, New York: Art Institute of Chicago-Rizzoli, 1986.

Franciscono, Marcel. *Walter Gropius and the Creation of the Bauhaus in Weimar: The Ideals and Artistic Theories of Its Founding Years.* Urbana: University of Illinois Press, 1971.

Friedman, Alan. "The Novel." *1900–1918.* Vol. 1 of *The Twentieth-Century Mind: History, Ideas, and Literature in Britain.* Ed. C. B. Cox and A. E. Dyson. 2 vols. London: Oxford University Press, 1972. 414–16.

Fullbrook, Kate. *Katherine Mansfield.* Bloomington: Indiana University Press, 1986.

Fuller, J. F. C. *Generalship: Its Diseases and Their Cure.* Harrisburg, PA: Military Service Publishing Co., 1936.

Fussell, Paul. *The Great War and Modern Memory.* New York: Oxford University Press, 1975.

Gardner, Brian, ed. *Up the Line to Death: The War Poets, 1914–18.* London: Methuen, 1964.

Gates, Barrington. "Enchantment." Rev. of *Orlando,* by Virginia Woolf. *Nation & Athenæum* 27 Oct. 1928: 148–50.

"German Trench Architecture." *Architectural Review* July–Dec. 1916: 88+.

Gilbert, Sandra M. and Susan Gubar. *The War of the Words.* New Haven: Yale University Press, 1988.

Godfrey, Walter H. "Peace and the Art of Architecture." Part II. *Architectural Review* July–Dec. 1919: 160–62.

Graves, Robert. *Good-bye to All That.* 1929. New York: Jonathan Cape, 1930.

———. *In Broken Images: Selected Letters of Robert Graves 1914–1946.* Ed. Paul O'Prey. London: Hutchinson, 1982.

———. "The Leveller." Gardner 93.

———. "Postscript to 'Good-bye to All That.'" *But It Still Goes On: An Accumulation.* New York: Jonathan Cape, 1931. 3–48.

———. "Trench History." Rev. of *Undertones of War,* by Edmund Blunden. *Nation & Athenæum* 15 Dec. 1928: 420.

"The Great Battle." *Times* [London] 3 July 1916: 9+.

Greene, Graham. *A Sort of Life.* New York: Simon and Schuster, 1971.

Gropius, Walter. *The New Architecture and the Bauhaus.* Trans. P. Morton Shand. 1965. Cambridge, MA: M.I.T. Press, 1989.

Haig, Douglas. *The Private Papers of Douglas Haig 1914–1919.* Ed. Robert Blake. London: Eyre & Spottiswoode, 1952.

Hellman, Geoffrey T. "A Varied Shelf." Rev. of *Good-bye to All That,* by Robert Graves. *Bookman* Mar. 1930: 121.

Hemingway, Ernest. *A Farewell to Arms.* 1929. New York: Scribner's, 1957.

Hill, Frank Ernest. "A Poet Went to War." Rev. of *Undertones of War,* by Edmund Blunden. *New York Herald Tribune Books* 31 Mar. 1929: 7.

Hitchcock, Henry-Russell. *Architecture: Nineteenth and Twentieth Centuries.* The Pelican History of Art. Ed. Nikolaus Pevsner. Harmondsworth: Penguin, 1958.

———. Foreward to the 1966 Edition. *The International Style.* By Hitchcock and Johnson. 1932. New York: Norton, 1966.

———. and Philip Johnson. *The International Style.* 1932. New York: Norton, 1966.

Howe, Irving. "The Idea of the Modern." *The Idea of the Modern in Literature and the Arts.* Ed. Irving Howe. New York: Horizon Press, 1967.

Hussey, Christopher. *The Life of Sir Edwin Lutyens.* 1950. Woodbridge, Suffolk: Antique Collectors' Club, 1989.

Hutcheon, Linda. *The Politics of Postmodernism.* New York: Routledge, 1989.

Hynes, Samuel. *A War Imagined: The First World War and English Culture.* New York: Collier-Macmillan, 1992.

Ibsen, Henrik. *Ghosts.* 1881. Trans. Michael Meyer. *The Plays of Ibsen.* Vol. 3. New York: Washington Square–Pocket, 1986.

"The Imperial War Graves Commission." *Times* [London] 10 Nov. 1928, War Graves Number: vi+.

James, Henry. "The Jolly Corner." *Selected Fiction.* Ed. Leon Edel. New York: Dutton, 1964. 544–84.

———. *Within the Rim and Other Essays.* 1918. Freeport, NY: Books for Libraries Press, 1968.

Jencks, Charles. *Le Corbusier and the Tragic View of Architecture*. Cambridge: Harvard University Press, 1973.

Johnson, Philip C. *Mies van der Rohe*. New York: Museum of Modern Art, 1947.

Joyce, James. *Finnegans Wake*. 1939. New York: Viking-Penguin, 1986.

———. "The Sisters." *Dubliners*. 1916. New York: Viking-Penguin, 1987. 9–18.

Jünger, Ernst. *The Storm of Steel: From the Diary of a German Storm-Troop Officer on the Western Front*. Trans. Basil Creighton. 1929. New York: Howard Fertig, 1975.

Keegan, John. *The Face of Battle: A Study of Agincourt, Waterloo and the Somme*. 1976. New York: Viking-Penguin, 1978.

Kern, Stephen. *The Culture of Time and Space: 1880–1918*. Cambridge: Harvard University Press, 1983.

Kipling, Rudyard. "The Gardener." *Debits and Credits*. New York: Doubleday, 1926. 339–52.

———. "Mary Postgate." 1915. *A Diversity of Creatures; Letters of Travel 1892–1913*. New York: Doubleday, 1925. 381–400.

La Motte, Ellen N. *The Backwash of War*. New York: Putnam, 1934.

Lawrence, D. H. *The Letters of D. H. Lawrence*. Ed. George J. Zytaruk and James T. Boulton. Vol. 2. London: Cambridge University Press, 1981.

———. "To Edward Garnett." 5 June 1914. Letter 732 of *The Letters of D. H. Lawrence*. Vol. 2. 182–84.

———. "To Lady Cynthia Asquith." 9 Nov. 1915. Letter 1045 of *The Letters of D. H. Lawrence*. Vol. 2. 431–32.

———. *Women in Love*. 1920. Harmondsworth: Penguin, 1981.

Le Corbusier [Charles-Édouard Jeanneret]. *Towards a New Architecture*. Trans. Frederick Etchells. 1931. New York: Dover, 1986. Trans. of *Vers une Architecture*. 1923.

Leed, Eric. *No Man's Land: Combat and Identity in World War I*. Cambridge: Cambridge University Press, 1979.

Le Queux, William. *German Atrocities: A Record of Shameless Deeds*. London: George Newness, Ltd., n.d.

Levenson, Michael H. *A Genealogy of Modernism: A Study of English Literary Doctrine 1908–1922*. 1984. Cambridge: Cambridge University Press, 1986.

Liddell Hart, B. H. *A History of the World War 1914–1918*. 2nd ed. London: Faber & Faber, 1934.

Lodge, David. *Working with Structuralism: Essays and Reviews on Nineteenth- and Twentieth-Century Literature*. Boston: Routledge & Kegan Paul, 1981.

Longworth, Philip. *The Unending Vigil: A History of the Commonwealth War Graves Commission 1917–1967*. London: Constable, 1967.

Ludendorff, General [Erich]. *My War Memories 1914–1918*. 3rd ed. Vol. 1. London: Hutchinson, n.d.

Lukács, Georg. *The Meaning of Contemporary Realism*. Trans. John and Necke Mander. 1957. London: Merlin, 1963.

Mahaffey, Vicki. *Reauthorizing Joyce*. Cambridge: Cambridge University Press, 1988.

Mansfield, Katherine. "Bliss." 1920. *Collected Stories* 91–105.

———. *Collected Stories of Katherine Mansfield*. Edinburgh: Constable, 1945.

———. "The Daughters of the Late Colonel." 1922. *Collected Stories* 262–85.

———. "Prelude." 1920. *Collected Stories* 11–60.

———. "To John Middleton Murry." 10 Nov. 1919. *Katherine Mansfield's Letters to John Middleton Murry 1913–1922*. Ed. John Middleton Murry. 1929. New York: Knopf, 1951. 380–83.

Marcus, Jane. "Corpus/Corps/Corpse: Writing the Body in/at War." *Arms and the Woman: War, Gender, and Literary Representation*. Ed. Helen M. Cooper, Adrienne Auslander Munich, Susan Merrill Squier. Chapel Hill: University of North Carolina Press, 1989. 124–67.

Matthews, T. S. "Farewell and Hail." Rev. of *Good-bye to All That,* by Robert Graves. *New Republic* 19 Feb. 1930: 23.

McHugh, Roland. *Annotations to* Finnegans Wake. 1980. Baltimore: Johns Hopkins University Press, 1982.

Meyer, Jacques. "Verdun, 1916." Trans. Sally Abeles. Panichas 54–65.

Middlebrook, Martin. *The First Day on the Somme: 1 July 1916*. New York: Norton, 1972.

Morgan, J. H. *German Atrocities: An Official Investigation*. London: T. Fisher Unwin, 1916.

Morley, F. V. "A Poet at War." Rev. of *Undertones of War,* by Edmund Blunden. *Saturday Review of Literature* 11 May 1929: 993–94.

Mortimer, Raymond. "A Good Beginning." Rev. of *Memoirs of a Fox-Hunting Man,* by Siegfried Sassoon. *The Nation & Athenæum* 27 Oct. 1928: 150–52.

Murry, John Middleton. Editorial Notes. *Journal of Katherine Mansfield*. Ed. John Middleton Murry. London: Constable, 1927.

Newton, Ernest. "Peace and the Art of Architecture." Part I. *Architectural Review* July–Dec. 1919: 160.

Owen, Wilfred. "To Susan Owen." 4 Feb. 1917. Letter 482 of *Collected Letters*. Ed. Harold Owen and John Bell. London: Oxford University Press, 1967. 430–32.

Panichas, George A., ed. *Promise of Greatness: The War of 1914–1918*. New York: John Day, 1968.

Pater, Walter. "Style." 1888. *Selections from Walter Pater*. Ed. Ada L. F. Snell. Boston: Houghton Mifflin, 1924. 86–108.

Pehnt, Wolfgang. *Expressionist Architecture*. Trans. J. A. Underwood and Edith Küstner. 1973. London: Thames and Hudson, 1979.

Pevsner, Nikolaus. "Finsterlin and Some Others." *Architectural Review* Nov. 1962: 353–57.

———. *An Outline of European Architecture*. 7th ed. Harmondsworth: Penguin, 1963.

Remarque, Erich Maria. *All Quiet on the Western Front*. Trans. A. W. Wheen. 1929. New York: Fawcett-Crest-Ballantine, 1987.

Roheim, Geza. *The Gates of the Dream*. New York: International Universities Press, 1952.

Rosecrance, Barbara. *Forster's Narrative Vision*. Ithaca: Cornell University Press, 1982.

Rybczynski, Witold. *Home: A Short History of an Idea*. 1986. New York: Penguin, 1987.

Sassoon, Siegfried. *Memoirs of an Infantry Officer*. New York: Coward, McCann, 1930.

Scarry, Elaine. *The Body in Pain: The Making and Unmaking of the World*. New York: Oxford University Press, 1985.

Scheerbart, Paul. *Glass Architecture*. Trans. James Palmes. 1914. Published with Bruno Taut. *Alpine Architecture*. Trans. Shirley Palmer. 1917. New York: Praeger, 1972.

Scheffauer, Herman George. "Hans Poelzig." *Architectural Review* Oct. 1923: 121–27.

Schmitt, Bernadotte E. and Harold C. Vedeler. *The World in the Crucible: 1914–1919*. New York: Harper & Row, 1984.

Schriftgiesser, Karl. "The Memoirs of a Fox-Hunting Man." Rev. of *Memoirs of a Fox-Hunting Man*, by Siegfried Sassoon. *Boston Evening Transcript* 2 Mar. 1929: 3.

Sharp, Dennis. *Modern Architecture and Expressionism*. New York: Braziller, 1966.

Shusterman, David. *The Quest for Certitude in E. M. Forster's Fiction*. New York: Haskell, 1973.

"The Silent World." *Times* [London] 10 Nov. 1928, War Graves Number: iv +.

Sinclair, May. *The Tree of Heaven*. New York: Macmillan, 1918.

Smith, Helen Zenna. *Not So Quiet . . . Stepdaughters of War*. 1930. New York: Feminist Press, 1989.

Stallings, Laurence, ed. *The First World War: A Photographic History*. New York: Simon and Schuster, 1933.

Stamp, Gavin. *Silent Cities: An Exhibition of the Memorial and Cemetery Architecture of the Great War*. London: Royal Institute of British Architects, 1977.

Stevens, Wallace. *The Collected Poems of Wallace Stevens*. 1954. New York: Knopf, 1978.

———. "The Noble Rider and the Sound of Words." 1942. *The Necessary Angel: Essays on Reality and the Imagination*. New York: Vintage–Random House, 1951. 3–36.

Terraine, John. *White Heat: The New Warfare 1914–18*. London: Sidgwick & Jackson, 1982.

Thompson, Leonard. "A Suffolk Man at Gallipoli." Vansittart 70–72.

Thomsen, Christian W. *Visionary Architecture: From Babylon to Virtual Reality*. Munich: Prestel, 1994.

Travers, Tim. *The Killing Ground: The British Army, the Western Front and the Emergence of Modern Warfare 1900–1918*. London: Allen & Unwin, 1987.

Tuchman, Barbara W. *The Guns of August*. New York: Macmillan, 1962.

Vansittart, Peter, comp. *Voices from the Great War*. London: Jonathan Cape, 1981.

Vaughan, Edwin Campion. *Some Desperate Glory: The World War I Diary of a British Officer, 1917*. 1981. New York: Henry Holt, 1988.

Warren, Whitney. "The Destruction of Churches in France." *Architectural Review* July–Dec. 1916: 19.

West, Rebecca. *The Return of the Soldier*. 1918. New York: Dial, 1980.

"What Happened Last Time." *Architectural Review* July–Dec. 1941: 3–5.

White, Hayden V. "The Burden of History." *History and Theory* 5 (1966): 111–34.

———. *Tropics of Discourse: Essays in Cultural Criticism.* Baltimore: Johns Hopkins University Press, 1978.

Whitridge, Arnold. "A Farewell to Youth." Rev. of *Good-bye to All That,* by Robert Graves. *Saturday Review of Literature* 8 Feb. 1930: 706–707.

Whittick, Arnold. *War Memorials.* London: Country Life, 1946.

Williams, John. *The Home Fronts: Britain, France and Germany 1914–1918.* London: Constable, 1972.

Williams, Tennessee. *The Glass Menagerie.* 1944. *The Theatre of Tennessee Williams.* Vol. 1. New York: New Directions, 1971.

Wilson, Trevor. *The Myriad Faces of War: Britain and the Great War 1914–1918.* 1986. Cambridge: Polity Press, 1988.

Woolf, Virginia. *Collected Essays.* Ed. Leonard Woolf. Vol. 2. 1966. London: Chatto & Windus, 1967.

———. *Jacob's Room.* 1922. New York: Harcourt Brace, n.d.

———. "Modern Fiction." *Collected Essays* 103–110.

———. *Mrs. Dalloway.* 1925. New York: Harcourt Brace, n.d.

———. "The Narrow Bridge of Art." *New York Herald Tribune* 14 Aug. 1927. Rpt. in *Collected Essays* 218–29.

———. "Solid Objects." *A Haunted House and Other Short Stories.* 1921. San Diego: Harcourt Brace, 1972. 79–86.

———. "To Clive Bell." 24 July 1917. Letter 852 of *The Letters of Virginia Woolf.* Ed. Nigel Nicholson and Joanne Trautmann. Vol. 2. New York: Harcourt Brace, 1976. 167.

———. *To the Lighthouse.* 1927. New York: Harcourt Brace, n.d.

———. *The Waves.* 1931. New York: Harcourt Brace, n.d.

———. *A Writer's Diary.* New York: Harcourt Brace, 1954.

———. *The Years.* 1937. New York: Harcourt Brace, n.d.

INDEX